Mr. Clark's
Big Band

ALSO BY MEREDITH O'BRIEN

Mortified: a novel

A Suburban Mom

Mr. Clark's Big Band
A Year of Laughter, Tears, and Jazz in a Middle School Band Room
Meredith O'Brien

ISBN: 978-1-942545-62-0
Library of Congress Control Number: to come

Wyatt-MacKenzie Publishing
DEADWOOD, OREGON

Wyatt-MacKenzie Publishing, Inc.
www.WyattMacKenzie.com
Contact us: info@wyattmackenzie.com

Mr. Clark's Big Band

A Year of Laughter, Tears, and Jazz in a Middle School Band Room

MEREDITH O'BRIEN

Wyatt-MacKenzie Publishing
DEADWOOD, OREGON

Dedicated to my son Jonah and to the Green family.

Table of Contents

(Chart of the Big Band to come)

Preface

In January 2012, a 12-year-old boy died in his sleep. Hours earlier, he had been playing basketball with the town recreational league in the Trottier Middle School gym. By morning, this seemingly healthy, smiling, warm-hearted boy was gone. Emails bearing the news were sent out by the Southborough, Massachusetts schools at around lunchtime. Parents, stunned, called one another but didn't have much to say because, what was there to say? What would they tell their children? When a parent tucks a child to bed at night, the parent usually breathes a sigh of relief, *This child is safe beneath my roof. All is well.* The death of seventh grader Eric Green upended all of that for Southborough parents, myself included. *If this could happen to Eric, could it happen to my child?* the question echoed. Learning, months later, that Eric had an undiagnosed heart condition did nothing to alleviate the local parents' worries.

The grief was like a wave washing over the small town of less than 10,000, in a western exurb of Boston. It kept crashing ashore like the incoming tide for the families of middle school children, students who knew Eric, who played baseball, lacrosse, basketball or soccer with him, or who played music alongside him at the Trottier. Teachers and students alike openly wept in school hallways. Parents found themselves crying in the aisles of Stop & Shop while picking out breakfast cereal, imagining their own sons or daughters, imagining what it must be like for Suzy and Peter Green who lost their youngest son.

At the time, I had two seventh graders, boy-girl twins, and a fifth grade boy. My older son Jonah had been forging a closer relationship with Eric. Eric attended my son's birthday party the prior August, a small affair where a group of boys had pizza, cake, played video games and spent most of the sleepover being goofy middle school kids. Eric arrived late to the festivities, still sweaty from soccer practice. As he shed his cleats at the front door, he asked me for some pieces of newspaper.

"Newspaper?" I asked.

"I can put it in my cleats so they won't smell."

Jonah attended Eric's birthday party in 2011 too. They stayed up late watching a movie, one of those ridiculous comedies that parents hate but kids love. He, Eric and a small group of boys got their first taste of freedom on the day school let out for December vacation in 2011 when they went to the Solomon Pond Mall in nearby Marlborough to have lunch and do Christmas shopping. Suzy had phoned all the parents days before, leaving detailed voice mail messages to assure us that she would remain at the mall, hanging out in the food court. Although she wouldn't be sitting with them, she'd give them some space because when you're a middle school boy, being seen at the mall with your mom is just embarrassing.

Less than a month after that outing, Eric passed away. The idyllic suburban lives his friends had been living were shattered. Suddenly, the boys were afraid, afraid of death, afraid of losing people. There was guilt that they were still here, that they would move forward in their lives, that they would celebrate more birthdays, finish middle school, get driver's licenses, grow up. But Eric wouldn't do any of that. Some of Eric's friends, including my son, didn't want to mark any milestones because to do so made them feel bad, as if, in some way, they were being disrespectful to Eric's memory, leaving him behind. How could they laugh or joke around when Eric had died? How could *anything* be funny anymore?

The weeks after his passing were dark ones, especially in my house. I didn't have the words to make my son feel better. I couldn't reassure him. I couldn't explain what had happened or why. I was having trouble comprehending it myself. One of my friends, whose eldest son was also a seventh grader and friend of Eric's, said she couldn't stop herself from creeping into her children's bedrooms at night, silently putting her hand on their chests to make sure they were still breathing. She wasn't the only one.

By June, a group of bereaved parents, teachers and students

formed the Eric Green Committee to start to discuss planning an event to celebrate Eric's life, although at first, the meetings were more support group than planning-oriented. The group decided there would be an event to celebrate Eric in the spring of 2013. Some of the money from the Eric Green Fund—whose proceeds the Greens had determined would be given to the Trottier Middle School music program because Eric loved music and his silver trumpet—would be allocated to commissioning two musical compositions in Eric's memory.

But before the 2011-12 school year came to a close, the students who played in the Trottier Big Band had to get through the second annual Jazz Night. Jazz Night was a concert given by this elite jazz band at the middle school. These young children would perform more than a dozen pieces, a major feat of endurance, and be accompanied by a professional musician. It was a showcase for the talented band and its ambitious director, Jamie Clark. All proceeds from Jazz Night were going to the Eric Green Fund.

As a mother, I was worried about how my son, a drummer in the Big Band, was going to get through the night and how the other kids were going to fare. Would they break down? Would this prove too much for them? They were all still pretty raw. We all were. With the color green everywhere—on the boys' ties, on the ribbons tied on the instruments or pinned to shirts, on the parents' clothing in the audience—it was expected to be an emotional evening.

"As you all know, we lost Eric Green this past year," Mr. Clark told the audience near the beginning of the performance. "And we are heartbroken. And we miss him and we miss him as a member of our band, a member of our school and a member of our community. But one of the things that music can do is console you when you are pretty much inconsolable. And that's why we're gonna play, 'A Band's Gotta Do What a Band's Gotta Do' ''cause that's what music is all about, to bring comfort and joy. He's dearly missed and we will always miss him. This is for him."

The Big Band kids played crisply and brightly, performing well beyond their chronological ages. They kept themselves together, even after Mr. Clark introduced "Swing Shift." Following a lengthy and weighty silence, Mr. Clark rubbed his hands along his white-gray beard on both sides of his face, pacing as he spoke: "Eric Green was a truly wonderful person, a wonderful athlete, a wonderful musician, wonderful student, a wonderful friend. We're all heartbroken at his passing. And we've been dealing with it the best that we can. We've been talking about it a fair amount during Big Band rehearsals. In December, we played a piece that was called 'Swing Shift.' It was last played here, and Eric performed a solo. We haven't performed it since, but we're going to play it right now, and we're going to take this moment to dedicate it in the memory of Eric and the way that he lived his life and the wonderful young man that he was, who was taken from us much, much too soon."

When it was over, the sounds of sniffling and a standing ovation filled the room, warm with love. The children stood and accepted their applause. Backstage, when it was over, a local reporter interviewed a few of the children and they burst into tears, tears that had been held back all evening. The students emerged from the band room into the arms of family members and well-wishers who were crowding the lobby. The children were smiling behind their watery eyes.

All weekend, I thought about Jazz Night, wondered about it. How were those children, my son Jonah included, able to play all the way to the end of that concert? Throughout the performance, I found myself sniveling into the wad of tissues. Other parents sitting there in the dark around me were wiping away tears as well, their eyes red-rimmed after the final notes of "Sweet Home Chicago" rang out at the show's conclusion. I didn't understand it. How were they able to play all those songs so powerfully, so full of splendor? All of those pieces? Then it hit me: Mr. Clark. Mr. Clark was the key. He had a big and boisterous persona, along with an obvious affection for and devotion to his students. His leadership guided the children through the initial days when Eric's music stand stood empty, when the children asked Mr. Clark why he was gone, why not them instead of him. Mr. Clark's students, along with their parents, adored him with a fervor that bordered on cult-like.

Having just completed my first novel, I was trying to figure out what my next writing project would be. I thought about Mr. Clark as the prototype for a fictional character but decided it wouldn't be believable. He was too over-the-top. People would think I was being overly dramatic if I crafted a character based on him. So why not just write about him as a real person, in a work of nonfiction? An idea started to quickly gel, a question really: How did Mr. Clark help those children overcome their deep sadness in order to perform? The question morphed: Why not follow the grieving members of the Big Band during the next school year—what would have been Eric's last year at Trottier—and see how their camaraderie, the music and Mr. Clark helped them heal, and if indeed they would heal? They would have to travel through the first anniversary of his passing. In June 2013, they would have to premiere two pieces commissioned in Eric's memory and play starring roles in whatever ceremony the Eric Green Committee organized. As the book idea developed, I consulted with Mr. Clark to see what he thought of having a writer shadow the Big Band rehearsals and performances for the next school year. Thrilled, he bought in immediately. The school principal approved the project, as I agreed that I would—like Tracy Kidder did in his classic *Among Schoolchildren*, when he sat in with an elementary school class for a year—change the names of all of the current Big Band students in the book I intended to write.

Next, I needed buy-in from my son Jonah (whose name is changed in the story that follows) and the parents of whoever would earn spots in the 2012-13 Big Band. My son proved to be the toughest sale. A very private person, and even more secretive about his grief, Jonah had pretty recently asked me to stop writing parenting columns and blog posts that mentioned him. The idea of having me observe Big Band rehearsals for his eighth-grade year did not appeal to him. At all. "You'll ruin it," he told me, fearful that my presence would alter what was special about the band room. His eventual approval of the project was conditional: He didn't want me to speak with him during rehearsals and didn't want me to call attention to myself. I agreed to his terms.

I spent September 2012 through June 2013 following the Big Band and Mr. Clark around. In January and June, I interviewed as many Big Band members and parents as would consent to speak with me. Not all of them did. Some initially agreed, then changed their minds. I interviewed Trottier teachers and former Trottier students. I logged many, many hours with Mr. Clark, got to know his wife, his daughters, his parents and his friends. I interviewed Suzy Green and the Northborough-Southborough school superintendent. I discussed music and the Big Band with musicians, composers and educators. I read books and articles about jazz and jazz education.

The result is this book which tells the story of how being a part of a middle school jazz band, led by a charismatic band director, helped students find peace with the death of one of their friends and bandmates. Here are some things you should know before we begin: I do not pretend to be a music expert, in fact I play no instruments and can barely carry a tune when I sing along with the car radio to the eternal horror of my sons. I am not an unbiased observer. I have been an enthusiastic fan of the Big Band and an admirer of Mr. Clark's since Jonah joined the school's beginner jazz ensemble, the Stage Band, in sixth grade. Jonah and some of my Southborough parent friends were part of the Eric Green Committee. Some of my friends were also Big Band parents. Despite my biases, I have tried to take a step back from my connections to the Big Band and simply chronicle the year in the life of this group, focus on the stories of select members and flesh out the who, the what and the why of Mr. Clark as fairly as I could, as best as anyone could describe the melancholy, joyous and silly year.

Prologue

It was the evening of Memorial Day, May 26, 2015 and the band room was filled with the raucous music made by former members of the 2010-2011 Big Band, the group which Mr. Clark said "put Trottier on the map."

"This is the band that set the bar for the rest of the Big Bands to follow. They took the Big Band on their backs and met every challenge," he told the sixty assembled family members and friends in the hot and humid room of the first Trottier Big Band to snare an Outstanding Award at the University of New Hampshire Jazz Festival. "I have missed them terribly. I love you guys. I love you dearly."

These twenty-seven teenagers—nine of whom were on the cusp of college—were drawn back to their middle school band room to soak in this warm embrace set to music. The high schoolers were the catalysts behind organizing what they called "the Mr. Clark reunion." Since they'd left Trottier Middle School, many confessed, they'd longed for the connection, the camaraderie, the joy of the Big Band. Nothing had been able to fill the space in their hearts that was once occupied by the experience of playing in this space with this man. So bereft that Mr. Clark wouldn't be able to be their band director beyond middle school, a number of these teens gave up playing music. This reunion, this playing of six Big Band pieces— whose sheet music some of the students still had in their possession—was the first time many of the teens had played jazz music in years. With only an hour of rehearsal beforehand, followed by a buffet smorgasbord pulled together by their parents, the Big Band graduates delivered a concert about which Mr. Clark later observed: "It was messy and raw, but God was it good."

"They just wanted to be with Mr. Clark," said Deb Keefe, the mother of Brian, a junior. Brian and his Southborough band friends had been aching to reconnect with Mr. Clark, to play with him just one more time. "Please make this happen," Brian begged his mother when he was trying to organize the gathering.

These were students I'd seen flock to the band room before Big Band performances with the express purpose of giving their old teacher an enthusiastic bear hug. The ones who formed the human tunnel after Jazz Night. They were the same people I witnessed embracing Mr. Clark before town parades, as the marchers gathered in downtown Southborough, including the boy who wept when I asked what playing for Mr. Clark in the band room meant to him. Their desire to revisit their middle school years, to be those awkward adolescents, was palpable. You could see a similar sentiment reflected in their parents' eyes which pooled in response to the bliss of their children's flushed faces as the students played "Groovin' Hard" like they'd just had rehearsal the day before. Their playing was explosive, jubilant. With just four trumpet players—all of whom could easily reach around their trumpets and cover the bells with their hands during "Dance Like No One's Watching" unlike their current middle school counterparts who had much shorter arms—they sounded powerful. And loud, like true Sonic Lords of Death. The former band members responded to Mr. Clark's gestures, sometimes before he'd even made them, like the entire saxophone section rising as one during that measure which showcased them in "Groovin' Hard." It was as if they'd stowed away the knowledge they accumulated during their middle school years and put it in a dusty box which they re-opened in the band room. Mr. Clark didn't even have to raise his voice. I take that back, he did raise his voice when he was conducting them in "Late Night Diner," the first chart the group played. He loudly grunted, *And!* in a way he might have directed a group of colleagues who'd really gotten into the music. He wore a droll smile on his reddened face. His tone wasn't that of a teacher leading a bunch of 11- and 12-year-olds. It made me think of something then-eighth-grade-guitarist Jesse said when I interviewed him a few days after his Trottier career came to a close: "It's almost effortless with him. That's what makes him such a great teacher, that's why everyone loves him."

After the parents made pleas for an encore, and Mr. Clark responded by having the students play the last few measures of "Late Night Diner" again, people remained in the stuffy room for nearly a half-hour. Group photos were taken by a bank of parent paparazzi. Photos were snapped of Mr. Clark and the nine high school seniors—almost all of whom were taller than their former conductor—as they draped their arms over one another. The teens queued up individually and waited patiently to grab hold of Mr. Clark with both arms, like they were grabbing onto their fleeting childhoods.

"That was one of the best nights I've ever had as a teacher, truly," Mr. Clark said, vowing to hold more Big Band reunions in the future. "I'm incredibly blessed far more than I could ever have imagined or deserved, actually. I have gotten so much more than I've given, at least in my mind."

As the members of the 2010-11 Big Band demonstrated, Mr. Clark and the Big Band are never quite in the past.

CHAPTER ONE

Bring Your 'A' Game

‖: The lead trumpeter was hurtling down the Massachusetts Turnpike en route to the hospital in the midst of a mid-June thunderstorm. He was supposed to be prepping to play a significant solo in the jazz piece "Kaleidoscope," a complex tune composed in honor of one of his bandmates who died the previous year at the age of 12. But instead of settling into their auditorium seats, Patrick's parents were rushing their youngest son to the hospital, hoping to get there before his appendix burst.

Back in the band room, Patrick's absence was sorely felt, especially by the sixth grade trumpet player who was to take his place. When Mr. Clark told Henry that he would have to take Patrick's top spot, Henry's round face grew a little gray as his mouth fell open and formed a soft, horrified "o." It was bad enough that the sixth grader was already terrified about whether he'd be able to make it all the way to the end of the Trottier Middle School Big Band jazz concert, the longest concert of his life, where the student musicians were expected to play sixteen pieces. Henry was already prepared for his lips to go numb by the time the final, bluesy notes of "Sweet Home Chicago" rang out into the night air. Numb lips were one thing, but stepping into Patrick's shoes as the top trumpet player for the unorthodox, trumpet-laden piece just seventeen days after its premiere at an emotion-drenched service? That seemed like a lot to ask.

Henry, who was physically smaller and slighter than many of the other thirty-three middle schoolers who comprised the Big Band, barely said a word all year during the group's thrice-weekly, before-school rehearsals. He usually tried to blend in with the other trumpet players in the back row, ducking behind his scratched, black metal music stand, hoping that the booming voice of the short and barrel-chested Mr. Clark would never be aimed in his direction. Most of the time, it seemed as though Henry wanted to hide, despite the fact that he was playing one of the louder instruments in the band. But on this hot June night, Jazz Night—when the audience would include former Big Band members and a professional saxophonist —Henry couldn't hide. Mr. Clark wouldn't let him.

As much as the performance meant to the students, this jazz concert was also a big deal for Mr. Clark, who was in his eleventh year of teaching middle school. It was the marquee event of the year, a chance to show everyone what his elite Big Band could do, how these kids—ranging from some who had yet to shed all their baby teeth, to boys who could shave—could play with astonishing maturity. These were students he hand-selected from an eager pool of sixty who auditioned back in September. Both Mr. Clark and his students wanted to demonstrate that the 2012-13 Big Band was just as good as the groups that preceded them, which won accolades at the University of New Hampshire Jazz Festival and the Massachusetts Association for Jazz Education competition. Although the band director attempted, in his intense-yet-nurturing Mr. Clark way, to reassure Henry that he would do *Just fine*, Mr. Clark couldn't camouflage his own nerves. The highly caffeinated, 44-year-old conductor, who'd been up since 3 a.m., patted Henry on the shoulder, a public show of confidence before he paced around the band room looking edgy.

Mr. Clark was painfully aware that the Southborough, Massachusetts middle school Big Band had endured many challenges during the academic year, more than just the absence of the lead trumpeter on Jazz Night, more than the garden variety woes of adolescence. Their biggest challenge? Making peace with the loss of

Eric Green in January 2012. The ache over his passing remained intense, not just when they played Eric's jazz piece "Kaleidoscope," but almost every day in the band room that year. It was in the green grosgrain ribbons that remained fastened to the shiny saxophones and flutes, evident during the very first Big Band rehearsal in September. It was in the green neckties and green hair ribbons band students wore at performances. It was in the thick, forest green rubber bracelets—which said, "Spirit of Southborough" on one side and "Eric" on the other, with musical notes next to his name—that nearly every band member, as well as Mr. Clark, sported. It was in the eyes of Eric's friends who attempted to find joy while also struggling with remorse that they couldn't share that happiness with the boy who would never leave his childhood.

Tonight, Jazz Night, was their final performance together as a band. For the eighth graders, it was the closing of a chapter; these students were ready to celebrate the fact that they'd made it through middle school and give themselves permission to move on. However, learning that not only would Patrick be absent, but another trumpet player, a mouse-quiet sixth grader, Brad, was ill as well made the night suddenly feel precarious. During the 7 a.m. rehearsal, hours earlier, Mr. Clark announced that Patrick was at home with what his mother initially thought was a stomach virus. Mr. Clark said he hoped Patrick would rally in time for the performance. "Everybody keep your fingers crossed," he said as a few students audibly gasped, knowing that Patrick's trumpet playing figured prominently in several numbers. "We've been working ten months to get to this point. Ten months. Bring your 'A' game."

Henry and his older brother, Harry, an eighth grader who was the number-two tenor sax player, arrived late to the performance, leaving precious little time for Henry to absorb the load that had just been placed upon his bony shoulders. Mr. Clark sent the brothers to the auditorium to make sure that their sheet music was open to the first number, "Back to the Basement" so the band could walk on stage and start playing almost immediately, with no introductions, just seizing the spotlight with a riot of explosive sound. While Henry, still in shock, checked his music, Mr. Clark informed the rest of the students that Patrick had appendicitis and was on his way to Boston

Children's Hospital, a little over twenty-five miles east of town. "The show must go on," he told them, quoting the old showbiz saw, but not looking like he entirely believed it, not at that moment anyway.

At least the fire from the smoldering electric keyboard hadn't started yet.

When you're at the Trottier Middle School when the foliage is thick and green, it can seem as if you're in the middle of nowhere, even though you're fairly close to Route 9, a busy, four-lane thoroughfare that ends in Boston to the east and in the Berkshires to the west. Less than a half-mile from Route 9, insulated by residential neighborhoods, Trottier itself is a quiet island surrounded by woods and wetlands, sharing a common, speed-bump-filled drive with the in-much-need-of-repairs, 1960s-era Neary Elementary School, some two thousand yards to the south. The combined Trottier-Neary educational compound is home to three outdoor tennis courts and a sandy volleyball pit as well as two baseball diamonds, four soccer fields and an outdoor track. There are only two exits from the property, one on the Neary side which empties out onto the residential Parkerville Road, leading to Route 9 on the right and Main Street on the left, and the Trottier exit which leads to a rural neighborhood on Deerfoot Road.

As classrooms go, the band room at Trottier is the biggest of the forty-eight and had the benefit of a sound consultant's input when it was designed, complete with an acoustics-friendly open-bar joist ceiling. It's also the only classroom space with air conditioning, something that the band director adores because he's perpetually feeling overheated. Although there are some who refer to the room as a sanctuary from the rigors of middle school life, it is, in fact, a peninsula. The 50 x 40 room was added onto the two-story middle school, at the end of a long hallway behind the auditorium, in 2004 during an $11 million renovation project, six years after the $49 million middle school was constructed. The space boasts its own, light blue, double-doored external exit to the front sidewalk, located at the back of the room. It has four double windows, which look out onto the front parking lot, the side parking lot where students exit from the buses in the morning, and a small basketball court.

When I entered the band room for a Mr. Clark-led tour in the summer of 2012 before the students returned, it was brimming with personality. Inside, there were the typical things one might expect to find in a middle school band room: rows of music stands, a wall of metal instrument cages painted beige, a white board with musicals staves, an American flag, posters featuring musical icons (three including Frank Sinatra, one which featured him in silhouette, in a spotlight with "Frank Sinatra My Way" at the bottom), drums— four timpani drums protected by black plastic coverings, along with a row of snares, cymbals on stands, a beat-up upright piano, a scuffed black wooden theater riser, a long red, white and yellow school banner which features the school's ram mascot, and a tan wall-mounted phone that, throughout the school year, would angrily blink red because Mr. Clark hadn't checked his voicemail messages.

There were, by my count, nineteen laminated inspirational posters on the walls as well as handmade posters, including computer print-outs in large lettering on white paper. "I CAN'T DO IT ... YET!!" read a long and thin sign taped above the front windows. "It's all legato, man!" was another extra-large quote that had been uttered by a musician and was meant to convey to the students that in order to play well, they need to play together. "Full tilt, full time," a phrase used by New England Patriots player Tedy Bruschi, was in the same cluster of quotes; it was there because Mr. Clark believes that football is "the ultimate team sport," second only to playing in a band. Above the wooden shelving unit, with its seventy-two slots for sheet music, were small plaques: Trottier's first top award from the University of New Hampshire jazz festival, the first gold and silver won by the Trottier seventh- and eighth-grade bands at the annual Massachusetts Instrumental and Choral Conductors Association (MICCA) competition, and the first silver and bronze won by the Trottier Orchestra at MICCA.

The loudest elements, however, were the voices of the students, both present and former, embodied by art work, photos and other memorabilia: several hand-drawn comics featuring a bearded and bespectacled man known as "Band Guy;" an art deco-ish black cardboard sign, edged with silver-colored duct tape that said, "Clark's Late Nite Diner Coffee Café," and four vibrant papier-mache masks —in the shape of a purple flower, the sun, Minnie Mouse and a face with funky, spikey hair—made in art class by students who left Trottier two years prior. Hung in the back corner of the room, above where the Big Band played: an entire cork board covered with multicolored bubble letters written on 13 pieces of 8½ x 10 white paper arranged to say, "Now property of King Jamie and the Bandies Empire," with a sinister-looking drawing of Mr. Clark, sporting a yellow crown. Nine, large, panoramic photos covered the chalk board in the front of the room, photos taken of the eighth grade classes from 2003-2011 when the students were standing in front of the Capitol building during the annual D.C. trip which Mr. Clark had chaperoned since arriving at Trottier. The faces of the old students facing those of the new.

The band room also served as an embodiment of Mr. Clark's quirkiness. Atop the wall-mounted TV: a stuffed *Toy Story* pig peeking down at the screen next to a straw cowboy hat topped with a pink wig and goggles. On top of a large speaker on the wall: a giant stuffed Tigger wearing a Santa hat with his paws around a large stuffed Yoda. An old black and white photo of Mr. Clark—he still had dark hair—adjusting the kilt he was wearing over shorts while playing a student-faculty game of field hockey was taped to a chalk board. Sitting on a small table in the front of the room was a framed 8 x10 photo of one of Mr. Clark's favorite spots on earth: Disney's Magic Castle.

On top of one of the instrument cages, over to the left, next to the air duct, was a cautionary tale forged in metal: a black music stand that, years ago, had been mangled in a fit of anger by Mr. Clark. Once the year began, I would, from time to time, see students eyeing is warily. They all knew the story. It was legend.

CHAPTER TWO

Pencils, Not Pens

‖: "Count Bubba," by the California-based Big Phat Band, was blasting. I could hear it as soon as I rounded the corner from Trottier's modest front entrance, walked past the auditorium and hung a left toward the music wing. The horn-heavy, devil-may-care recording engulfed me.

Mr. Clark was wearing black jeans, brown and tan Merrel boots—built for comfort, not fashion—and an untucked pink, oxford shirt that was frayed at the tip of the right side of his collar. He was happily swinging his left hand along with the music while holding his red, metal travel mug of coffee in his right. He had a fresh haircut.

As the members of the Big Band gathered for their first 7 a.m. rehearsal in September 2012, Mr. Clark immediately distributed the sheet music for their first piece and made it quite plain, up front, that the kids needed to have their pencils ready during these sessions. "If a pencil doesn't have a point, what is it? A stick!" he said, answering his own question.

He told students where they were to stand in the back of the band room. The Big Band set-up wrapped around him as he stood in the open-ended front. He had sketched out everyone's positions soon after he decided on the relatively diverse group of students who would be accepted into the ensemble.

The kids' reedy and smooth notes during their instrument warm-ups clashed with those from the Big Phat Band recording that was still emanating from the speakers. Some of the students wore very serious faces as they warmed up. As of 7:10, not everyone had arrived. It bugged Mr. Clark when kids were late, something that wound up happening all year long, no matter how many warnings he issued. Mr. Clark poked his head out the band room doors. "Hurry up! Hurry up!" he told the band members who were strolling down the hallway. Ethan, the eighth-grade lead tenor saxophone player and de facto Big Band student leader, sauntered into the room wearing a black fedora, a tuft of his dark, gelled hair poking out from beneath the front of the hat. All jazz. He was late but he is Ethan. He needed to make an entrance.

Despite the fact that the window shades on all the windows were drawn, it was extremely bright inside the white- and cream-colored room. Between the blinding light seeping through the gaps in the white shades and the waves of sound coming from different directions, coupled with Mr. Clark's booming voice, it was impossible not to be WIDE AWAKE. "Good morning!" Mr. Clark said to them, a thread of giddiness in his voice. He was as excited for the first day of Big Band rehearsal as kids usually are on the last day of school. He had been waiting for this moment since school let out last June, what he called the worst month of the year. He hated the summers but loved September.

The students responded with a tepid, dragged out, "Good morning, Mr. Clark." They sounded tired and looked sleepy, except for Ethan and his hair gel. This was the first time they had to show up at school this early in the morning after a summer of sleeping in.

Dissatisfied with their reply, he demanded that they try again, only louder. "Good morning, Mr. Clark!" shouted nearly all the children at maximum volume.

Mr. Clark handed the sheet music to two stragglers who came in after his greeting: Angelina, a popular eighth-grade clarinet player, and Natalie, a seventh-grade violinist with boundless enthusiasm. Including a violin in the jazz ensemble was unusual. Some band directors would not allow a violinist to join a jazz group. At the local high school, flute and clarinet players were excluded from the jazz ensembles, too. Mr. Clark was more open-minded about what instruments he allowed in his Big Band than other band directors. After Natalie asked Mr. Clark about adding a jazz violin to the Big Band, he decided to give it a try. "I've never had a violin player," he told me. "This is an experiment."

On this first morning of the jazz violin experiment, the students were on their best behavior. Though they looked a tad drowsy, they gave the impression of being organized, at least initially. There was no noticeable goofing off amid the tentative energy in the room. It was as if they were waiting for something.

They commenced the new school year by playing their audition piece, "Groovin' Hard," the Buddy Rich Band's signature 1970 chart, described as "hard-driving blues" by a music website. Mr. Clark characterized "Groovin' Hard" this way: "It's all about attitude, just attitude that, *We're better than everybody and it's not just that we know it, you know it too.*" After telling Noah, a studious eighth-grade drummer, and Richie, a melancholy eighth-grade bassist/drummer, how to establish the rhythm for the song, Mr. Clark instructed the two boys playing the trombone—eighth-grader Brandon, the tallest person in the room, and seventh-grader Henry, whose voice I don't think I heard all year—and two of the sax players—seventh-grader chatterboxes Danny and Derek—that he expected them all to come in "huge" on this. Within weeks it would become evident that Danny, whose personality was nearly as gigantic and loud as Mr. Clark's, would come in huge all the time, and not just during songs.

To my amateur ears, it wasn't a bad first attempt at a powerful, in-your-face piece. The three flutists were stooped over their fresh sheet music, seeming to know what to do without being told. Mr. Clark encouraged them with emphatic hand motions that caused him to break into a bit of a sweat. Looking over at the rhythm section, he started vigorously clapping—one hand vertically above the other—to demonstrate the time he wanted them to keep. Predictably, there were hiccups, like having to wait for the kids who moved in slow motion. Halfway through "Groovin' Hard" for example, Richie, who had large, haunted brown eyes, was still working on setting up the bass. He didn't seem fazed that the band started

without him. The Big Band had to sight-read the piece without a
bass line for guidance. Mr. Clark was noticeably exasperated with
Richie's leisurely motions. But it was only the first rehearsal.

"Overall, nice read for the first run-through," Mr. Clark told
them. "Nice playing."

After making their first bit of music, Mr. Clark took care of
some business. "Congratulations on making the Big Band. There
were sixty people who auditioned for these spots." He elevated a
list of the members of the 2012 Big Band. "Why am I holding this
in front of you?"

Kyle, a curly-haired, eager-to-please seventh-grade trumpet
player, offered, "Because we have to work hard to make it to get to
2013?"

"Yes!" Referencing the dozens of students who didn't make the
elite band, many of whom opted to play with the Stage Band—a
jazz band which took all comers and rehearsed on Monday and
Wednesday mornings before school—Mr. Clark said he had a deep
bench of reserves from which to pull if the current Big Band members
didn't pull their weight. "If you're not gonna work, I'm gonna make
them happy."

"We have a huge amount of potential," Mr. Clark continued,
pausing before he read aloud from the "Hard Work" poster hanging
in the room. "I am going to push you and push you and push you.
Sometimes, I won't be your favorite person in the world. And that's
okay."

Very briefly, he gestured in my direction and explained why I'd
be attending their rehearsals and performances, leaving out the fact
that my son was one of the Big Band drummers, before quickly
swerving back to the music, to "Groovin' Hard." He asked them to
half-say, half-sing the first three notes of the piece, *Dat-dat-dat*. A
handful shyly complied but many sat in awkward silence and moved
their lips without actually making sounds.

Mr. Clark asked if the group knew who the Sonic Lords of
Death were. Dark-haired Patrick—seventh-grade lead trumpet player
who lingered in the shadow of his older brother, a wildly talented
musician—suggested that the Sonic Lords were the trumpet players
in the back of the band room, at the farthest spot away from Mr.

Clark. He was correct.

"Would you be afraid of a Sonic Lord of Death who played like this?" Mr. Clark asked as he hunched his shoulders, drew them inward toward his chest, slouched, ducked his head and pulled his elbows to his sides, pretending to play an imaginary trumpet with the bell end pointing toward the floor. He contrasted that petrified-looking posture with the one he wanted to see from his Big Band Lords. He stood up tall—as tall as his 5-foot-8 middle-aged frame would allow him—his shoulders pulled back, his head up and the bell of his pretend trumpet aloft at a 45-degree angle like he was signaling the arrival of a queen. "I need power!" Mr. Clark bellowed, eyeing the very young trumpet section as a few of the students tried to hide behind their music stands. Some weren't all that much taller than the stands. They had heard all about Mr. Clark's propensity to holler with a sound that seemed to come from the tips of his toes and gained velocity as it traveled upward, bursting forth from his mouth as though electrically amplified.

Mr. Clark turned his sights to the large, all-male saxophone section. "I'm gonna need attitude ... like the coolest person you've ever known." Ethan smiled knowingly.

The band played "Groovin' Hard" for a second time. To empha-size certain notes, Mr. Clark jabbed his finger into the air so hard that if someone had been in the way, his jabbing would've left a bruise. He stopped the band before they got to the end of the piece. First of all, Mr. Clark said, the ends of the trumpets weren't pointed up toward him so he couldn't hear them. Second, he told Noah, the drummer on this piece, to *Boom-BAM!* more forcefully on the down-beat. "The drummer's job is to set it up."

When the students went home, their job was to work on the notes, Mr. Clark said. Learning their individual parts would have to be done on their own time, not during band rehearsals. He urged them to practice.

He slid into motivational mode: "Sixth graders, you are not sixth graders. You are members of the Big Band. Don't be afraid of those eighth graders in the band because I'm much meaner than them." In what would become a pattern—have the kids play music, throw out advice and encouragement, toss in a little news, joke around, then go back to the music and provide tough criticism—Mr. Clark returned to another section of "Groovin' Hard" and asked them to tackle it with verve. They played it substantially better, more as a unit than they had at the beginning of the rehearsal. As they reached the piece's crescendo, Mr. Clark did a little dance: in a half-crouch position, he bounced his upper body up and down, extended his right index finger out and moved it in a circle as if he was winding a temperamental crank-start car. He said he would look silly if they didn't crescendo at the moment he cued them to crescendo. And he didn't want to look silly, at least not for that reason.

Mr. Clark zoomed to another topic, like he was trying to stuff months of knowledge and advice into the kids in fifty minutes. "What happens in the band room stays in the band room," Mr. Clark read from another one of the posters in the room, where "stays" is twice the size of the other letters. That segued into his plea for them to signal to him if an adult entered the band room because his back was usually facing the door. Mr. Clark tended to say a lot of things he would prefer that people not hear out of context. Context was everything when it came to understanding Mr. Clark. The kids nodded in solemn agreement. They were making a pact.

They played "Groovin' Hard" a third time. Mr. Clark turned his conducting into an aerobic activity. When the drummer struck or the sax players were supposed to punctuate a note, he punched in the air like a boxer. Air punches equaled musical punches, fierce emphasis. When they finished the three-and-a-half-minute piece, he made suggestions for tweaks and techniques, however several students just sat there, immobile. Mr. Clark noticed this and asked them to write down his chestnuts of melodic wisdom. In pencil. Pencil was key. Pen was permanent. There was nothing permanent in music, thus the pencil. Which could be erased when the conductor changed his mind. Nearly all the saxophonists sheepishly confessed they didn't have pencils with them. "Go get them!" Mr. Clark said. The boys silently fetched their writing implements from the backpacks they'd thrown atop one of the many blue plastic chairs at the front of the room.

As the band took another shot at "Groovin' Hard," Mr. Clark

took to stomping his right foot like an angry horse and clapping so hard that his palms turned cherry red. "You've got to build it and then come crashing in. You want the audience to be surprised that you've still got the capacity to create such volume at the end of the song."

Frighteningly red in the face, Mr. Clark wound up his imaginary crank-car again with his right hand and roared, *Whoooah!* as "Groovin' Hard" hit its crescendo. But Mr. Clark wasn't satisfied. Their playing had no oomph; it was bloodless, he said, while his own blood poured into his ruddy face. He had them play the last note. Four times in a row. "Hit it harder! Harder!" By the fourth try, the students finally concluded the song with the auditory punctuation their director was seeking. They were spent and Mr. Clark was winded.

Having exhausted himself with "Groovin' Hard," Mr. Clark asked the students to tune up again before their second piece. A minute or so went by—a chance for the kids to catch their breath—before Mr. Clark distributed the sheet music for "Dat Dere," a 1960 Bobby Timmons tune rearranged in 2011 by composer Erik Morales. There was mass confusion. While the conductor's score, which contained all the instruments' measures, was on Mr. Clark's music stand, the students were only supposed to have the sheet music for their specific instruments. The process of handing out music was proving difficult and took longer than the impatient Mr. Clark had expected as students shuffled the papers at a glacial pace. Although the kids seemed older when they played jazz with attitude, they were really young and not necessarily as on top of things as Mr. Clark might have wanted them to be, like being able to easily hand trumpet sheet music to trumpet players and not to sax players.

Once the "Dat Dere" parts were resting on the correct music stands, Mr. Clark cued them to sight-read it. The only thing that emerged from their instruments was a jumble of auditory soup. Very quickly, he called a halt to their playing. Curious students who had just arrived to school wandered down the Music Department hallway and peeked into the band room to see what all the noise was, something that proved distracting to the Big Band members. Mr. Clark focused his attention on the flute and saxophone players, urging them to tap into the feel of the music. "Technically, this is a very hard piece," Mr. Clark told me. "It changes color from light, or bright, and dark. It's big. It's warm, enveloping sound."

As he prepared to close the first rehearsal, Mr. Clark gave them their assignments, to be completed in less than twenty-four hours: practice all of "Groovin' Hard" and the first forty measures of "Dat Dere." Sensing the students were starting to tune him out—they were already jamming papers into folders—he raised his voice, "Write this down! Everybody, write this down!"

Surveying the group, Mr. Clark realized that Jesse, the gifted eighth-grade guitarist, did not have a pencil. In fact, Jesse hadn't been writing anything down throughout the entire rehearsal, despite the saxophonists' earlier walk of shame. "Jesse!" he shouted. Blushing deeply, Jesse—a solidly-built kid who would go on to play freshman football and focus seriously on music—made his way out of the back of the band formation, squeezed around the drums and the bassist, passed behind the piano player as he skulked over to his backpack which was slumped on the floor against the metal instrument cages. Although he did get a pencil, the likelihood that he would actually write anything down when he was behind his music stand, which also shielded him from the eagle-eyed gaze of his band director, was slim. Throughout the year, he did a lot of pretend-writing in the back row.

"Frank Sinatra," Mr. Clark continued, as if the interlude while waiting for Jesse to get a pencil never happened. "Count Basie. B-A-S-I-E. Write it down! Write it down!"

Despite the repeated emphasis on note-taking, some students were still ignoring him and not writing down his directives. This caused Mr. Clark to grow ominously quiet. "We are *not* having this conversation after today," he said. "You. *Will*. Have. Pencils." He paused. "Big Phat—P-H-A-T—Band. Why am I telling you to write this down? Part of your job is to start listening to this music. These musicians will be exemplars, awesome examples of what we're trying to do."

With a few moments remaining, Mr. Clark decided to have one more go at "Dat Dere," during which they fared slightly better than they had all morning. About a third of the way into the song, he stopped them and asked them to pick it up at a later spot. He stopped them again. The band was a stalling car. Mr. Clark didn't explain why he was starting and stopping at all these intervals, but it appeared as though he was calculating, measuring and assessing the music, trying to figure out who and what was off, who and what was on, and where the strengths and weaknesses were.

Now they heard his assessment of their first hour of work together as the 2012-13 Big Band, the band in mourning, the band trying to get past its sorrow by making music together. On "Groovin' Hard:" "It's not anywhere close to where we want it to be." However, Mr. Clark admitted it was "pretty good." "You're here to make music at the highest level you can reach," he told them, reminding them that for the next rehearsal he wanted them in the band room at 6:50 a.m. with sharpened pencils in hand. Although the end of the rehearsal had grown somewhat tense, band members lingered instead of heading directly to home room. They chatted or played riffs on the piano and guitar. They wanted to joke around with their band director. "Goodbye!" Mr. Clark said sternly, like he was giving the boot to particularly tenacious members of a fan club. He pointed to the double doors, "Goodbye!"

Mr. Clark was wearing baggy jeans and a gray, zip-up fleece, looking as relaxed as his faded denim, much more so than yesterday. Kids were shuffling in, looking and sounding tired. And it was only the second day of rehearsal. They were still in summer mode where they could sleep in late. Guitarist Jesse was the last to arrive, traipsing in at a little after 7:15.

He cued them to play "Groovin' Hard" and slapped his hands together—his right hand thundering down onto his left as he leaned his torso to the side so that he resembled a human question mark. The clapping seemed to serve dual purposes, to help them keep the right tempo ("so they internalize it") and to wake them up.

It accomplished neither.

One look at the green trumpet section—only one eighth grader among them, Eric would have been the other eighth-grade trumpet player—standing atop the scuffed-up wooden risers, would say as much. The inexperienced group seemed to be shrinking behind their music stands, shoulders curled forward, heads down. Some of them were so diminutive that I could only see eyes and the tops of their bed-head hair above their stands. Their timidity made them appear even smaller. They were aiming the bells of their trumpets at the floor, driving their music into the ground.

This would not do. Not for Mr. Clark. And not for "Groovin' Hard," a loud, aggressive swing tune that called for the trumpets to really earn the moniker which Mr. Clark had bestowed upon them: the Sonic Lords of Death. He encouraged them to pull their bodies upward and erect, to confidently plant their feet about hips' distance apart, pull their shoulder blades back and hoist their trumpet bells upward, toward the back of the room, explaining that the sound would go wherever the bells were aimed.

"Make sense?" he asked to no one in particular, waiting for someone, anyone, to just nod or say, "Yes" so he could continue.

The next run-through only made it a few measures further than the first dive into the piece. Mr. Clark stopped them with a wave of his right hand, like he was lazily shooing away an annoying fly. He grimly stood in front of them. He was silent. When Mr. Clark is silent, students tend to pay attention. His silence is as loud a message as his normal bellowing. After taking a swig of coffee from his travel mug, he aimed his annoyed bright blue eyes through his wire-rimmed glasses at them and asked the children to pick it up at measure 86. "I'm glad we had that conversation," he grumbled.

This time, the trumpets—several of which bore thin, emerald green memorial ribbons—improved. Incremental improvement. At least they weren't blowing the horns directly into the music stands, though they were still hunched over and weren't very loud. "Groovin' Hard" required volume. Searching for an approach that would get through to the students in that section, Mr. Clark ripped off his fleece, even though it was chilly in the room. (Throughout the year, I would learn, the room was a veritable ice box as Mr. Clark's internal thermostat ran hot.) He tossed his fleece onto an empty stand, where it promptly slipped off and fell to the floor. He left it there. In his clunky brown hiking boots, he trekked to the center of the room and cupped his hands around his ears, shouting to the trumpets that they had to be louder. Mr. Clark stood, left hand curled in front of his mouth, and tapped his left foot as if testing to see if they were keeping up the proper tempo. Without warning, he darted to another part of the room to assess … something. What he was assessing? No one was quite sure. Volume? Sound quality? The feel of the bass guitar?

Then he revealed the answer: He couldn't hear the saxophone section because the rhythm folks—the drummer, the guitarist, the bassist and the pianist—were too loud. Mr. Clark waited for them to write down on their sheet music that they had to dial back the volume. When it finally dawned on the kids in the rhythm section that he was waiting for *them* to note his words of wisdom on the paper in front of them, everyone but the guitarist complied. Jesse didn't have a pencil. Again.

"Rehearsal starts at seven. With a pencil. At seven," Mr. Clark said pointedly, arching one of his salt-and-pepper-colored eyebrows.

He unceremoniously shifted from the swinging beats of "Groovin' Hard" to the icy measures of "Dat Dere," a funky jazz tune with an emphasis on the jazz flute section and playful piano riffs. But first, the middle schoolers had to sit back and listen to a recording of the piece, actively listen, Mr. Clark admonished. "Focus on the music, not the holes in the ceiling," he said, recounting one student who once spent study hall trying to tally the number of holes in the ceiling. The story, meant to entertain, only served to distract the students as they started debating how long it would take to get an accurate count of the tiny marks in drop-ceiling tiles in any given room. This would become routine, this tendency of Mr. Clark to use humorous tales—frequently about bodily functions, poking fun at himself or relating some bizarre bit of trivia—to break the tension and relax the students, something he hoped would transfer to their playing. This particular band required, he would learn, more comic relief than prior ensembles. Though he typically arrived at rehearsals with a list of goals he wanted to achieve, sometimes his aim was to keep his students "loose and confused. That makes the kids pay attention because they don't know what's coming next." More often than not, they went on discombobulated tangents that twisted and weaved around and between topics that took them far afield from the original anecdote Mr. Clark shared with his pupils.

Mr. Clark cranked "Dat Dere" on his iPod, animatedly directing Art Blakey & the Jazz Messengers, if only in his imagination, as the group listened to the piece they were to play. Finally, at 7:37, after having been in rehearsal for thirty-seven minutes, the kids were awake. The volume they created with their first "Dat Dere" run-through was stronger than it had been with "Groovin' Hard," though they weren't playing together and their timing was noticeably off.

"Bracket it," Mr. Clark said, voice gravelly as he pointed at the sheet music on the stand in front of him. Most, but not all of the students marked the measures where they'd been having trouble on their sheet music with the requisite brackets. He suddenly pivoted from issuing directives to a playful riff: There was something about "Dat Dere," something about its slinky, playful beginning that he said reminded him of the Pink Panther sneaking around, or perhaps a cat burglar of some sort, plotting to scale roofs before stealing jewels.

"Why a cat?" asked Ashley, a seventh-grade flutist with a long mane of blond hair who was struggling with her music stand, which kept sinking lower than she needed it to be.

Sharing his first authentic laugh with the select band in which he had so much hope and optimism, Mr. Clark pantomimed being an abnormally large, slightly frightening cat, tip-pawing around, its front paws up in the air over its head, although it was hard to imagine Mr. Clark being able to slink any place with a hushed feline dexterity. Hushed. Dexterity. Didn't really scream Mr. Clark.

CHAPTER THREE

Every Note Matters

|: As soon as I turned the corner, veered away from the administrative offices, and passed the auditorium, I entered the Music Department wing on the second week of Big Band rehearsal. I could hear it before I could see it. Unlike during the first day of Big Band rehearsals, when I simply heard music blaring from the band room once I was about a third of the way down the hall, today, I could hear the hodgepodge of notes like a wall of sound, students warming up, competing with the various jazz selections coming from Mr. Clark's iPod.

Mr. Clark commenced the class by belting out, "Good morning!" to the students.

Indecipherable murmurs.

"Good morning!" he shouted at a louder volume.

He was getting frustrated now. "Good! Morning!"

Finally, they responded in kind.

Satisfied, Mr. Clark said simply, "Groovin' Hard." Within ten seconds, they began to play. It was not to his liking. "No bell! No bell! No bell!" he barked. "And that's not a prize!" The wisecrack went over their heads. The trumpet players had the bells of their trumpets pointing downward again, apparently having forgotten all about the directives about standing tall and pointing the ends of their trumpets up and out.

At 7:07, already annoyed, Mr. Clark roughly wriggled out of his dark gray pull-over and then spotted Ethan, the lead sax player, holding a pen, precariously close to putting ink on the sheet music on the stand in front of him. With surprising swiftness, the stout Mr. Clark snatched the pen from Ethan's hand and, without looking, hurled it over his right shoulder to the other side of the room where it landed beneath a chair and slid into the base of a music stand. "Go. Get. A. *Pencil*."

Mr. Clark had a thing about pens and sheet music. To me— someone who ducked when he tossed the pen across the room, worried that he'd forgotten I was sitting behind him—his antipathy against the implement I held in my own hand, poised over my note-book was a mystery. Had he spilled ink on a trombone in his past? Had a bad experience with a pen and a tux? Had he been doused with ink in a prank gone awry? Later he told me, unconvincingly, that having the kids use pencils was simply a matter of pragmatism. As the students became more comfortable with playing a piece, he tended to change the directions he gave them on this measure or that measure. Without the ability to erase his earlier suggestions, the sheet music would become an indecipherable mess. However, during the entire year I followed the Big Band, I would never once hear him tell anyone to erase anything from their sheet music. At the end of the year, when I looked at some students' sheet music, they were covered in indecipherable pencil markings that looked thoroughly confusing.

Ethan's pen hurling through the air, however, was the least of the Big Band's worries on this particular morning early in the school year. To determine who had practiced over the weekend and who didn't, Mr. Clark went over measures instrumental section by instrumental section. Saxophones. Trumpets. Other brass. Flutes and clarinets (although there was hardly ever a problem with this all-female section of the band, other than over-exuberant chatting). Rhythm. This was a surprisingly effective yet painful exercise, nakedly exposing which section was in serious need of practice. The result of his examination: the sax section needed a lot of work.

It was 7:10 by the time guitarist Jesse arrived, three rehearsals in a row in which he was late. "Make sure you have a real pencil this time," Mr. Clark said to the kid who didn't have a pencil during prior rehearsals. (Jesse later admitted that he never wrote anything down on his music the whole year. Did Mr. Clark know this? What would he have done had he discovered that not just Jesse, but several members of the Big Band pretended to write notes on their sheet music when he ordered, "Mark it in" or "bracket it"? I didn't want to narc on the kids—I was observing their year, not their teacher—so I didn't tell him until the academic year ended. Upon being told this, he burst out laughing.)

The section that had clearly practiced "Groovin' Hard": Rhythm. Throwing both of his arms out to the side as though he were air-hugging the pianist, bass player, guitar player and drummer, Mr. Clark cooed, "One of the best rhythm sections in New England! ... And they look *fabulous*!"

Not so much the rest of them. "Some of you don't know this piece," he said portentously. "You're faking it. I can tell." This was a Mr. Clark tactic I noticed fairly quickly: playing sections against one another and trying to foster the idea that when one section failed to flourish, their lack of effort reflected back on the entire group. *Team*, he would tell them, *we are a team. Don't let the team down.*

As he ordered the band members to practice over the next couple of days—except if they were going to be celebrating the Jewish high holidays in a temple, of which maybe a handful would—Mr. Clark spied a pen in Jesse's hand. Sometimes it seemed as though Jesse was oblivious. *Hadn't Mr. Clark just made a theatrical point about pens the other day? He mentioned having a pencil when Jesse came in late,* I thought as I watched Mr. Clark push his way to the back row where the red-headed guitarist was nestled among the back window, the drums and the trumpet section. He snatched the pen out of Jesse's pale, freckled hand and threw it across the room, but this time, he was facing in my direction and threw it overhand so I didn't have to worry about being hit in the eye. *Was this for my benefit?* I asked myself. I couldn't tell if this is how Mr. Clark always behaved or whether this was because I was in the room. The students would later say he always acted like this.

"Get a pencil," Mr. Clark said calmly as he made his way back to the front of the group, to his perch on the gray metal stool that he stole from the Tech Ed room. "*Real* musicians mark everything in."

And after the praise he'd lavished upon the rhythm section, Mr. Clark blamed Jesse for holding up rehearsal, and said several sections, the brass in particular, had fumbled through the measures and were in dire need of practice.

Although the school year was still young, Mr. Clark wanted to set the tone. *You're in the Big Band. This is voluntary. You practice. You learn the music. You do your part for the team. You don't let your section down.* Thus the rationale for the grilling that the trumpet section received next. He asked each individual trumpet player to play measures. One. By. One. Mr. Clark tried to never call the students by name when he did this. He used their position names instead, like "third trumpet," "second trumpet" and so on. It made for an uncomfortable few moments, listening to the squeaking and squawking of mangled notes made by blushing children who had not yet practiced. I felt badly for the kids, particularly the sixth graders who tried to hide their crimson faces behind their instrument and music stands. By the time he reached the third and fourth trumpet players, it was clear that, overall, the trumpet section did not know the piece. Mr. Clark was silent for a moment.

"You musically pants-ed them," he finally told the wayward trumpeters, referring to the rest of the band whose sound they were affecting. "I will continue to pick on the trumpets ... You can't hide and you can't fake it in this band."

With that, he moved their attentions to "Dat Dere." But first, he offered an apparently random critique of pop music, calling it unsophisticated, consisting of only two speeds. "It typically only has two emotions," Mr. Clark said. Anger: his eyes went wide as he angrily screamed, "Argh!!" Love: he wrapped himself in a self-embrace, closed his eyes and smiled. With jazz, however, "every emotion is at one's disposal. I like pop music," he said, as his gigantic playlist—over 6,000 songs—on his iPod could attest, 473 of which were cotton candy-ish pop songs and 1,100 were rock. "I like ice cream, too. Clearly." He put his hands on his belly, which was not large, but not flat either, kind of Philip Seymour Hoffman-esque. Mr. Clark kept all that energy, enthusiasm and insanity packed within a dense frame fueled by vast quantities of caffeine and sugary junk his students gave him.

As the middle schoolers delved into the music, the trumpets meandered, as if lost, awash in discordant notes. Several trumpet bells were pointed toward their music stands. From my seat off to the side of the band room, I wanted to remind them, *Put your bells up! He's told you numerous times!* But I was only an observer and shook my head as I waited for the inevitable boom to be lowered on their heads by Mr. Clark. If I was already getting impatient with their failure to lift their bells up, to be on time, to bring in pencils and not pens, I could only imagine how Mr. Clark must have felt.

Meanwhile, the brass and trombonists were having difficulties articulating their notes. Much to their embarrassment, Mr. Clark insisted that the members of the brass section *say* their notes aloud, *Dat-dah, dah, dah, dat!* After that tutorial, the group sounded more cohesive, at least timing-wise. "I'd rather the notes be wrong and the rhythm be right," Mr. Clark said. "Now go home and learn those notes."

But the brass and trumpets weren't alone in the difficulty they had with the material. The sax players weren't together either and, given the prominent place the saxophones had in the groovy tune, it was extremely noticeable, even to neophyte musical ears like mine. "Didn't I ask you guys to work on that for this time?" Mr. Clark snapped. "It's gotta be better than *that!*"

Maybe it was something in the way he said "that." He did it with a little twang, like a teenager mocking an adult. It prompted ill-advised laughter among some in the back row. "No!" Mr. Clark growled. "That's not funny. Bad music," he paused for effect, "is *never* funny." And he meant it. The room was silent.

I squirmed in my seat. *If this was how the rehearsals are going to be, it's going to be a long year*, I thought.

At the end of the session, he distributed two new pieces, Brad Zvacek's "Back to the Basement" and Frank Sinatra's "Fly Me to the Moon," a song that, a year later, Mr. Clark would say the Big Band was never really able to capture, despite the fact that Mr. Clark worshipped Sinatra and played the crooner's version repeatedly in the band room.

"You need to make sure you listen to 'Fly Me to the Moon,' the Mark Taylor arrangement, particularly with the sax," he suggested. "We've got some of the best arrangements out there. ... And don't try to play the piece faster than it is meant to be played."

"Back to the Basement," by contrast to "Fly Me to the Moon," is a shuffle, he declared, a type of swing music that's very laid-back, and whose tone is hands-in-your-pockets/I'm-totally-all-that. (Between "Back to the Basement" and "Groovin' Hard," those two summed Mr. Clark's predominant personality traits. It was only once you got to know him and were privy to his inner softie that his affection for sentimental pieces like "Fly Me to the Moon" made sense.) The students needed to know the difference between the feel of the two pieces and they needed to know it by the next rehearsal. In two days.

♪

Early in the 2011-12 school year, Mr. Clark told his students, "Everything I say is profound, funny or profoundly funny." Therefore, he reasoned, someone should write down everything he said. Then-eighth-graders Emily Gordon, Riley Casey and Christina Forrest did just that. Here are some of the best ones from the 728 quotes they gathered in the Trottier band room.

o The more I yell, the more I love. It is kinda sick and twisted isn't it?

o I have never actually eaten a kid.

o Where's my coffee?

o Do any of you ever hear a voice in your head? [Students reply, "Yes."] Has it ever sounded like me? ["Yes."] Now you should be really scared.

o Be careful what you wish for, because you might just get it. You might have a new band director tomorrow.

o Soft and gentle don't have to go together. I'm neither.

o I have a faculty meeting later and I'm not allowed to sit near Mr. Griffin any more.

o Seven-oh-seven a.m. and I'm already a jerk.

o I am amplified and I am not using a microphone.

o I ate a lot of pizza and candy. Now I'm ready.

o If I was looking for perfection I would look in the mirror.

o Music is the endless pursuit of perfection.

o Less talk, more tune.

o Can you believe I get paid for this?

o I'm not as evil as people say I am.

o This is me, short and fat. This is Mr. Felo [a gym teacher], long and loud. What's Mr. Griffin [a math teacher]? He is x and no one cares what x is.

o "Sweet, gentle, caring." Doesn't sound like you're describing me.

o Do you often just randomly fall over?

o There are many things that I do better than you.

o Better teaching through insults.

o Embrace the weirdness. ... I'm not asking for a hug.

- Now play it so the old, deaf lady can hear it.

- I love animals. [Big pause. Some kids say, "Aww!"] They are tasty.

- Early is on time.

- There is no running in the band room.

- Is that decaf?

- That's what I do. I squash dreams.

- I've never worn contacts because I'll poke my eye. Eye jelly. It tastes like strawberry.

- There's a whole lot of attitude up there with nothing to back it up.

- Trombone players aren't afraid of trumpets, but they run in terror from piccolo players.

- When I say I teach middle school, people either take a step back or say, "Poor you."

- You hear that music right? … Okay, I don't have to boost my medication.

- Just do it my way. There might be a better way, but it's unlikely.

- I'd be a really bad mime.

- A dot is short, like me.

- Come to my concert. You'll see the whole symphony orchestra accompanying me.

o I'm in shape. Circle is a shape.

o Oxygen would be good now.

o My cat came back to life again.

o If you hit one out of every three balls in your baseball career, you get into the Hall of Fame, but if you play one out of every three notes correctly, you are an awful musician.

o Finja = fat ninja = me!

o Without the earth, I wouldn't get sandwiches.

o I'm so tired of my own voice right now.

o More Rottweiler, less Chihuahua.

o I know you came here for the bad jokes.

o I'm comfortable with you people being mad at me.

o Coda: Yoda's little brother.

o [Coughs loudly.] Hairball! I ate my cat ... no, she only weighs, like three pounds. Not even a meal.

Reservoirs cover about a quarter of Southborough, which boasts an abundance of stone walls and rolling country sides adjacent to residential neighborhoods. New developments of single-family colonial homes dot the landscape, usually set back away from extremely narrow, rural roads. Mailboxes that sit on the end of driveways frequently become casualties of snow plows which accidentally run them down during New England winters. Two interstate highways slash through the town, the north-south I-495 and the east-west Massachusetts Turnpike (I-90), not including the east-west Route 9 which creates a barrier between the north and south sides of town. Families of wild turkeys are fond of loitering in the middle of Main Street when they're not fleeing the random coyotes or occasional fisher cats that amble through town. A granite marker stands in the center of the town, a silent testament to the fact that General Henry Knox traveled through Southborough to transport artillery from New York to Boston during the Revolutionary War.

As of 2014, Southborough had seventeen restaurants, a yoga studio, two fitness centers, three spa/salons, two public golf courses, a used car lot and a Cadillac and a Volvo dealership. There were three private schools (one for autistic students), four public schools and six churches (two of them Catholic) in a town that likes to get together and celebrate. There's an annual jack-o-lantern event held during Columbus Day weekend where residents place their carved gourds atop the historic stone wall that surrounds the colonial-era cemetery in the town center and then return, hours later, after volunteers light all the candles. Annually two parades—for Memorial Day and for Heritage Day, Southborough's birthday— take over the town's streets, in addition to a Thanksgiving morning 5K called the Gobble Wobble. There's an annual fireworks display, Summer Nights, on the grounds adjacent to the Neary Elementary School, usually preceded by a concert and booths selling fair food.

The image of Southborough, established in 1727 and home to nearly 10,000, is one of a sleepy suburb, nestled between Worcester and Boston, with its own stop on the east-west commuter rail. The community is located along the outer rim of Route 495 that hugs Boston in a wide "C," making Southborough more of an exurb of Boston—twenty-five miles west of it—than a suburb of it. Many perceive this town as a place to hang your hat en route to Boston, particularly those professional, white collar workers who overrun this once-thriving farming community. These days, Southborough is often labeled affluent, given that per capita income exceeds $100,000, as compared to the rest of Massachusetts citizens whose per capita income was $67,000, according to 2014 government data. (The nation's was at $52,000.) In 2009, CNNMoney.com named

Southborough the 31st best American small town.

Its residents cotton to Southborough's deep Yankee roots, celebrating the fact that all of its 7,000+ eligible voters can participate in its open town meetings held each spring in the Trottier Middle School auditorium (where Mr. Clark, who does not live in town, runs the AV equipment), where folks vote on things like the municipal budget, although only a couple hundred usually show up, despite the promise of an open microphone where voters can speak directly to town leaders. It's at these town meetings where one can catch a glimpse of the changing nature of its residents, with the "townies" who speak with hard Boston accents, dwindling in numbers. Town meeting members might spend an hour debating an issue worth a few thousand dollars "on principle," but then approve a multi-million-dollar school budget with minimal discussion.

Southborough is an overwhelmingly white community—89 percent white, 9.5 percent Asian, 1.2 percent African-American and 1 percent other races, according to federal statistics. It has a vocal and very active group of parents who populate the volunteer ranks of the town's vigorously competitive youth sports leagues—soccer, baseball, football, lacrosse, hockey and basketball—and run the Southborough Organization for Schools (SOS) events. The biggest population group in town, in 2010, consisted of people in their mid-to-late 40s, many of whom live in the community's single-family homes, ranging from modest ranch homes and newer colonials, to some palatial manses on the north side of town on streets like Sears Road and Presidential Drive.

When it comes to politics, nearly 60 percent of Southborough's voters are not registered with any political party—unenrolled is the official designation, with a capital "U" on the voter lists—though residents oftentimes vote more conservatively than those in other Bay State communities. For example, in 2012, Southborough narrowly voted to reelect President Barack Obama instead of putting former Massachusetts governor Mitt Romney in the White House; however, town voters wanted to see Republican Scott Brown reelected to his U.S. Senate post instead of the victorious challenger, Democrat Elizabeth Warren. That year, Southborough voted in favor of legalizing physician-assisted suicide although the rest of the state's voters rejected it.

When it comes to education, parents flood into town meetings to make sure that the school budget is passed unscathed so they can assure that Southborough schools excel. On Massachusetts' standardized tests, known as the MCAS (Massachusetts Comprehensive Assessment System), the town's students fare much better than the state averages. In 2014, Southborough's elementary and middle school students scored about 20 points higher than students across Massachusetts. For example, by eighth grade, 91 percent achieved advanced or proficient scores in English, contrasted with 79 percent in the state. By the time Southborough's students are ready for high school, they can attend the Algonquin Regional High School in the neighboring and larger community of Northborough, where the student body exceeds 1,400. The home of the Tomahawks—the T-Hawks—was named one of *Boston Magazine's* top 50 public high schools. In 2014, *U.S. News & World Report* ranked Algonquin number 502 nationally and 23rd in the state, noting that 100 percent of Algonquin's tenth graders were proficient in English and 96 percent were proficient in math. However, if Southborough students don't opt to attend Algonquin, they attend one of the many private or charter schools in the greater Boston area, including the famed St. Mark's boarding school whose campus dominates Southborough's downtown area and serves as the staging ground for Southborough's Heritage Day festival each fall.

Southborough is a small enough community that social circles tend to overlap like a Venn diagram. Among parents of school-aged children, particularly if those children play on town sports teams or participate in extracurricular activities together (band, Boy or Girl Scouts, dance, gymnastics, religious school), many know one another. If a dad runs into another father whom he hasn't met, chances are, he knows another father or mother who knows this guy. At times, it can seem almost claustrophobic.

This building of a band, building the camaraderie, building the trust and cultivating an atmosphere of excellence within a safe place in which students could express emotions, took time. It felt like an eternity to me as I silently wished the kids would just do what Mr. Clark asked. For the first several weeks of rehearsal, there was a lot of the same old, same old: drilling the musicians, section by section or child by child if need be, to drive home the point that not only did they need to learn their parts, but that they couldn't or shouldn't let their bandmates down. Forcing the children to play alone and to show the rest of the group their weakness and their lack of dedication was a painful yet necessary part of the process.

At exactly 7 o'clock, Mr. Clark cued the saxophone section of the Big Band—the only section that was there in its entirety as other band members were still arriving on the last Friday of September—to start "Dat Dere." The results weren't terrible. Mr. Clark had them work on their precision, go through measures boy by boy, as there were only boys in the sax section. "That's not anywhere close, gentlemen," he said, shaking his head.

Flutes—who had a starring role in this song whereas in other songs were largely overshadowed— were next. As usual, the section shined. Their precision was razor sharp. They beamed under Mr. Clark's adulation. If only the rest of the sections were like their section. When it was the trumpets' turn to demonstrate where they were in "Dat Dere," I braced myself. Thankfully, they were significantly stronger than they had been. Several players, though not all, had their bells up nice and high.

At 7:12, when Mr. Clark was telling band members not to noticeably react if someone makes an error during a performance because the audience likely wouldn't notice, Jesse crept into the room, late again. He was already blushing, but at least he had a pencil in one hand, his guitar in the other.

"Jesse, I want you to see me after practice."

Mr. Clark took another approach with the Sonic Lords and Lady of Death today: confidence building. Praise was effusive, maybe because they hadn't booted their playing of "Dat Dere" and had earned it. He told them there was a "whole world of difference from yesterday to today." Even when they missed notes or cues, he did not appear irritated, although he did comment on the miscues matter-of-factly, "I can tell if you practiced because if you practiced, you play it with confidence."

Instead, Mr. Clark directed his critiques to the saxophones, to Josh, the sturdy, shaggy-haired brunette, eighth-grade baritone sax player, who also played as a lineman on the local youth football team. Although very quiet during rehearsals, on occasion he would come up with some oddball non sequiturs. Josh wasn't playing with much power this morning, at least not enough for Mr. Clark's taste who liked his Big Band music loud most of the time.

"That might work for a band made up of mere mortals," he told Josh, "but not this one." Pointing to Harry—the tall, thin, redheaded, popular-but-reserved tenor sax player—who was sitting next to Josh, Mr. Clark said, "When I look over, I should see a little blood coming out of Harry's ear." After the next run-through, Mr. Clark put his hand on Harry's chin, gently turned Harry's head away from Josh to "look" for blood. He dramatically shook his head "no" when he didn't find any. It was somewhat unsettling to have a forty-something man who looked like Santa Claus, with his prematurely whitened beard, encouraging one child to make another's ears bleed.

"How good was it at rehearsal?" he joked. "People were bleeding. Yeah, man."

This was the first time a rehearsal had an air of comfort with no edginess. The man who stood in front of them was starting to once again resemble the good-natured Mr. Clark of legend, the one who students adored enough to came back to Trottier, many years after leaving, to visit and wrap in a tight embrace. Here was the infamous sense of humor, that warmth. While he was always generous, kind, open and wittily funny with me, I hadn't yet seen him fully allow himself to show this part of his personality to his Big Band this year. He seemed, during this rehearsal, as if he had consciously granted himself permission to just be himself, more like Mr. Clark than a band director who had to whip the band into shape, a drill sergeant during boot camp. The kids didn't seem to be gripping their instruments in a terrified hold. They held them assuredly, even when they moved to "Fly Me to the Moon," the mood remained loose.

Through a series of funny faces and hammy voices, Mr. Clark played the Sinatra recording again and told them to pay close attention while listening to recordings of Sinatra's smooth ode to a lover, to realize that they needed to play together and listen to one another. "If you don't do it together, it sounds like one of the sax players has diarrhea," he joked.

He put his hands to his cheeks, in an almost bashful fashion, and extolled the virtues of Sinatra, the musician: "Frank Sinatra was the best musician because everything that came out of his face had a purpose ... If you want to be a great musician you need to study Frank Sinatra."

Things got even stranger than mentioning diarrhea in the same breath as Sinatra and telling an eighth grader to make a classmate's ear start bleeding. Rapper Flo Rida started to boom from the speakers. Flo. Rida. During Big Band rehearsal. Mr. Clark, who'd just moments prior been waxing poetic about Sinatra, started to dance to the popular song, "Low," one of those terribly awkward dances you might see a drunk uncle do at a niece's wedding, his hands elevated above his head while all the youngsters in the room cringed with embarrassment. The students buzzed with a "What will he do next?" excitement. Mr. Clark grinned broadly, his fluffy, steely gray and white hair not moving an inch while the rest of his body bobbed around haphazardly. The strains of the rapper were abruptly replaced by the gentle rap of a drum, tweeting flutes and slick, sultry vocals. He'd switched over to "Fly Me to the Moon." On top volume. The girls in the clarinet and flute section giggled, amused. At this moment, Mr. Clark was simultaneously a performer, teacher, musician and court jester. When the song ended, he bowed at the waist, then rose upright and slowly raised his arms over his head. Whatever it took to reel them in, to connect, to team-build, to practice, to trust.

CHAPTER FOUR

Origin Story

Jamie Clark aspires to be the human equivalent of LinkedIn. He works to draw all of his worlds together—childhood friends, colleagues, former students, band parents—into one, big melting pot. His wife Colleen, a quiet homebody, says he's "the master of small talk," one of "those people who can walk into a crowded room, not know anyone in the room, and walk out with ten friends." He's most at home when he has people surrounding him and who are laughing at his jokes.

Though his oldest friends will admit he sometimes "rubs people the wrong way" with his attention-drawing behavior—he tends to be the loudest person in any given room—they describe him in kind and loving terms. An unbreakable glue. A game-changer. A gift that makes lives richer. A man with his own gravitational pull. The best man at seven different weddings. Jamie has been the epicenter for his friends' social lives dating back to when he was a teenager living in Madison, Connecticut. That was during his Dungeons & Dragons years, a time when he and his friends could be found hanging out at the Clark family's house, occasionally racing their cars down the narrow, tree-lined Madison streets or drinking beer in the lean-to they built in the woods at the end of Sperry Road.

This guy—who his students often describe as loud, crazy ("in a good way"), sometimes scary, funny and energetic—is unabashedly emotional. He cries with only the slightest of provocations. His daughters, Meghan and Bridget, like to make bets as to when during the movie they're about to watch he'll start to cry. This is the man who ate soup for six months in an effort to save enough money for an engagement ring after reading in David McCullough's biography that Harry Truman believed buying an engagement ring "with borrowed money would be bad luck." He presented an engagement ring to Colleen while he was in the middle of performing during a concert, taking the microphone and proposing, just before his ensemble played "Danny Boy." He has been known to scoop up copies of *Tuesdays with Morrie* at secondhand bookstores and yard sales so he can give them away. (He gave me a hardcover version within months of starting this project.) Jamie collects inspirational quotes, keeps pages and pages of them on his computer. Periodically, he posts them on Facebook or writes them out in his cramped handwriting on slips of paper and gives them to students who need the emotional boost.

Among the pop cultural obsessions that inspire him, which he says explain who he is and what he values: *The Lord of the Rings* trilogy and *The Hobbit*, about which he is passionate (he sees himself as Frodo's loyal friend Sam, although his friends disagree with that characterization because Sam isn't on center stage); *The Last Lecture* about a dying professor's quest to find the meaning of life; *The Five Secrets You Must Discover Before You Die* whose secrets involve connections between people; *Mr. Magorium's Wonder Emporium* particularly its quote, "Your life is an occasion, rise to it;" *Mr. Holland's Opus* about the impact a music teacher had on students' lives and *It's a Wonderful Life*, the classic film about the "rich" man who lacks money but considers many people as friends. Cynicism and apathy are sentiments Jamie wholeheartedly rejects as he can be almost unrelentingly hopeful and cheerful.

To some folks who perceive him as a softie with a fondness for bad jokes, it might come as a surprise that Jamie has struggled with his temper his whole life. In his younger years, he was an easy mark for classmates who teased him until he flew into a rage, lashed out, and was sent to the principal's office. Although Jamie is mostly able to curtail his temper, he says he has difficulty not becoming irate when someone is in trouble. Of the fistfights he had from when he was a child through his early 20s, most involved protecting a female. In the 1980s, when the vice principal of the Daniel Hand High School in Madison said that "violence is never the answer," Jamie disagreed, saying he was right to slam a male student's head into a cafeteria table to stop him from striking a female friend of his. The offending boy, who had left a red mark on a girl's neck after ripping a necklace off her, had raised his hand to slap her when Jamie stepped in. "I will never say to you that what I did was wrong," he told the vice principal. His father would kill him if he *didn't* stand up for that girl, the teenager said.

When he married Colleen O'Brien—whose name Jamie's mother saw in the local newspaper when she was heading to Boston University to study music, just like Jamie, prompted the comment, "You should meet her and bring her home"—Jamie's explosive anger had not yet been tamed. Following a blow-out fight over whether to use plastic or regular plates for a Christmas gathering, the pair decided to institute what they called "Rules of Engagement" for future disagreements: No pointing. No name calling. No sarcasm. No walking away. No one is allowed to mention something from a previous fight. So far, so good.

"He's always very excitable," his mother Maureen says. Jamie agrees, calling himself the proverbial apple to her tree: "She's just this little, tiny Irish woman who grew up in the Bronx who takes zero crap." However, Maureen adds that when he was a small boy with white-blond hair he was exceedingly sweet, "He always looked like sugar would melt in his mouth." Within the Clark family, Jamie, the middle child, freely admits that he revels in his "most favored child status," the clown to his older brother Brad's stoicism and his younger sister Laura's even-temperedness. Jamie grew up idolizing Brad, a 6-foot-3, 225-pound high school athlete who, as an adult, wound up making a lot of money while his kid brother—barely 5-foot-8 and not at all athletic—struggled financially.

Although the town he considers his hometown, Madison, is an affluent community along the Long Island Sound where many famous people have and still live—like celebrity chef Jacques Pepin and former *New York Times* editor Jill Abramson—Jamie says his family didn't live on the "fancy side" of town, nor did his family belong to the swim club like the "fancy people." His family went to the public beach, although the upper-middle-class Clark family considered itself comfortable. It was in Madison, where Jamie moved when he was in fourth grade that his musical career blossomed, although there were early inklings of musicality when his nursery school teacher alerted his parents that there was something really "wrong" with him because he described sound as either light or dark as opposed to loud or soft. It was in the fourth grade that he selected the trombone as his primary instrument simply because the music store was all out of saxophones, which was the instrument his paternal grandfather played in swing bands to earn enough money to put himself through law school.

By the time he was in high school, Jamie racked up awards for his trombone playing, participated in a number of symphonic groups in which he was the lead trombone, and even played at Tanglewood in the Berkshires one summer. Dozens of yellowing news clippings from local papers from those years commend Jamie's musical talent, with the bushy-haired, dirty blond teen standing, almost always smiling, trombone in hand in the accompanying photos. All of that success earned him a full music scholarship to Boston University in the fall of 1986. After a year of college, Jamie was offered the chance to join a professional quintet, which would mean quitting school and traveling extensively. The young trombonist joined Epic Brass in 1987 and went on to perform at Carnegie Hall, traverse the world, and visit nearly every U.S. state. He earned $6,000 his first year, although as the number of concerts increased, so did Jamie's income. On the road, he developed a taste for black coffee and it became his life blood, a vital substance that kept the manically ener-getic Jamie functioning. Throughout his work with Epic Brass, he said he loved engaging the audience, which he did by hamming it up. That routine didn't go over so well when Epic Brass was reviewed by *The Los Angeles Times* in 1993 and it was called the "F-Troop" of musical groups whose performance was labeled "stale shtick." "The audience loved it though," Jamie said in Epic's defense.

In the meantime, the traveling musician set up a home base

with his friends in the back half of a duplex on Burnham Street in Belmont, ten miles outside of Boston. At times, the Burnham house was akin to a big, beer-filled man cave where a parade of pals would crash, occasionally for months at a stretch. His pals handled Jamie's bills for him while he was traveling, and when he returned home, they told him how much he owed them. It was during this time, the winter of 1990, when Jamie found his way to Colleen O'Brien, the girl whose name his mother saw in the newspaper, who grew up in the town next to his and who was also a musician, a classically trained vocalist. Before they started dating, the two had heard of one another and had friends in common. Colleen, who did not pursue a professional career in music after graduating from BU and went on to become an executive assistant for a power company, was supportive of Jamie's musical career, even when it took him away from her.

In 1999, he quit Epic Brass and resumed his college education, earning his bachelor's degree in history by taking classes at then-Bridgewater State College between driving all over eastern and central Massachusetts to teach music lessons, sometimes thirty lessons per week, including teaching trombone and euphonium at two small Massachusetts colleges. He earned his degree in 2002 and successfully acquired a preliminary teaching license for K-12 music and grades 5-12 history/social studies.

With his hectic schedule, Jamie was fearful of becoming the dad in that Harry Chapin song, "Cat's in the Cradle," the one who never saw his kids. Colleen and Jamie would meet at a location between her work and his work or his classes and hand off the girls to the other parent. "Jamie went gray quickly during this time," she said.

At first, he hated teaching. "Playing the trombone is pretty natural for me," he says. "I was never big at practicing and you can't tell a kid to 'just do it.' I had to come up with different ways to teach the kids how to play … and I had to learn to experiment with teaching techniques." This was the beginning of his if-a-lesson's-not-working-flush-it teaching philosophy.

Jamie didn't give up performing completely. He was invited to become the principal trombonist with a local symphony orchestra in

Milford, Massachusetts in 2000 at the same time that he was serving the identical role for the Plymouth Philharmonic. In 2001, he and four friends founded Brass Venture, a brass quintet, which continues to perform periodically. He also subbed for other trombonists from time to time. It was one of those last-minute substitutions that led to Jamie's arrival in the Southborough middle school. During a break from *Joseph and the Amazing Technicolor Dreamcoat* at the Foothills Theater in Worcester, Jamie was standing next to the show's music director, Dennis Wrenn—also the music director at the Algonquin Regional High School—at the urinals, when Jamie told him he needed a job that would provide benefits. Within days, Jamie had an interview for a benefitted, half-time position at the Trottier Middle School in Southborough, most of whose students move up to the Algonquin Regional High School in ninth grade. Wrenn told then-Trottier principal Linda Murdock that Jamie would grow into the job, despite his lack of a teaching degree. Murdock, a musician herself, agreed, saying she was most impressed with "what he wanted music to do for kids." A key question she asked during his interview, *What would you do if you had a student with a degenerative muscle disease who desperately wanted to play trombone?* Jamie's answer: He'd encourage the student, rewrite the musical parts as necessary, maybe suggest another instrument if arm strength and mobility became an issue. This is exactly what Murdock wanted to hear. "The ensemble is for the kids," Murdock said. "The kids aren't for the ensemble. You include everyone who wants to make music." Not everyone she interviewed believed that. "I thought that Jamie had two things we needed: 1) intelligence 2) determination."

At the end of his first year at Trottier in June 2003, Jamie decided he could no longer work part-time. He needed to work full-time for full-time money. A charter school in a nearby community offered him a full-time music post, but he didn't want to leave Southborough, having already fallen in love with the school and his students. When he told Murdock about the other offer, they struck a deal: if Jamie could learn how to teach orchestra students, as well as the concert and jazz band students, he could have the job, full-time. For three months, Jamie immersed himself in string instruments, got a violin, cello and viola, and consulted with fellow performers from Milford's Claflin Hill Symphony Orchestra regarding hand and bow techniques. By the end of the summer, he was ready. "He was a ball of fire," said Keith Lavoie who took over the principal's job from Murdock in 2009. "He won over Linda. He just gets it. He has a with-it-ness, a real understanding for what the kids are giving you and he can make adjustments on the fly."

No longer the globe-trotting musician nor the private instructor driving around to tutor as many students as he could in order to pay for diapers and a mortgage, Jamie made the Trottier job his own, throwing his passion, temper, talent and enthusiasm at the music students, starting the school's first marching band in 2010 and making sure that the students participated in regional music festivals, which they hadn't done before. Charles Gobron, then-superintendent of the Northborough-Southborough school district, said of Jamie: "I think he's phenomenally talented. What I really admire as a teacher, is that he makes everything look so easy. He is so incredibly invested in everything he does."

But Jamie wouldn't be Jamie if he didn't push things a bit, put his own stamp on his evolving teaching style. A student-teacher who once spent a semester observing and teaching alongside Jamie, said he was astonished when he saw the Trottier band director—who he initially thought he was a "buffoon" although he quickly changed his opinion—repeatedly flout conventional teaching wisdom, doing things like shouting, "Play better!" at his students, using sarcasm and making poop jokes. "He broke all of the teacher rules," said Scott Morrill, now a middle school band director in a Boston area suburb. Morrill feared that his mentor was putting his job in danger when he saw Jamie being forthright with the students, refusing to sugarcoat his reactions when they didn't play as well as Jamie thought they could. Plus, he hugged everybody.

Rule-breaking is a given for Jamie at Trottier. Many of Jamie's colleagues liken him to Robin Williams and Williams' genie from the movie *Aladdin*. Eighth-grade Language Arts teacher Steve Brady suggested, "Imagine the biggest class clown you've ever seen and that's him at faculty meetings. ... As goofy and out-of-the-box as he is, he is the most dedicated person in the building. He's always here, and with that, you take the eccentricity." Friend and coworker Lisa

Klein, Trottier science teacher, said that on occasion, Jamie needs to be reined in. "I wouldn't say he's disruptive, but we wouldn't put up with that in my classroom," she said of his antics in faculty meetings. Another teacher, who said not everyone appreciates his sense of humor, observed, "He's definitely of the mindset of asking for forgiveness rather than permission."

Like when it's his turn to do morning announcements to the entire school over the loudspeaker and he says things like, "Remember, if you're in band, you don't have math homework tonight." Or in 2012 when Jamie and his Big Band students conducted an early morning guerrilla operation, moving the furniture from his faux rival's classroom—math teacher Tom Griffin—into the lobby next to the gym. They placed the band room furniture inside the math classroom, taking over the classroom like it was a piece of contested territory in a boundary dispute. "One morning, as I was walking in and I heard the band in my room," Griffin said. The desks had been arranged into the shape of musical notes and a sign declaring that the "Bandies" had conquered was on the board. Jamie's trouble-making behavior appears to be mostly tolerated by his genial principal, the thirty-something Lavoie, who likes to reference their relationship to the 1970s show *The Odd Couple*, calling himself the uptight Felix to Jamie's slovenly Oscar. "I've told him he has to dial it down a few times," Lavoie said.

Ironically, the loquacious instigator chooses not to eat lunch in the faculty room with his colleagues, preferring instead to camp out during lunch and study periods in the band room, where he keeps a stash of snacks (Pop Tarts, ramen noodles, M&Ms, Wheat Thins and oatmeal packets), plays music and welcomes band and non-band students alike. He is plenty friendly with many of his colleagues after school, going on day trips with some of their families, or enjoying a laugh between classes, during bus duty and on field trips, of which Jamie's a big fan. Five different women who work with him in various capacities (three teachers, one administrator and one parent volunteer) joke that they are his "work wives."

According to his youngest daughter Bridget, Jamie's decision to teach at the middle school level was perfect because, inside his head, he is somewhere between the ages of 8 and 14. One of his students observed, "He's like a kid in an adult body, only he's responsible." In the Trottier band room, Jamie plays up his role of being the "big kid," acting like the goofball. "No one's going to be a bigger idiot or fool in this room than me," he said. "You can't do it. It's impossible. I'm the biggest idiot in the room." He once told his students to write, "Look at the big ugly freak at the front of the room" at the top of their sheet music so they wouldn't be so serious and would loosen up.

In and out of the band room, he's a blur because he's almost perpetually running around doing something—like taking graduate classes in music education, practicing with the Claflin Hill Orchestra and his brass quintet, or volunteering to help conduct a local symphonic group, New Horizons, composed of amateur musicians 50+ years old—or because he's too busy yakking with people. "I'm constantly going," he said. "I don't know where this came from. I'm exhausting to other people." The only time he's silent is when he's reading or sleeping. But even when he's sleeping, he's still kind of loud, given that he wears a wheezing, heaving, Darth Vader-esque CPAP contraption strapped around his head at night. (After he told me about it, he texted me a frightening selfie of him wearing the sleep mask.)

It's highly appropriate that his Facebook avatar is Tigger, the always-bouncing, ever-jovial cartoon character. Klein said, "He definitely is Tigger. He roars when he needs to. He just makes people happy."

CHAPTER FIVE

Faking It

Perhaps it was wishful thinking that prompted Mr. Clark to play "Fly Me to the Moon" as the Big Band members entered the band room for the first time in October. Despite prior warnings—which were largely filled with empty threats of arrive-on-time-or-else, only "or else" never actually materialized—students were still arriving well after 7 o'clock. For the clarinet and flute sections, it seemed like word had spread virally to arrive at school looking like you just stepped out of a fashion magazine. They wore brightly colored jeans, draping scarves, floral skirts and dangling earrings. Significant thought had been put into what the young girls—some of whom were starting to look like women, donning makeup and, occasionally, heels—wore to school, unlike most of the rest of their male counterparts who wore shorts through December, T-shirts, expensive sneakers, sports jerseys and sweatshirts. Under Armour, with its conjoined "u" and "a" logo, was the brand of choice for the boys, most of whom looked very, very young. The only ray of fashion sunshine for the boys came when fedora-wearing Ethan opted to go all hipster, wearing a button-down shirt open over an ironic T-shirt.

When they played the first few measure of "Fly Me to the Moon," it was not as flashy as the girls' clothing. They were weak and fairly shaky. Had they practiced? That wasn't clear. But, at least for the beginning of this rehearsal, Mr. Clark didn't seem as though he was going to blast them. Not yet anyway. *Was this his plan all along? Be hard in September but softer in October? Was there a plan or was Mr. Clark just winging it?* I frequently found myself vacillating between feeling like a protective mom who wanted the kids to do well and not invite Mr. Clark's wrath, and a detective, trying to parse Mr. Clark's teaching techniques, which were vastly different than my own, which were playing out at a local university where I taught writing and journalism. *If he is able to crack open these kids emotionally when they're petrified of the crushing loss that hangs over the band room, certainly I could use some of his moves to coax writing students into writing something powerful and personal,* I thought.

"Don't try to overplay," Mr. Clark said gently. "You don't have to be the [Count] Basie-man all by himself. He had friends."

He drew his breath in deeply. "What kind of song is this?"

Someone blurted out, "He loves someone."

Mr. Clark said it was about the feeling of longing that was precisely articulated by Sinatra throughout the song. More than anything, Mr. Clark wanted the students to allow the music to get inside their hearts, to move them, and for them to express those feelings through their instruments. With this piece, I wondered if they were having difficulty locating the feelings about which Sinatra was crooning because very few of them had dated or were dating anyone. Or maybe they didn't want to think about who they longed for who was not there. Someone who would never stand among them. Someone whose name they seemed afraid to mention. Maybe all those feelings were still too raw, too jumbled up inside their adolescent hearts. And they hadn't yet gelled as a group, hadn't reached a point where emotional vulnerability felt comfortable, making an expression of longing too much and too soon.

Mr. Clark talked at the sax players, the trumpet players, offering pointers, tweaking here and there, leaving the rest of the band to sit and stew in their emotions. Seeking something to occupy her attention, clarinet player Angelina started openly chit-chatting with other clarinet players and the nearby flute players. They used their music stands to block them from Mr. Clark's view. Meanwhile Carol, one of the band's three seventh-grade piano players who also played clarinet, sat on the piano bench with her hands in her lap. She slumped over slightly. Waiting for the sax and trumpet players to get their acts together. She never had to worry about getting corrected by Mr. Clark. Ever.

Perhaps it was boredom or the avoidance of difficult feelings that prompted some of the kids to start horsing around while Mr. Clark was busy with the trumpet section asking them to mark something in on their sheet music. Out of the corner of his eye, Mr. Clark noticed that Lauren—the lone female trumpet player and the only eighth-grade trumpet player, a popular, athletic girl—had gum in her mouth. Gum was verboten in the band room. However, Mr. Clark didn't call Lauren out on it, just like he rarely called her out for being late to rehearsal although he routinely gave guitarist Jesse a hard time in public for his mistakes. *Why no sharp comments for her?* I wondered.

Before commencing with a whole-band playing of "Fly Me to the Moon," Mr. Clark directed a stern look to the trumpet section, urging them to "kick the parc out of it," "parc" being Mr. Clark's code word for "crap." "Bells up," he said. "Stand tall and PLAY!"

The transformation between the 7 a.m. version and this one, a half-hour later, was remarkable. There was a sonic explosion. "Most middle school jazz bands are going to get here for their concert," Mr. Clark said. "… But this is where we start."

This surprisingly successful rendition of "Fly Me to the Moon" led to a decent spin through the beginning of "Dat Dere," however, as they went deeper into the chart, something seemed off. Actually a lot of somethings seemed off. It got weaker as they played, sloppier. Perhaps that practicing they did over the weekend didn't extend through to the end of the song. They knew the beginning and the chorus. The rest was a mess.

"We're getting there," he declared. "Was this a better rehearsal?"

A murmur from the students, "Yes."

"Why?"

"Practice," one student mumbled.

"Because you practiced."

♪

The Big Band members appeared to be in a chipper mood, thoroughly energized before the beginning of the Columbus Day weekend. Perhaps selecting the quiet, emotive "Fly Me to the Moon" wasn't the best piece to kick off this rehearsal with a group of antsy adolescents who were eager for a mini-vacation. The first time Mr. Clark stopped their playing, it was to tell the lead alto sax, "You can't be shy!" He tried to illustrate the absurdity of the boy's shyness by pretending to bow to invisible people standing next to him, "'No you go first.' 'No, YOU go first.'" He wanted the boy to seize his notes.

Mr. Clark grunted as he stripped off his maroon Trottier Middle School hoodie, revealing a short-sleeve maroon Trottier Middle School T-shirt beneath. "I'll stop there," he said. As with most of the bizarre verbal voyages on which Mr. Clark was apt to travel, he offered a tiny glimpse into the thought process that goes on in his over-caffeinated brain as he regaled the musicians with a story about a professor who had a nervous breakdown, cursed at his students and then stripped off all of his clothes.

"Why did you tell us that?" asked Danny, the student who many agreed was the most likely to become Mr. Clark when he grew up.

No answer came forth, although the tale seemed to take the sting out the earlier criticisms he had leveled at the group's efforts, a brief reprieve. Once the students resumed "Fly Me to the Moon," the trumpet section was asked to play select measures. Then individual players had to play the measures, starkly alone in their quivering notes. A couple of the students were earsplittingly off-key. None of the other students—who later told me watching their peers play solo like this when Mr. Clark knew the kids didn't know the piece, made them very, very uncomfortable—overtly reacted. Students were poker-faced while the kids who either hadn't practiced, or were in over their heads with this piece, musically floundered. Unflinching, Mr. Clark told the trumpet players to raise their music stands so they wouldn't have to lower the bells in order to read the music, a hazard for several of the shorter trumpet players. "There's a visual element to performing," he said as he demonstrated a self-assured posture in front of them, holding an invisible trumpet aimed high, with his shoulders back, chest forward and feet firmly planted widely.

The mood shifted in the room when saxophonist Owen—a petite, whip-smart dollop of musical perfection—correctly fielded a question about "Dat Dere." Mr. Clark trotted up to Owen and bear-hugged him, saying that hearing him provide the right answer was "better than eating a doughnut. Or a sandwich! Or a doughnut sandwich! Oh! Do you remember last year when Kentucky Fried Chicken had a sandwich with chicken and ... other bad stuff? I had twelve of 'em and I was unconscious for a week."

Smiles spread through the rows, particularly among the trumpeters who were relieved that the hot spotlight of scrutiny was no longer on them. The smile that popped onto sixth-grade trumpeter Henry's face caught my eye. His smile was brilliant and altogether too infrequent. Henry, a small slip of a boy with dark hair and deep dimples, seemed eager to placate Mr. Clark, making emphatic faces when saying the notes, opening his eyes widely and nodding ardently when given direction.

Capitalizing on the lightness of the moment and the whimsical nature of "Dat Dere," Mr. Clark implored them to put themselves out there, emotionally, into the music, "Even if it's wrong notes, don't ever, ever, ever, ever play wimpy. ... Play it strong even if it's wrong." I was skeptical about whether he would really accept that in a band rehearsal, strength in the wrong key or at the incorrect tempo, whether the kids were ready to put themselves out there yet. But, in the moment, the kids seemed to lap it up.

"Some of you are faking it," he added. "That's okay for now. For. Now."

♪

Days later, Mr. Clark was still correcting the same mistakes. Students hadn't practiced. They weren't listening to one another. They weren't *feeling* the music yet. The trumpets were stressed out. It was a pivotal time for the Big Band. Mr. Clark, who was frequently mulling how to motivate and help them, tried to remind them of the cost of not pulling their own weight: they would let down the team.

"You *volunteered* to be in this group," he said solemnly one October morning. Although he said "academics come first," he said the students had to be dedicated to the band too. A handful of musicians had recently left the rehearsal to attend a Spanish extra help session when Mr. Clark was convinced those kids had excellent grades and didn't need the help. "People have been telling me they were too busy to practice. Is that ever a good excuse? No."

"What kind of boat is this?"

They responded in rote fashion, "A rowboat."

"*Everybody* has an oar," Mr. Clark declared as he strode in front of the band. "What kind of a boat *isn't* this?"

"A cruise ship," the students said, sounding distinctly bored.

"A cruise ship," he parroted, a bit of sarcasm creeping in. "There aren't any drinks with little umbrellas in them. ... If you don't play your parts, you'll be thrown overboard."

"I know you haven't been practicing," Mr. Clark said. "How many of you have not practiced?" Did he really expect the 11-, 12-, 13-, and 14-year-olds to be truthful when they knew he could take their admissions into unpredictable comedic territory at the kids' expense? Surprisingly, a few students tentatively raised their hands. Mr. Clark glanced at the beleaguered members of the trumpet section, kids who it was clear had not practiced, but none of them raised their hands. He asked the rest of the band to render their judgment: How many of them thought the trumpet players had run through these pieces over the weekend? No hands went up.

The seven-member trumpet section received no relief from Mr. Clark's scrutiny when they turned to "Fly Me to the Moon." Whereas he said the sax section played plenty loud enough, the flute section, composed of high-sounding instruments, was even louder. The trumpets were nowhere to be found in the mélange of sound.

"Trumpets," he said, "you just got your butts whipped by the flute section." Mr. Clark—who always seemed kinder and gentler with the female Big Banders, perhaps because he had two daughters the same age as these girls—lavished compliments upon them, told them they were awesome. The trumpet section, however, "was the opposite of awesome," he said, half-joking, half-not.

Despite his humor, coupled with his carrot-and-stick approach, he seemed to be losing them this morning. Several were easily distracted. The mere entrance of a handful of music students into the band room so they could stow their instruments away in the metal cages for later use in the orchestra, sixth-grade band or the seventh- and eighth-grade band, riveted the Big Band members who appeared eager for something else to look at other than Mr. Clark, and for this particular rehearsal to be over.

Mr. Clark finally gave in and released them, but not before telling them that the Big Band "isn't like an episode of *Glee*. Everything doesn't magically come together in an hour. Find time to practice because it isn't going to happen on its own. The work's gotta happen."

CHAPTER SIX

The Mayor of Fortissimo

By 7:10, most of the band members had arrived. Mr. Clark told the students to grab the battery-operated tuners from the cardboard box sitting next to his stool in front of the Big Band set-up and make sure their instruments were ready to play. As bleats and blasts of instruments were played into the tuners, he told Cassidy he wanted the eighth-grade bassist/drummer Richie to play "Fly Me to the Moon." The subdued Richie, however, tended to move at a snail-like pace, the antithesis of his hyper-charged, sleep-deprived band director who was under the influence of multiple cups of coffee, oftentimes, with extra turbo shots of caffeine for good measure. Richie was taking an extremely long time to set up his bass equipment, while Mr. Clark was itching to start the Sinatra tune. Mr. Clark's gruff impatience, complete with exaggeratedly loud sighs, did nothing to speed Richie along.

When the band resumed playing, notes were still off. The placid, happy-go-lucky countenance Mr. Clark had worn when he greeted arriving students in the hallway before rehearsal was gone. He used the tip of his brown boot to kick the box of tuners toward the flute section. He grumbled that someone there had clearly not tuned, although no one would admit to having shirked tuning duty.

A lecture about volume followed the mandatory tuning. This

piece, Mr. Clark said, isn't about playing loudly all of the time. If they played loudly and intensely—all fortissimo—throughout the entire piece, there wouldn't be a dramatic crescendo. There couldn't be. All the sections of this love song would be of the same intensity. They needed to pull it back, curb the volume in order to musically express power, nuance.

The trumpets, into which Mr. Clark had been attempting to instill some fire on "Fly Me to the Moon," remained problematic. He isolated each part of the section by first trumpets, second trumpets and the like and asked each to play a measure: Patrick and Henry, the lead trumpets, Kyle and Lauren, the second trumpets, Brad and Tim, the third, and Justin and Jeffrey, the fourth. It was another painful listening experience as he sought to pinpoint the erroneous notes and paucity of volume shifts. Those listening fidgeted in their seats, making a silent plea for those kids to just practice so this wouldn't keep happening.

Mr. Clark grew uncharacteristically poetic as he discussed the importance of dynamic range in music, explaining "fortissimo," an Italian word that means "very loud," when playing a musical piece. He might as well have been explaining himself. His whole life was fortissimo. Glancing around for an example to show the kids what he meant, he pointed to Noah and told him to play the drums really loudly. "Imagine you're playing on your brother's head," he said, referring to Noah's brother who played in the sixth-grade band.

Mr. Clark turned to Richie, who was playing bass on this piece, and asked him to say the notes aloud. Richie's voice wasn't at all audible, at least from my vantage point. Mr. Clark refrained from commenting on Richie's anti-fortissimo recitation, yet another example of his varied approaches to students, some of whom he was willing to publicly push (like Ethan and Jesse) and some of whom received a lighter touch (like Lauren and Richie). There were times, I began noticing, when it didn't seem as though he was certain which approach he should take and had to guess. On a few occasions, he guessed wrong.

As Mr. Clark attempted to get the band back on track, he had them move on to "Dat Dere," Danny asked if anyone had seen the TV ad for LED lights that featured a deer with really wide, bulging eyes. When no one responded right away, Danny started talking faster, providing more details about the ad until his classmates drowned him out in a cacophony of high-pitched, disconnected, adolescent observations about current television advertisements. It was not clear what prompted the deer-in-the-headlights ad discussion.

Although Mr. Clark paid lip-service to trying to refocus the band, there was no stopping the storm front of silliness that had overtaken the band room. Sax players Harry and Ethan started complaining that the band room was the coldest room in the school. "It's the middle of October and you're wearing shorts," Mr. Clark pointed out. Eighth-grade clarinet player Anisha—who, along with clarinet player Angelina received the most "stop talking" admonitions from Mr. Clark—said Mr. Clark should shut off the air conditioning in the room, which ran practically all year. Mr. Clark demurred, saying that the room would become too hot if he turned off the AC and refused to consider that perhaps he was the one who was overheated. (I, for one, agreed with Anisha and Angelina. I spent most of my time in the band room shivering and, a few times, had to borrow a jacket from Mr. Clark.)

It was at this point in the rehearsal that Mr. Clark took the subject between his teeth and ran with it. "If we were all fat, we could use less heat and have a smaller carbon footprint," he said, patting his belly. "Eat doughnuts and save the environment! Love Mother Earth! Eat chocolate éclairs." An environmental message wedded between doughnuts and éclairs was exactly what the Big Band needed. When they started playing "Dat Dere," it felt as though its disparate pieces were starting to come together. The trumpet players successfully managed to make their way through a tricky passage. Pleased, Mr. Clark smiled and said, "It's not magic. It simply appears to be magic to the audience."

This morning was different. Felt different, tone-wise, confidence-wise and even temperature-wise. In a room that is chilly all year round, on this morning in mid-October, it was warm. Mr. Clark was so ebullient he could barely contain his emotions within the confines of his body; excitement and goofiness exuded, despite the fact that his gravelly-sounding voice indicated he was coming down with whatever bug was making its way around Trottier Middle School. I should've known that he was going to be a bit wired today when he texted me at 6:44 a.m. with this message, "VIENNA!!" in all caps and two exclamation points.

He was referring to what he calls the Vienna Playlist, comprised of 200+ songs from a variety of musical genres. Its name was inspired by the 1977 Billy Joel song "Vienna," which promotes slowing down and not getting so lost in the business of life that you forget "what you need." During his second year of teaching, Mr. Clark was regularly arriving to school feeling grumpy. He realized after spending his 20-minute commute to school listening to the news, he was getting discouraged with the world and wound up spreading the grouchiness to the students like a viral infection. So he switched things up and created a list of songs to listen to on the way to school, "songs that remind me of what's important and what matters," tunes as varied as Carole King's "Child of Mine," Dan Fogelberg's "Leader of the Band" and the Muppet movie soundtrack song "Pictures in My Head," to Sawyer Brown's "Thank God for You" and Israel Kamakawiwo'ole's "Somewhere Over the Rainbow." Many are sentimental tear-jerkers.

The first rendition of "Dat Dere" during this morning's rehearsal was solid. The kids sounded as if they were actually enjoying themselves rather than being dragged through the measures by the scruffs of their necks. They weren't playing like the children that they were. If you closed your eyes, they sounded like older musicians, more experienced. After weeks of awkward forced marches through measures, admonitions about practicing at home, about learning the songs deep within their marrow, the music was falling into place.

"Do you hear how much better we are than we were on Tuesday?" Mr. Clark said, sucking the remnants of the cold coffee from a black travel mug, not his usual red one. He was clearly disappointed that, at only 7:13 in the morning, there was no more left.

It's hard to provide a logical explanation for what transpired next or how the conversation wound its way from the whereabouts of Mr. Clark's usual red travel mug (the students seemed to notice everything about their director and asked where his usual mug was—dirty and at home), to his declaration, "There's some part of your body that doesn't have any nerve endings." I did not catch the detail about to which body part he was referring. I hadn't had nearly enough caffeine that morning to keep up with Mr. Clark or these middle schoolers. At one point, after waving his arms and shouting, "Stop! Stop!" to try to tamp down the chaotic, fractal conversations that broke out around the room, Mr. Clark complained that his retinas were being singed by having to look directly at the fluorescent, yellow highlighter-colored sweatshirt worn by Ethan who was sitting in the front row. Perhaps it was the fact that Mr. Clark was blinded or somewhat disoriented by the flashy duds that prompted him to join a conversation about monsters, specifically being chased by them. Mr. Clark pretended he was being chased by an unseen monster, clomping his feet loudly in his hiking boots, running in place, flopping his arms loosey-goosey at his sides, looking over his shoulder, eyes bulging behind his glasses. For the first time this year, the band room was electric with energy. Even the normally well behaved girls in the flute and clarinet sections were bursting with enthusiasm. Mr. Clark took an imaginary empty bottle, scooped up the lightning in the room and transferred it back into his charges. They took another stab at "Dat Dere." And it was just as good as their first try of the day. Mr. Clark wore a wry smile as he nodded along.

Mr. Clark attempted to move onto "Fly Me to the Moon," but bari sax player Danny, whose hair was standing up on end like he'd just woken up, wasn't done fooling around. He somehow missed Mr. Clark's redirection and continued making silly, rubbery, Jim Carrey faces for the amusement of the students sitting in his near vicinity. When Mr. Clark tried to bring them back to the playing of the Sinatra tune, Danny loudly belted out, *To Jupiter and Mars, and the stars!* Mr. Clark continued smiling and explained that the piece was about "unbridled joy," which, during this rehearsal, was unmistakably present. For a moment, the students forgot that they were in mourning and were instead kids who could deliver quality music if only they allowed themselves to do so. Insistent that they absorb "Fly Me to the Moon's" sentiment, he compared the piece to the feeling they might experience if he announced that a bus pulled up in front of the school and they were told they were all going to Disneyland.

They began "Fly Me to the Moon," but it wasn't right. They were playing in the same way they'd been talking: really loudly with no nuance. To drive the point home, Mr. Clark said they sounded like they were getting right up into someone's face and shouting, "I! Love! *You!*" Pantomiming the creation of a large round ball in front of him, Mr. Clark said their playing needed to be "softer and rounder."

"Like you!" a voice from the band volunteered.

He started poking himself in the belly. Then he looked down and poked the right side of his stomach, encased in a long-sleeved, moss green T-shirt, and declared that he could see the left side moving, comparing it to having an earthquake in California which causes a tsunami in Japan. Unfortunately, a tsunami of sound washed over "Fly Me to the Moon." Nothing gracious, none of the subtle notes Mr. Clark was seeking were evident. He interrupted them mid-measure with an insistent, "No!" To demonstrate what he wanted to hear, Mr. Clark cued up Sinatra on his iPod at the front of the room.

Fill my heart with song
And let me sing for ever more
You are all I long for
All I worship and adore.

"I don't think you could rush that man to do anything," he said, as seventh-grade violinist Natalie swayed back and forth, her bow in the air.

CHAPTER SEVEN

Good Enough

𝄆 Mr. Clark had just issued the rhythm section specific orders about what parts of "Dat Dere" to work on for the next day, singling out chords that really needed work, when he noticed guitarist Jesse wasn't writing anything on his sheet music. While his fellow musicians were writing, or pretending to, eighth-grade guitarist Jesse was boldly staring at his teacher.

"Who else plays chords in this band?" Mr. Clark asked.

"I already know the chords," Jesse replied, defiant.

"But you need to practice," Mr. Clark said.

Jesse said nothing, blinked, then looked away, a brave move considering Mr. Clark's cranky disposition.

A silent standoff ensued between Jesse and the band director, who saw shades of his own temperamental, authority-challenging, detention-getting middle school self in the guitarist. Playing in school ensembles had saved the young Mr. Clark from himself, kept him focused or at least doing the bare minimum of school work that was required in order to remain a member in good standing in music ensembles. Looking at Jesse, a naturally gifted musician who was easy to rile and occasionally talked back to his teachers, Mr. Clark experienced an uncomfortable déjà vu.

While Jesse clashed with Mr. Clark on a number of occasions, mostly over the boy being late or routinely forgetting to bring his sheet music and a pencil, Jesse credited his band director with turning him on to the instrument with which he could no longer live without. During his seventh-grade year, Jesse had tried out for the Big Band as an alto sax player when the competition for spots in the saxophone section was stiff. Instead of cutting him from the Big Band, Mr. Clark told him he should play guitar for them instead. "I learned the sax part and sucked at the guitar then," Jesse told me later. "I only knew three chords. I was way over my head in the whole thing. I look at it and it was Egyptian." (Jesse's interpretation of the cliché "It was all Greek to me.") After asking his mother to sign him up for some private guitar lessons, Jesse soon became hooked. "I have to thank Mr. Clark for guitar because now I play guitar all day."

Mr. Clark believed Jesse had a musical soul. He could see it in the boy's face when he played. He loved music. Although Mr. Clark frequently, loudly, and publicly held Jesse accountable for his missteps, he had a soft spot for the boy who he thought needed firm direction. And Jesse didn't find Mr. Clark's sharp comments intimidating or as intimidating as some of his fellow students did. "I'd say Mr. Clark likes me, deep down, but he sometimes thinks I'm a bonehead," Jesse said. "I understand him I guess. He's loud, but he's not the loudest I've ever heard. I've had my fair share of adults yelling at me."

The tension between Jesse and Mr. Clark was broken on this particular morning when the teacher decided to give the guitar player a silent pass, but not before sending a hard-to-read grimace Jesse's way.

Mr. Clark swiftly directed the students' attention to a brand new piece, "Back to the Basement," a bluesy shuffle that was not intended to be rushed. It was too cool to hurry. To dramatize what he meant, Mr. Clark put his hands in his pants pockets and strutted around in front of the band, as much of a strut as the deeply uncool Mr. Clark could pull off while wearing clunky Merrill boots, bulky cargo pants and a charcoal gray, fleece vest. Mr. Clark looked like Santa Claus, hugged everybody and was prone to uttering phrases like, "Okie-dokie." Didn't exactly scream "cool," especially to middle school students.

The students seemed to like listening to "Back to the Basement," a fresh tune published earlier this year, composed by American jazz musician/music professor Bret Zvacek. It blasted from the speakers in the front of the band room and made them forget about the taut Jesse-Mr. Clark moment that preceded it. There were smiles, bobbing heads and tapping feet, something you didn't see when Sinatra's "Fly Me to the Moon" was playing from Mr. Clark's iPod.

"Do you hear how awesome that sounds?" Mr. Clark asked. He turned his head and furtively looked over his right shoulder, on the lookout for authority figures who might have suddenly appeared in the room. In an ersatz whisper, he said, "That's bad ass." He smirked knowingly, as if hoping to spark something inside the kids by using profanity. The students looked delightfully surprised as they smiled conspiratorially back at the resident bad-ass-in-chief.

Amidst the bad assery, seventh grader Carol raised her thin arm at a perfect right angle as she sat silently on the piano bench on the left side of the room. She had her arm elevated for some time, but in a room filled with the likes of Mr. Clark, Danny, Ethan and other animated personalities, when the music wasn't playing, Carol's hushed elegance was lost. She wasn't willing to raise her voice along with her limb. Some students were energetically chatting, but Carol—with her silky, long, black hair perfectly in place—sat there, flushing slightly as she observed that a few other bandmates noticed that her arm was raised. She said nothing.

Meanwhile, Mr. Clark asked the band to imagine that they were in a gang and that the five members of the rhythm section were their enforcers, which was comical because, with the exception of Jesse, the rhythm section was populated by wiry, shy kids. Regardless, Mr. Clark wanted the students to imagine that the percussionists were tough. Perhaps drummer Noah, who could easily be knocked down by a stiff wind, could ward off bad guys with his drumsticks, with Jesse serving as the muscle. Maybe then, Mr. Clark hoped, the Big Band would get into the right frame of mind to play "Back to the Basement." The students started playing the piece, but were interrupted only a handful of notes in. Mr. Clark asked the brass and percussion sections to play again. Jesse's guitar playing was innately soulful but too loud. It swallowed up the rest of the band. Carol, who tried again to silently get Mr. Clark's attention by raising her hand, finally gave up.

♪

Mr. Clark had tennis elbow, even though he wasn't a tennis player. He had a black fabric and Velcro brace around his right elbow because he had some kind of repetitive motion injury. He did, after all, spend hours waving his arms around in front of the sixth-grade band, the seventh- and eighth-grade band, the orchestra, the Stage Band (which also played jazz two mornings a week) and the Big Band, as well as the New Horizons band he helped conduct a couple evenings a month in Wayland, a 20-minute drive east of Southborough. There was also his own trombone playing, which he did for his brass quintet, Brass Venture, and for the Claflin Hill Symphony Orchestra, a 12-year-old group which performed in the MetroWest region outside of Boston.

He donned the elbow brace reluctantly—in fact he only wore it to a handful of rehearsals before he dispatched with it entirely after saying he'd "solved" the problem on his own by changing his sleeping position—as he led them in playing their new tune "Back to the Basement." Mr. Clark stomped his hiking boot-clad left foot on the floor to count to four to start them off, whereas he would normally use his hands, clapping or pounding flat-palmed on his chest to establish the beat he wanted them to follow. It was very odd to watch his bull-like stomping.

The trumpet playing on the next piece, "Dat Dere," caught Mr. Clark's ear, necessitating another uncomfortable spotlight moment where, one by one, the students had to play a handful of measures alone. Most of the kids' individual playing made me wince with pity. Patrick, the lead trumpet player, was the exception; he was always ready. His playing didn't make me flinch inside. As for everyone else … I wanted to ask Mr. Clark to stop, to plead with each kid to do his or her job already instead of having to endure this embarrassment. *He's the expert and knows how to motivate these kids*, I kept telling myself. *The kids adore him so there must be a point to this shaming exercise. It must be part of the process.* Had I been witness to a season's worth of football or basketball practices, I told myself I would likely see a lot worse.

The atmosphere in the band room began tightening like strings on a violin on the precipice of breaking. The discomfort grew as each subsequent trumpet player dismally attempted to tackle the measures Mr. Clark had named. The spotlight was scorching and revealed that most of them didn't know "Dat Dere" all the way through. I hoped they learned their parts. Soon. The tension was starting to get to me and I didn't even have an instrument.

They ended the rehearsal by playing "Groovin' Hard"—the band's loudest, most in-your-face piece—at top volume. "The whole piece can't be screamin' loud," Mr. Clark said. "You don't have the chops to get through it." During their second attempt at "Groovin' Hard," Mr. Clark noticed that mild-mannered Cassidy was simply standing there, not playing her sparkly fuchsia Ibanez bass guitar. Why not? Because "Groovin' Hard" was Richie's tune on bass and Richie wasn't there. Mr. Clark scrunched up his face. Cassidy was under the mistaken impression, as a sixth grader, she'd never be expected to replace an eighth grader on the bass. To distract the band while Cassidy retrieved the music, Mr. Clark revisited one of his favorite topics: explosive diarrhea, a subject that rarely failed to elicit laughter from the adolescents in the room. Perhaps Richie wasn't here because he had it, Mr. Clark suggested, in which case, Cassidy, the only other bassist in the room, had to fill in for him. Reluctantly, as though she felt as though she was doing something wrong by playing Richie's part, Cassidy settled in to play. But even with the addition of the bass line, "Groovin' Hard" really wasn't.

"You're doing a version of 'Guitar Hero,'" Mr. Clark said. "There's no life. You're not making *music*."

Harrumphing, he trudged to the front of the room, pulled out his iPod and played the bold 1970 Buddy Rich Band version of the piece. Some of the kids were listening, or at least they were nodding their heads, while others were zoning out. It was hard to tell if they were thinking about the music. When the song concluded, Mr. Clark shut off the iPod, walked to the front of the band and started counting, *One, two, one, two, three ....*

Mr. Clark stalked around in front of them. The groove seemed to infect him as he attempted to draw it out of the children. He mim-icked the song's up-tempo punches with gestures. He wanted his enthusiasm to be contagious. He shouted, red-faced. He pin-wheeled his right hand. And they responded. After they'd concluded, Mr. Clark, ever the showman, took a dramatic step backward, the back of his neck tinged a sweaty pink. He was pleased. "*There's* my band," he said huskily, a proud papa. "Did you *feel* it? Did you *hear* it? You just became a band. You just became the *Big Band*. That was awesome."

I couldn't tell, since I was sitting behind him, but he sounded as though he might have had tears in his eyes. He could get very emo-tional when talking about his students. A few months earlier, he had shown me some of his cherished mementos from former students that he kept in a special box. He had been reading aloud to me a stu-dent's essay about the Trottier band room when he abruptly went silent after drawing in a big gulp of air. I looked up from the essay and at his face and saw tears. Mr. Clark strongly believed in putting his emotions on display, right out there, and tried to coax those around him, students especially, to do the same, to show the world an authenticity of feeling. He once told me, "I don't know how you can create art with a façade." I knew that this moment in the band room—when the kids gelled as a band, allowed themselves to show their authentic selves, trusted themselves and one another—was something he'd been eagerly anticipating. And here it was. Here they were.

"*That's* a team. Yes, yes, yes, yes! Holy cow. Yes, yes, yes, yes!" he shouted like a child on Christmas morning. "What's the date? October 23?" He sighed loudly. "*This* is what I have been waiting for. That's why you get up at 5:30 in the morning … For most bands, this is where we get to in June."

Almost trying to press his luck, he had them play "Groovin' Hard" again. I crossed my fingers, unconvinced that the next version would be as good as the one they just played, worrying they would disappoint him. I was wrong. "Yes!" Mr. Clark yelled again, stomping his left foot three times in joy upon the song's raucous conclusion. Their playing: precise and teeming with life.

♪

Danny could not sit still. He was bouncing up and down in his seat, singing the dreadful 1990s Vanilla Ice pop song "Ice, Ice Baby" to himself. Perhaps this was an unusual tune for a garden variety middle school kid to be singing in 2012, but not for Danny, or the band room version of Danny who was unconcerned about what others thought about him. During this school year, it seemed as though Danny—who participated in school plays and sang in the chorus—was struggling with who he was and who he wanted to be, trying to decide which persona fit him best: the lovable jokester who wanted to be the center of attention or the athletic dude who was in with the in crowd. In the band room, he seemed comfortable, welcomed, accepted, despite his tendency to sometimes be annoying.

This was a sanctuary for kids to explore the blurry edges of their personalities because in the band room, cliques were non-issues. Coolness didn't matter. The musicians were in a family, Mr. Clark liked to say. Their unofficial theme song, played every year by the seventh- and eighth-grade band, was Sister Sledge's 1970s hit "We Are Family." The members of the Trottier school bands were also members of football, soccer, basketball and lacrosse teams, as well as involved in visual arts, drama, and the math team. The quietest, most conventionally geeky students played music next to popular kids, very attractive kids next to the students who were afraid to look at themselves in the mirror. In middle school, their identities were still in flux, evolving and maturing as they tried on a variety of identities to see what fit best, as their bodies changed in front of them. As Mr. Clark watched them bloom from sixth grade through eighth, his rule was that everyone in the band room had to treat each another as family members, albeit in a family where the papa bear sometimes got hopping mad. Students told me that while they might never speak with fellow band members of different social strata outside of rehearsals, when they were in the band room, they were teammates. Teammates have one another's backs.

And yet Danny, who frequently wrapped Mr. Clark in enthusiastic embraces, seemed to be at odds with his own desires to be himself and to be liked, particularly when he sought out the attention of the elusive trumpet player, Lauren. Today, he was Danny, the goofy band kid who wanted everyone to look at him, entertaining the group with a series of non sequiturs, from one-hit-wonder Vanilla Ice and a discussion about the lyrics of "Somewhere Over the Rainbow," to Danny's father "forcing" him to listen to an acoustic radio show on Sunday mornings on a Boston station.

"They always play 'Somewhere Over the Rainbow,'" he said. "And they say that the leaves are *green!*" He paused and widened his large eyes as he looked around to see if everyone else got it, because, at this very moment, on October 26, what remained of the leaves on the trees outside the window were red, orange and yellow, not green. No one else quite understood his objections, or didn't care. It was just Danny being Danny.

One of the problems with having rehearsals early in the morning with a group of pre- and young teens was that they were not all that energetic. It could be challenging to rev them up, get them to groove when they still had sleep in their eyes. Mr. Clark tried a combination of approaches to draw their emotions out of them, to do for them what coffee and his go-to-work Vienna playlist did for him. Today, it seemed like the kids needed their own Vienna playlist, or an espresso, or something to get them going. Mr. Clark used trial and error to figure it out.

On the upbeat "Back to the Basement," the first tune he had them play, he tried yelling and cajoling: "Trumpets, count your rests!" Mr. Clark admonished. He followed that up with, "You get to the solo section, then you crap out."

Later: "You're not playing well together."

Pointing directly at Brandon, the bashful lead trombonist and only eighth grader in his section: "Lead your section! You can play louder than that."

To the whole band: "You're really playing jazz well, but you're not playing from here," he said as he pointed to his heart. "It's all

correct, but it's not interesting. Stop thinking and start feeling ...
Feel it. Feel it! Feel it! Make it more than marks on a page!"

As they played "Back to the Basement" again, Mr. Clark
shouted, *More attitude! More attitude!*

Then: *More, more! ... One! Two! Three! Four! One! Two!*

He seemed as though he was trying to use his body language to
prod them into action as he jabbed at the air like he was poking
someone in the chest, picking a fight. His face started to grow damp.
"Do you hear how it's changing? How it's ... *MORE?*"

He directed his flushed face toward the young trumpet players
on the right side of the risers. "Third and fourth trumpets! You were
leaving the lead trumpets out to dry!"

Here was where the mood shifted. The stick was put away. It
was time for the carrot portion of the lesson, the fun part, where,
after he got their blood pumping through their veins, he made them
laugh and forget about their self-conscious adolescent selves. How?
For a reason I didn't quite catch, Mr. Clark decided to explain the
history of flipping someone off with a middle finger, which, confus-
ingly, led him to comment that the band's playing had been slowing
down and was, "Bo. Ring." And, if you possess the mindset of a
middle school boy, this would naturally lead to a discussion about
B.O. and joking that sax player Ethan was likely the source of the
B.O. smell in the room. (There was no B.O. smell, none that I could
detect anyway.) Ethan, always game to mess around, declared that
he had, in fact, applied deodorant before rolling into rehearsal late.

"Did you put it under your armpits, or behind your ears like
you used to do?" Mr. Clark asked.

"I put it on my face," Ethan said dryly.

"You know what I need? Visual deodorant." Mr. Clark pretended
to rub stick deodorant across his eyes. Remembering that parent-
teacher conferences were scheduled for this evening, he speculated
about how the conversations with "parental units" would go if they
heard that he'd been discussing "visual deodorant."

The joking continued as the band prepared to take another stab
at "Dat Dere." Shortly after telling the baritone sax players to play
louder and with more precision, Mr. Clark realized they weren't
paying attention to him, and were not discussing how to improve

their playing, but were instead discussing *SpongeBob SquarePants*. "Stop! Talking!" he shouted as he stomped around in front of the group. Was this genuine annoyance or part of some idiosyncratic Mr. Clark teaching method? "I *hate* SpongeBob!" he added.

Off the surprised and questioning looks the students gave him, he said, "Because it's moronic."

The bass amplifier started crackling loudly as Richie fussed with it. He couldn't get it to stop. The hum of the uncontrolled electricity prompted a discussion about what to do if someone's getting electrocuted. In the event that someone near them was being electrocuted, their fearless leader urged the middle schoolers to knock that person off his or her feet.

As bizarre as it sounds, the combination of the simplistic directorial admonition to "play better" and to "stop thinking and start feeling," mixed with poetic musings on the history of flipping someone off, body odor, visual deodorant, SpongeBob and electrocution was precisely what these kids needed to wake them up and focus them because when they played "Dat Dere," it was, indeed, electric. The students glowed with pride as they recognized that they'd played remarkably well, even as Richie's amp continued to misbehave and send inadvertent, staticky bleats into the air.

"So Mr. Clark," Danny shouted, "you're saying that if you're getting electrocuted, we have permission to wale on you?"

CHAPTER EIGHT

Sorrow in a Shade of Green

‖: For the first time during this year's Big Band rehearsals, I noticed the first blossoms of young seventh-grader romance in the form of Danny using his expressive eyebrows, wise eyes and cute plump cheeks to try to woo Ashley, the flute-playing-girl-next-door who looked much older than she was. Throughout the hour-long practice, Danny kept staring at her and, when she met his glance, he held it for a full second before playfully looking away. She, however, did not turn away, almost like she was daring him.

It seemed as if the sweetness of the flirtation had been transformed into magical pixie dust that was sprinkled throughout the room and everyone had inhaled it. Mr. Clark was in a pleased and positive mood and was much gentler than he'd been with the kids during the past couple of weeks. Even the 7:20 arrival of Richie, who then spent what seemed like an eternity tuning his bass guitar so he could play "Dat Dere," didn't appear to ruffle Mr. Clark, who had other things on his mind. Like Eric Green. Bringing up the subject of Eric Green to this group of students, two months prior to the first anniversary of the 12-year-old's passing, was potent. Mr. Clark's heart remained heavy with loss and with the responsibility to take care of all of these children who were still hurting, wearing their pain on their instruments in the form of green ribbons, in their reluctance to channel their emotions into the ballad they'd been practicing. Mr. Clark wished he could shoulder their suffering, which wasn't possible of course, although he tried. He'd studiously avoided mentioning Eric.

The school had had a strange vibe from the very start of that day in January 2012 after the principal had been notified of Eric's passing by his mother, Suzy Green. There were a lot of closed doors and huddles of stone-faced people in the office. Then the announcement came over the loudspeaker: Teachers in Team A were to head to the teacher's lounge while Team B teachers were to cover for their colleagues. Upon entering the lounge, boxes of tissues were being placed on the tables as the principal, vice principal, guidance counselors and the team leaders gathered. The boyish-looking yet stern principal, Mr. Lavoie, would not make eye contact with anyone. When they were told, the tears flowed. "I was stunned," Mr. Clark said later. "[Eric] was supposed to be in Big Band. I just saw him the day before." The faculty brainstormed about how to inform the students. Before students could be told—by teachers reading from a statement distributed building-wide—Team B teachers had to be informed while Team A teachers returned to classrooms, red-eyed and dazed. Students started asking, "What's wrong with all the teachers?" Rumors flew. Mr. Clark had to stand in front of the seventh- and eighth-grade concert band and look at Eric's empty chair without letting on what he knew. Meanwhile, word was leaking out in the other Southborough schools. Parents who had Mr. Clark's cell phone number were texting him asking him what was going on. Unsure of what to do—"I can't hide my emotions, *ever*."—Mr. Clark asked the band to play every song they had.

The students were summoned to their homerooms as their teachers clutched printed statements to read aloud. Many struggled to push the words out past the lumps in their throats. Some of the seventh graders—in a town that was graced with non-existent violent crime and was relatively free from the loss of their children—openly wept. Others sat there, dumbfounded. Some felt compelled to do something, anything, to prove that Eric mattered, that he was here. Eric's friends were offered the opportunity to go to the guidance department, an option some took, although walking into a room of sobbing classmates seemed too much to bear for a number of them, my son included. Though the students continued to move from classroom to classroom as they normally would, their teachers didn't follow any lesson plans and instead asked the kids if they wanted to talk or watch a video. Mr. Clark had a free period after his seventh- and eighth-grade concert band members left, and he didn't know what to do with himself. He walked to the back of the empty band room, back to that black wooden riser where the trumpet players stood for the Big Band, where Eric had stood earlier that week. It was in that spot where he did what he routinely asked his students to do: Let their emotions out, to feel them. He wept alone.

At lunchtime, the students brought their food to the seventh-grade hallways and ate there together or in seventh-grade classrooms; that's if they ate at all. The school was filled with grief counselors dispatched to Trottier to offer help. Teachers who were parents themselves had a strong desire to lay eyes on their own children, to encircle them in an embrace that they prayed would keep their progeny safe. Lauren and another eighth-grade concert band member headed for the band room. Lauren, a fellow trumpeter, sat in Eric's concert band seat and the two girls bawled in great, messy heaves that teetered on the edge of hyperventilating.

The eighth-grade brass section of the concert band was scheduled to have the last class of the day in the band room. While a couple of students expressed dark thoughts—as in, "I wish it had been me"—others were angry. "Some of the kids were mad at this point, saying, 'This is wrong.' 'This shouldn't have happened.' 'This is crap.' They were looking for answers," Mr. Clark said. As he tried to explain that sometimes in life, things happen that we don't understand, he started crying again in front of the students. "I have to be honest with them."

The mourning also flowed through social media, through Facebook and through a local news blog where people posted memories and shared their grief. "Eric was one of the most amazing kids I knew," an anonymous Trottier student wrote. "Every day, he would come to school with a smile on his face. He was a complete genius. … School is going to feel empty without him there."

"Eric was the most positive kid I knew," another Trottier student wrote on the local blog MySouthborough. "He was always happy. I can't remember a time when someone was angry with him or the other way around. ... I had the pleasure of being in Big Band and Concert Band with him. He always was ready to go with a cheerful attitude. His athletic and academic ability just put him over the top. With him playing four sports and being an A++ student he was the ultimate role model. Everyone in school was his friend, no matter who they were. In honor of Eric, everyone in Trottier should wear green tomorrow."

For the parents, the news came in the form of emails from school principals bearing the ominous subject heading, "Sad News."

The day after his death, students who attended not just Trottier, but the Northborough and Southborough regional high school—Algonquin Regional High School—where Eric's older siblings attended, the Northborough middle school, and two private schools attended by Southborough kids, Worcester Academy and St. John's, wore green, an idea germinated by Eric's seventh-grade classmates. Boys and girls who played town and travel basketball wore green socks. Emerald green ribbons, affixed with safety pins, were distributed throughout the student body. Parents bought bright green duct tape that kids playing all manner of sport stuck onto their jerseys, a green slash over their hearts. Parents in the stands ripped jagged stretches of tape off shared rolls and applied them to their jackets, explaining the reason for the green to the befuddled parents for the opposing teams. Members of Eric's club lacrosse team put stickers, "Eric 37"—for Eric's number—on their helmets. Anything to keep busy, to do something active to mark Eric's memory, other than stew in sadness.

It was standing room only at St. Matthew's Church for Eric's funeral. The sanctuary was filled, as was the overheated meeting room in the basement, where I sat with my elder son, as the service was shown on a closed-circuit television. We had arrived too late to get seats upstairs. A couple of Eric's classmates grew dizzy in the steamy basement and were escorted outside. Dozens more people who couldn't fit inside the church spilled outside onto the sidewalk next to the building. Mourners tugged their long winter coats and scarves around themselves to ward off the January chill, listening to audio on speakers through which they heard the eulogies, the prayers and a recording of Eric's last trumpet performance with the Big Band, where he played a solo in Carl Strommen's "Swing Shift," an upbeat, swing piece with an emphasis on the horns, particularly the trumpet.

After the funeral, green—the color of spring, of new growth, new life—remained omnipresent at Trottier and any place where Trottier seventh graders were present. It was in the forest green rubber bracelets that had Eric's name on them, bracelets adorning the wrists of his classmates. It was in the green ribbons on lapels, backpacks and Trottier middle school instruments. On the green duct tape that the adolescent athletes didn't want to remove from their jerseys, no matter how battered it got after going through the washing machine. Eric's locker nameplate had been colored in with a green marker, transformed into a place where students left flowers and into which they slipped notes that were later delivered to Eric's mother Suzy.

Five months later, during their annual Jazz Night performance in June 2012, the Big Band opened up the wound that was "Swing Shift." Tissues were clutched and there were real concerns about whether the student musicians would be able to make it through the performance wearing a heavy yet invisible cloak of sorrow. The pressure was really on then-eighth grader Brian Keefe, a thin boy with dark hair and intense eyes, who was designated to play what had become known as "Eric's part" on the trumpet for the first time since Eric passed away. Brian delivered. The children, buoyed by their performance, stood tall while the adults in the audience were openly emotional, sniffling and dabbing at reddened eyes, raising more than $1,100 for the Eric Green Memorial Fund, a fund the Greens created to benefit the Trottier music program.

In an email to parents of the Big Band the next morning, Mr. Clark wrote:

What they were able to do last night was astonishing, consider-ing the level of playing, the concentration, the endurance and the emotional strain that was required. Astonishing for musicians of any age and the fact that they are so young makes it even more remarkable.

This year has been difficult to say the least. The kids have shown amazing resiliency and an enormous capacity to care for one another that far surpasses their playing ability...which is at an incredibly high level as you know!! I could not be prouder of them as a team or as individuals.

For the rest of the student body, there was no solace, no release. In fact, three months after Eric passed away, over a pizza lunch, a group of seventh-grade boys told Mr. Lavoie that they were angry with him because nothing had been done to honor Eric. Behind the scenes, administrators and faculty had been mulling how to process Eric's passing, but they didn't share their deliberations with the students until they formed the Eric Green Committee, composed of emotionally crushed students, faculty and Trottier parents. While the committee began its work, Mr. Clark set about using some of the more than $9,000 that had been contributed to the Eric Green Memorial Fund to commission two pieces in Eric's name, one for the 2012-13 seventh- and eighth-grade concert band and one for the 2012-13 Big Band. Each would be played at some kind of memorial/celebratory service slated for the spring of 2013.

Now, ten months after Eric's death, Mr. Clark needed to broach the subject with the Big Band, the fact that they would be asked to play a piece that was being written by composer Erik Morales, in their classmate's honor. "One of the things we're going to be doing is celebrating Eric Green's life," Mr. Clark said, asking if they'd ever noticed if any of their pieces had been dedicated to someone.

No one else said anything. Not even Danny.

"The concert band piece will be remembering that he's gone," Mr. Clark said. "The Big Band piece was supposed to be exciting and happy, like Eric," he added. "We're not going to need to play it perfectly," Mr. Clark said.

"Will people actually buy the song?" Danny asked.

"Yes," Mr. Clark said. The sheet music would be available for people all across the world to purchase. Once it was completed. But the piece wasn't ready yet, so they had to focus on the music in front of them, like "Dat Dere," which they proceeded to play well, the flute section particularly. They got a double thumbs-up plus a heart shape that Mr. Clark made with hands.

♪

A love song was playing, "Fly Me to the Moon"—again—at the same time a very intense staring contest was being waged. Patrick was losing. His opponent, Ashley, who had an unfair advantage because she could hide behind her music stand, whereas Patrick, who was taller than his stand in the back row of the trumpet section, was more exposed. Ashley also could make a scarier stern face than the young-looking Patrick, with his boyish fringe of dark brown bangs skimming his forehead above his glasses. Watching him try to stare her down was like watching a golden retriever puppy try to look ferocious.

"Nothing's fast," Mr. Clark said from the front of the room near his laptop, lazily snapping his right hand slowly as he sipped his coffee. "All laid back, all connected."

Ashley's eyes bored into Patrick's, not letting up. When Patrick gave it his best, harshest look, she turned red and ducked behind the stand. Patrick, triumphant, broke out in a kooky smile.

"Trumpets, we've gone over this," Mr. Clark said, sounding like a nagging parent. "You've got to play soft and warm and pretty."

Ashley stood up and looked at Patrick. He seemed conflicted. He was clearly enjoying the attention, but, with Mr. Clark walking back to his position in front of the band, Patrick seemed worried about getting called out. Ashley wouldn't give up.

After continuing to advise the trumpet players that they need to play longer and take sufficient breaths in order to have enough air "in the tank" by the time they got to the end of the piece, Mr. Clark veered into an early, random tangent, "I have been called an energy vampire. I suck the life out of people."

At 7:35, Richie silently slunk into the room, toting his bass guitar case. Trombonist Brandon and guitarist Jesse had yet to arrive either.

Mr. Clark returned to his iPod to play the Buddy Rich version of "Groovin' Hard" again to help them hear the difference in tone and tempo between this piece and the Sinatra one. The students played well, despite not having their guitarist and lead trombone.

"Overall, very, very good," Mr. Clark said, pleased. But he wanted more. Wanted the trumpet players back on their heels. "I want you to kick the crap out of that," he said.

As they were pulling their sheet music for "Back to the Basement," Ashley stood ramrod straight, donned a cross expression and stared Patrick down. When Mr. Clark looked over at Patrick, Ashley flashed a toothy "I'm innocent" grin. When Mr. Clark looked away, Patrick made faces back at her.

Mr. Clark had a Band-Aid on his left hand. He had been on the losing end of a battle with a basement window the prior day, accidentally breaking the window when he attempted to push the frame back into its proper place. It added a bit of visual variety to his conducting, though it was surprising that, Mr. Clark being Mr. Clark, his Band-Aid was just a boring tan one, and didn't have any cartoon characters on it. Spotting SpongeBob on his hand would've been fun, as fun as a flesh wound can be. Mirth was what Mr. Clark had on the agenda today, at least for sixth-grader Cassidy, whose bass playing on "Back to the Basement" lacked merriment.

"You've got to have fun," Mr. Clark said. "They're going back to the *basement*, where serial killers are, and you're shuffling because no one knows that you're a serial killer and you *don't care*."

Thus began the start of a "being a serial killer is fun" thread. Ethan and Danny started turning the phrase on its head. The notion of killer cereal tickled the group of middle schoolers, as did using cereal boxes as weapons, murder by paper cuts. Who redirected the conversation away from this lively subject? Jesse, who had an actual question about the music, a question about a section of "Back to the Basement."

After he answered Jesse's question, Mr. Clark noticed that the kid didn't have a writing implement. "Get a pencil, Goober," he said.

Jesse didn't take the gift he'd been given and responded he didn't need to get a pencil because he'd remember the advice. Mr. Clark insisted that Jesse get a pencil and write on his sheet music.

Jesse refused. Mr. Clark told him to play two concert Fs, adding, "That's a letter you should be familiar with."

"Oooh," members of the band taunted in a sing-song tone.

Pretending as though he was unfazed despite the color on his cheeks, Jesse responded, "What? That's not a diss."

Mr. Clark let the pencil issue drop. They turned to "Groovin' Hard," which they played exquisitely. Mr. Clark walked into the band area and stood atop an empty chair, looking like Robin Williams in *Dead Poets Society*. From his perch, he yelled for "more" from the trumpet players, stomping his left foot as they approached the huge shout chorus, its crescendo.

Before they could get started on the day's rendition of "Dat Dere," the conversation started to go rogue again. Sixth-grade drummer Martin wanted to discuss *Skyfall*, the latest James Bond movie, but Mr. Clark stopped him because he didn't want to hear any spoilers. Danny wanted to talk about torture, specifically whether putting someone into a box with a scorpion was worse than quartering, which Mr. Clark said was "so 15th century."

CHAPTER NINE

Play is a Verb

Mr. Clark had been stewing. *What should I do about this band? How can I motivate them? How can I help the trumpets?* He experienced an epiphany during a night out with friends at the British Beer Company in the nearby town of Framingham when he figured out "how to untie this knot" of the Big Band. Said epiphany was trotted out on a Thursday morning in late November.

As the students settled into their blue plastic seats, Mr. Clark brusquely kicked aside the worn metal stool in front of the band, declaring, "Two weeks from today, the concert will be over, so we've got to put the finishing touches on. It's time to get to work. Take out the music for 'Back to the Basement,'" they were told.

Although I thought their playing sounded crisp, Mr. Clark stopped them about a minute into the chart. He spent a minute, stooped over, messing around with the microphone and amplifier for the upright piano. Once he appeared satisfied with the microphone, he called for the piece to be played from the top. This time, he silenced them earlier than he had the first time. Trouble with the trombones and bari saxes. He left the Big Band area and walked to the opposite end of the room. I couldn't see what he was doing. The strains of Harry Connick Jr. and his jazz band playing "Supercalifragilisticexpialidocious" filled the air. Mr. Clark had a Kris

Kringle-like twinkle in his eyes as the infectiously jubilant, New Orleans-jazz tune marched along. The students looked puzzled. Bari sax player Danny, who initially knit his dark eyebrows in confusion, started bopping around in his seat. Mr. Clark abruptly cut the song off. Had it been the vinyl record era, there's no doubt that he would've dragged the needle across the record for effect. He started playing Connick Jr.'s upbeat "Do Ri Me," performed with unrestrained excitement.

"What? What's the difference?" Mr. Clark asked. "What? What? What?"

"More laid back?" a student offered, more a question more than an answer.

The drum quality better, someone else added, a statement with which their band director disagreed.

"See, see, see, *this* is what we're missing!" Mr. Clark said. "You don't even *know* what you're missing. ... You're not having any *fun*." In private conversations with me, Mr. Clark posited that they weren't enjoying themselves because they didn't think they deserved to have fun because Eric wasn't there to join them.

He compared their playing to trying to get an A without enjoying the subject matter, to relishing a book they read for pleasure but then having all that enthusiasm sucked out of it by a bad teacher. "That's what you're trying to do with this music, you're trying to get an A. All of you, trying to get an A. ... Knock it off! Listen. Have fun. *Play*! It's a verb."

The third time they began "Back to the Basement," Mr. Clark stood in front of them, clapping out the fast tempo of this thunderclap of a piece that grows roaringly louder as it progresses. He seemed like he was having fun, or was doing a good job of pretending he was. It worked. Their playing was lively, even if it wasn't perfect, which was his point. It was if he'd figured out the way to pull the joy out of them.

"Yes or no?" Mr. Clark asked.

"Yes!" the students replied.

Their zeal wasn't the only thing that was stirred. At that moment, sixth-grade trumpeter Brad announced that he didn't feel well. As he quickly exited the band room, the tiny boy began loudly vomiting.

I could hear the lumpy splash hit the linoleum. Mr. Clark shouted to sax player Ethan to start the music again as he ran out to the music hallway after Brad. There was a lot of crosstalk and uncertainty as Ethan didn't take to the leadership role right away or with any kind of authority. Anisha, the clarinet player, was able to muster a consensus with her suggestion that Noah, the drummer, should lead.

"All right, stop talking!" Noah said, his seldom-heard voice cutting across the din. Brad continued to get sick in the hall. "One, two, three, four, two, two, three, four!"

They played unexpectedly well, energetically and even through the solos, with Ethan providing guidance. Mr. Clark came back three-quarters of the way through the song—Brad had been led to the nurse's office—and, after the music stopped, the band leader picked right up where he had left off with his lecture about how they cannot let their quest to be perfect destroy their love of the music and their enjoyment in creating it.

"Richie, are you going to have fun playing the bass?" Mr. Clark asked.

"I guess," Richie said, his voice flat, his expression one of disinterest.

After Mr. Clark shared a tale about a fellow teacher who had asked him how he hadn't been fired yet for his behavior—joking that faculty members take turns over who has to sit next to him at meetings because he always gets into trouble—he directed them back to "Groovin' Hard."

If Richie showed any joy while playing bass on this piece, it was hard to tell because Mr. Clark said it was difficult to hear him. He wanted Richie to turn the amp up.

They began playing their signature tune again. Mr. Clark yawned in a showy fashion, then reclined on the dirty floor and pretended to be asleep. Students—who were playing in a slow, tired fashion—peered over their music stands to see what he was doing. Those trumpet players and clarinet players in the back stood on their tiptoes in order to get a glimpse. It was pretty clear from their smirks that they got the message.

"Okay, I started doing that because you guys were boring me. I literally could have fallen asleep," he said, "I wouldn't recommend lying down on the band room floor, that's just kind of a bad plan."

He smiled and said, "What's really awesome is that when I laid down you were thinking like, 'Jerk!' Then you played with such intensity, that I could actually feel the vibrations of the music through the floor, like ... like one of those chairs, from, what's that store?"

"Brookstone!" a couple of kids shouted.

They'd been playing "Dat Dere" for weeks, struggling with it. Not today. Not after the British Beer Company epiphany. Mr. Clark treated the song as if it was the first time he'd introduced it to them: "This one covers a range of emotions, kind of cat-burglar kind of cool, small, held back and then it grows into this enormous thing, then it comes back. You've got to kind of embrace all of that. ... One of the cool things about music is that it allows you to experience things that you normally couldn't, wouldn't or shouldn't experience."

A lofty notion, particularly for 7:30 in the morning on a Thursday.

Enter the cat burglars and doughnuts.

"You probably won't ever be a cat burglar. Danny, that would be a bad career choice for you." He pretended to be Danny as a cat burglar, tiptoeing around then getting easily distracted. "Ooh! Look! Doughnuts!"

Then Mr. Clark thought of the worst job for motor-mouth Danny: a mime, a discipline that would also prove impossible for the equally chatty band director. As the conversation pinged back and forth, with Danny chiming in on pastries, baking and mimes ("I am *so* good at miming!"), Mr. Clark smiled and started snapping to the "Dat Dere" tempo, telling the kids, without explicitly saying so, to channel their delight into their playing. The room felt charged, until measure 24 when he told them they needed to go from a softer sound to "an explosion of sound" and "full-on, in-your-face."

One of the saxophonists interrupted the director to ask if he could use the bathroom.

"Are you gonna puke?" Mr. Clark asked.

The boy shook his head, "No."

"Don't puke in your saxophone."

To cap off the puking element of the rehearsal, Mr. Clark treated the class to an even more grotesque tale:

"I was giving a concert one time. And I was in a quintet, so there were only five of us. Even if you're sick, you have to play. So every time I bowed, my stomach would kind of go *blerg*. So one time I bowed and went [*he made a vomiting sound*]. Puked all in my mouth." He paused for dramatic reaction. When the kids asked him what happened to the vomit, he said, "I swallowed it."

I started searching my bags for a plastic bag in case I needed to vomit. Not finding any, I hoped maybe I had some Tums rolling around the bottom of my purse.

Mr. Clark was talking about survivor's guilt again. Not to the students, but about them, wondering aloud to me for the second time this school year whether the kids still weren't allowing themselves to have fun when they played because Eric Green wasn't standing amongst them. Maybe the shadow cast by Eric's death combined with the particular makeup of this Big Band, he suggested, was preventing them from throwing themselves into the music. Or maybe it was because many were high-achieving, serious students who sought musical perfection rather than emotional authenticity. Or maybe their hearts had been so broken that they were reticent to voluntarily make themselves vulnerable again, at least not while their wounds still felt fresh.

Mr. Clark need not have fretted about where they were emotionally, at least not now. On this day, the members of the Big Band seemed like they were posing for stock photos depicting warm camaraderie. Popular kids and jocks were laughing and chatting with straight-A students, those who preferred to blend in with the wallpaper. In interviews with band members, they repeatedly told me that the band room was unlike any other place in the middle school. In here, it was a safe place, a refuge. The cool girl talked with the nerdy boy. The outgoing athletic boy joked with the bookish girl. Everybody was welcomed. Everybody supported one another or at least respected each other.

This was something that Mr. Clark—a self-described band geek in middle and high school—nurtured. Kids were encouraged to hang out in the band room during studies, to eat "Band Lunch." And even when students graduated from the fellowship of Mr. Clark, the protections and emotions of the band room lived within them. The kids were *always* his students; he would have no part of the phrase "former students." To many, the days they spent during early morning Big Band rehearsals, during Band Lunches and extra help instrument sessions left a yawning gap in their lives once they finished eighth grade. A gap that would likely never be filled.

But for the students who were sitting in front of him on this December morning, days away from their debut performance, their chief concerns were playing under the soloists, instead of drowning the soloists out, whether professional wrestling was real, the best way to eat raviolis (Danny said it was eating the "pointy parts first"), tales about their grade-school music teacher who reportedly threw things and what it would take to get the exercise-allergic Mr. Clark to actually chase someone ("Steal his coffee," Noah offered.). Danny started making very strange sounds with his mouth, an odd combination of scales, yelling and yodeling. "I'm talented at everything," he said.

Mr. Clark sustained the lightness of spirit. When he called for the students to pull out the music for "Dat Dere," he imitated a cat, slowly reaching his hands outward like feline paws, then curling them back toward him. After the students finished playing for the morning—only actually getting to "Dat Dere" and "Back to the Basement," because most of the time they were messing around, bonding with each other, something Mr. Clark tolerated more and more as their playing grew stronger—Mr. Clark turned to me and mouthed the word "Check!" as he wrote a check mark in the air. They were becoming a cohesive unit; the kids were finally learning their parts so as not to let down the team. (I hoped this meant there would be fewer shaming sessions making single kids play measures Mr. Clark knew they didn't know.) This was *his* band. And, he was their director, their leader.

There were two lessons that Mr. Clark wanted to bestow upon his young charges during the first week of December.

First, he wanted them to understand the gravity of the loss the music world sustained the prior day when jazz legend Dave Brubeck—famous for "Take Five" among many other pieces—passed away at age 91. "When he was about to graduate from college, they learned he didn't know how to read music," Mr. Clark, who loved history and graduated with a bachelor's degree in it, told the kids. When Brubeck was in the Army, he played piano, and because he was so good at it, didn't have to fight in the Battle of the Bulge. Indeed, when I later looked up Brubeck's bio, I found that Mr. Clark's tale was true, not merely a classroom yarn. "Music literally saved Brubeck's life," a PBS website, "Rediscovering Dave Brubeck with Hedrick Smith" said. "Right before his unit was to be sent to front lines in the deadly Battle of the Bulge, a Red Cross show came through and asked for volunteer pianists, so Dave signed up. He was such a hit that the next day, he was pulled out of his unit and ordered to organize an Army jazz band." Left unspoken: How much Mr. Clark hoped that the music they created in this room would help these particular students heal their wounds.

Lesson number two: Learn how to behave as members of the Big Band during their first public performance. "The Big Band wears all black," Mr. Clark told them. Specifically, they were to don black pants, black dress shirts. Girls could wear the same or a black dress or skirt. One student asked if they should wear green neckties like the Big Band did in June when they honored Eric Green during Jazz Night. "Only if you want to," Mr. Clark responded hesitantly. To the boys he added, "Guys, if you're wearing dark pants and dark shoes, wear dark socks if you ever want to get a date." Another rule for concert night: "Don't go running around like morons on the night of the concert. I want the Big Band to set the example for the rest of the bands."

Were they ready for their first concert? I wasn't sure. Then again, I had no experience with assessing whether young musicians were ready to stand on a stage in front of hundreds of people while the kids were wearing uncomfortable clothing and deliver. On some days, the students played very well. On others, it was a mixed bag.

Today, the bass guitar player for "Fly Me to the Moon," Richie, missed half of the rehearsal. Sax player Danny and flute player Ashley were flirting again when Mr. Clark was talking, pretending to shoot their instruments at each other or use them to mock-bash one another on the head. The Big Band's rendition of "Groovin' Hard" was flat compared to the version the band had turned out a few days ago.

By the time they got to "Dat Dere," Mr. Clark evidently thought some comedic relief was in order. Violinist Natalie handed Mr. Clark a policeman's cap and black, fuzzy cat ears, which he promptly put on his wide head. *Voila!* A cat burglar. "Play well, or I shall wear spandex and everyone will vomit," he warned. The cat ears came off midway through the 1960s jazz tune because Mr. Clark said the elastic was cutting off the circulation to his head.

It was freezing in the auditorium, like it normally was in the band room that was just down the hall. Unlike the band room, however, the lighting was dim. There were no windows and the setting was much more formal. As the Big Band students warmed up in their spot in the pit in front of the stage—the sixth-grade, seventh-eighth-grade concert bands and the orchestra would all perform on stage, while the Big Band and the Stage Band would play from the risers and the pit in front of the stage—their notes carried with them more gravity as they bounced off the walls in the empty room. Their music was less contained and bursting-at-the-seams in here than it was in the band room. It seemed easy for these kids—some of whom still looked like grade schoolers—to get swallowed up, lost in the expanse of the auditorium.

Having rehearsal in the auditorium also did something to Mr. Clark, who didn't seem like his usual Mr. Clark self. He wasn't messing around. Caffeine and adrenaline propelled him around the room in an almost manic fashion. Aside from the fact that their first show was the next week, Mr. Clark himself was trying to work his way through more grief he hadn't shared with his current students. The previous day, while listening to the radio, Mr. Clark heard on the radio that a 23-year-old Boston University graduate student had been killed in a bicycle accident involving an 18-wheeler. Later in the day, a local newspaper reporter called Mr. Clark, asking for a statement because the photojournalism student who died, Christopher Weigl, had been one of Mr. Clark's first students at Trottier. He played the clarinet. "He was an old soul," Mr. Clark told the newspaper reporter about Weigl. "He was kind. He was sweet. He was smart." Weigl grew up a few streets away from Eric Green's family.

After cueing "Dat Dere," Mr. Clark swiftly strode up a side aisle and stood in the middle of the honey-colored wood paneled auditorium, in the center of the middle row of the maroon cushioned seats atop the gray concrete floor. He cupped his hands around his ears. "Stop!" he screamed. "Jesse, go get a tuner." The flutes needed to be louder, he shouted. Some trumpet players still had their bells pointed toward their music stands. He told them to go directly to the crescendo of the piece, the explosively groovy shout chorus and play. The result was a handful of measures played with no energy, no pop, not even close to their best effort.

Mr. Clark stomped to the back of the auditorium to assess the sound quality from the cheap seats. His verdict: They sounded good but weren't in tune. Oh, and he told Martin that the drums sounded as though they were loose. It was also problematic that the flutes and clarinet sections couldn't hear the piano. On the positive side, he asked the students to "show appreciation for the best flute section in the Commonwealth of Massachusetts" for their smooth "Dat Dere" introduction. Overall, he declared that they sounded solid but lacked articulation. "You have to exaggerate," said the master exaggerator.

They responded by amping up their volume. "You just went from a very good band to being a *great* band," he said.

The weak spot in their four-piece set list: "Fly Me to the Moon." Mr. Clark played the Sinatra song on his iPod in the control booth in the back of the room. Sinatra warmly oozed from the auditorium's loud speakers. Other than a small snafu with the drums stepping on the piano solo and the trumpets messing up on measure 64—Mr. Clark responded to that trumpet measure with a juicy raspberry— the rest of the band played the way he'd asked. "Listen to this song once a day until the concert," he said.

"You're playing well as individuals," he said, "but you aren't listening to one another. You're going on autopilot."

Their strongest piece, "Groovin' Hard," came next.

Once again, he ran up the gray, carpeted aisle to the control booth and put Buddy Rich's lively "Groovin' Hard" on the speakers. When the song concluded, he trotted back down the aisle, the way a football coach paces around the sidelines. He cued the band, which had grown in power and confidence during the short period of the rehearsal. When they got to the triumphant, crashing end of "Groovin' Hard," there was a giant cackle from the back of the auditorium followed by Mr. Clark saying with a smile in his voice, "That'll do."

♪

If Mr. Clark was on edge on Friday, his feet were dangling over it on Tuesday. He was hanging on by his fingertips. Dressed in a loose-fitting Tedy Bruschi Patriots' jersey, he was roaming around the auditorium, swerving back and forth from being pleased with his charges to being supremely annoyed with them. Ten seconds into "Groovin' Hard," he silenced them with a dismissive flick of his hand. "You didn't tune! Go find tuners. Go! Trumpets particularly!" The second time they started the piece, the beginning seemed, to my neophyte ears, much better than their first run-through. However, it was clear from Mr. Clark's lion-like stalking that he wasn't satisfied. "Trumpets! Did you warm up the way you normally do?"

No response.

They were ordered to do their breathing exercises as he barked that the beginning of the piece "did not have any energy." He thumped his open right hand on his chest, making a loud, hollow sound to establish the tempo, the tempo. But there was still a problem. The adolescent musicians should have been playing mezzo forte. They weren't. As the band approached the last shout chorus, Mr. Clark made his way back to the front of the auditorium to goad them along, *Go! Go! Go!* When the last note rumbled out of their instruments, he said, "Good morning! [*Big pause*] There you are. *My.* Band."

Too bad they didn't maintain the momentum for "Dat Dere." The miscues multiplied. Ethan needed a new reed for his sax and was taking a long time to locate his back-up. "How long does it take to get a reed?" Mr. Clark asked.

"Why am I wearing this shirt?" he asked, pointing to the Bruschi jersey. "Why did the Patriots win last night? Because everybody played their game. The *whole* game." He was referring to New England's dismembering of the Houston Texans 42-14 at Gillette Stadium in Foxboro in a Monday Night Football contest. Quarterback Tom Brady threw four touchdown passes in the offensive triumph.

"You're standing there like lumps and expecting great music to come out," he said, likening them to the Texans of middle school bands. For about five seconds, there was an eerie silence. The eyes of some of the younger band members widened. Even Ethan seemed chastened.

"Do your job. Every marking on your music has a reason. Every note matters."

With that, he cued them to start "Dat Dere" again. They got as far as Ethan's solo before Mr. Clark pulled the plug. It was the rhythm section again. They hadn't been using the tempo Mr. Clark had set for them. "Honestly?!" Mr. Clark said, frustrated. When guitarist Jesse sought to borrow a pencil from someone because, as usual, he didn't have one, Mr. Clark directed a glare at the boy, "I noticed the guitar didn't go home last night."

Another uncomfortable pause hung in the auditorium. It felt as though the barometric pressure in the room was dropping.

"People play badly because of arrogance and I am sensing a whole lot of arrogance from this band," he said.

Their playing didn't seem bad to me, a little lackluster perhaps, but not insanely wretched, certainly not horrible enough to warrant such a tongue-lashing. That's why I began to suspect that this angry conductor bit was a strategy to get the students focused and motivated for the performance, snap a few of them who tended to space out to attention. Later, when I spoke with students to ask them their thoughts about this rehearsal, many said they were baffled and didn't understand why Mr. Clark seemed so annoyed. Others suggested that he gets worked up before every performance, nonchalantly adding, "He always does that."

Mr. Clark wanted to try "Dat Dere" from the top as he crossly flipped the pages of his score on the music stand in front of him. He stopped them the first time they got to the shout chorus. "Why does the shout chorus sound so good?" he asked. A number of students looked at him in confusion, surprised that a compliment came wrapped in a hostile tone.

Derek, a brave seventh-grade tenor sax player, proffered: "Because we're playing together?" His classmates held their collective breath, wondering if Derek was right, curious as to how Mr. Clark would respond.

"I can't believe that this rehearsal is going this way," Mr. Clark sputtered, looking away from them. "This shout chorus is the hardest thing you'll play, so why not play *everything* like this? ... Guys, you've got to play like it matters."

He appeared to be deep in thought for a moment or two. "You know what it is? You haven't practiced in four days. You haven't looked at this and this is what we've got, a decided lack of leadership."

How many cups of coffee had Mr. Clark consumed that morning? I wondered. *How much sleep had he gotten last night?* During the time I'd been shadowing him and his Big Band, I had never seen him this worked up. It was something that constantly surprised me, the fact that Mr. Clark was among the most popular teachers at Trottier, and he was a yeller, a yeller who could also be a giant teddy bear, but still. He was frequently seen lavishing affection—hugs, jokes, food—on the students. He got to know them really, really well because they were in his classroom for three years, unlike other teachers who only had a student for a single year. It was that tight emotional bond he forged with most, but not all, of his students, which seemed to inoculate him from criticism, from students complaining about his shouting.

I asked a number of his students to list three adjectives which describe Mr. Clark. Inevitably, almost every one of them put "loud" on the list. They said that he yelled at them more than their other instructors. Given the type of town and school district he taught in, one would expect that there would be a stampede of parents lining up at Mr. Lavoie's office door to complain if a teacher scolded a student, never mind outright screamed at a kid. Yet most of the band parents adored Mr. Clark, encouraged him to challenge their kids. They did not darken the principal's doorway, demanding that the band director tone it down. Mr. Clark loved their kids, the parents told me, and he does this for *them*. Instead, parents threw money and adulation at the looks-older-than-he-is band director. Parents were eager to do things to help out Mr. Clark. I had two sons take band classes at Trottier during that school year. And, despite my attempt to keep a professional distance from Mr. Clark because I was working on this project, I found myself lured into the cozy Mr. Clark circle, and on occasion, found myself bringing him a cup of coffee or helping him chaperone a trip.

Mr. Clark seemed strangely immune to parental criticism, except at the beginning of the year when some students don't make the Big Band and parents call to find out why. They were usually pacified when he offered that their children could play jazz in the Stage Band. As for his penchant to be football-coach-like tough on the kids—coaches tend to be afforded more license when it comes to shouting at children than classroom teachers are—Mr. Clark usually got a pass. The kids said they didn't take his shouting personally because they believed that he only yelled because he cared deeply. He wasn't phoning it in. He was pushing them. And they knew they needed to be pushed.

In the auditorium, Mr. Clark picked up his pile of scores and held them to his chest. He rubbed his forehead with his left hand, then placed a hand on his hip. His silence was deafening. "If you're not gonna do it, I can't make you do it."

He placed his left index and middle finger on his lips. "Well, you certainly haven't chosen to do this the easy way," he concluded. The band that was playing right notes, didn't "sound like the band that was here on Friday." *That* band had demonstrated a "love of music, and joy," he said. "This is not how it's supposed to happen."

CHAPTER TEN

Love Made Audible

𝄆 By 6:20 p.m. on December 12, the band room was bustling with the sixth-grade concert band, the seventh- and eighth-grade concert band and members of the Big Band. The orchestra members were in the adjacent chorus room. It was a sea of black and white, with the color green prominently dotting the landscape. It must have been a while since some of the boys had tried on their "good" clothes because many had outgrown them. Some were wearing black pants that were way too short for them, falling well above their ankles, exposing white ankle socks, despite Mr. Clark's recommendations that they wear black socks. A few of their neckties also came up short, not even close to skimming their waistlines. Then there was the matter of tying them properly. A number of these young boys didn't arrive with the ties already around their necks and they lacked the knowledge and experience of how to tie a tie. Several boys, clutching the accessories in their small hands, held them out to Mr. Clark like an offering, asking him for help. Mr. Clark, dressed in a black shirt and suit with a navy and forest green tie, patiently took each boy's tie and put it around his own thick neck and created a knot. The trick was to successfully maneuver the tiny ties off his neck and over his large head without untying them. His face reddened every time he worked a boy's tie over his own neck. He gently pulled the ties over the boys' smaller noggins and adjusted them, just so, beneath their collars.

The girls had no such fashion emergencies. Their attire was much more varied than their male counterparts. Some wore skirts or sophisticated dresses. Others, pants. While most donned cute flats, a few sported mature-looking heels, which coupled with their apparel, made them resemble more sophisticated young women. One girl in a concert band stood out from the pack in her short blue and white dress along with a pink cast encased in a walking boot on one foot and a one-and-a-half-inch white wedge sandal on the other foot.

Mr. Clark stood in front of the band room, where the chairs had been arranged width-wise in the room, and spread his arms out like the iconic Brazilian Christ the Redeemer statue in Rio de Janeiro. He looked like he was going to take off, but was, in reality, simply gesturing to get the noise-level to decrease to a buzz while the students warmed up and tuned their instruments. Two of his former Big Band members—a male freshman from Algonquin Regional High School and a female sophomore at the private St. Mark's school—entered the band room to give their old music director good-luck hugs. They made themselves comfortable in the band room, forever their "safe" place. The girl took her container of yogurt and settled into a window sill in the front of the room, tucking an Uggs-clad foot beneath her. Two more former students, now much taller than their former teacher, popped in to lay monster embraces on him. When it was time for the alums all to leave, they wistfully looked around at the clutch of current band students before reluctantly departing to take their seats in the auditorium. They would later tell me that music just wasn't the same without Mr. Clark.

The band members had been told to arrive by 6:30. But given the experience thus far with the Big Band, I didn't expect they'd all make it in time. There were many, including the usual suspects— like Jesse, Harry and Henry—who arrived nearly fifteen minutes late. Nervous chatter and big smiles filled the room before Mr. Clark led them all in the musical scale, sung in the beautiful voices of 157 middle schoolers, a technique that opens their throats and got them using "serious amounts of air," Mr. Clark said, adding that it also got their "ears working so it helps with intonation." They played the scales in a three-part round. After exhorting them only to tune further if asked to do so, a group of drummers carrying drumsticks who had nothing to do started playing energetic games of Rock, Paper, Scissors while talking up two female tuba players. One of the male concert band drummers initiated a drum stick dual with the female concert band drummer standing next to him. A female tuba player—with pin-straight, streaked strawberry blonde hair and makeup—tossed her hair around, getting the attention of one of the Rock, Paper, Scissors drummer boys. The collection of students in the room revealed a wide variety of middle school students, the tiny ones who were goofy little kids and the ones who wore shaggy Justin Bieber-like hair, to one eighth grader who sported the dark shadow of a burgeoning mustache and a minuscule oval spot that one could argue, if pressed, was the nascent beginning of a goatee. Some were chill, looking at their phones, while others were having slap fights.

As showtime neared, Mr. Clark delivered his typical, off-the-cuff, pre-performance pep talk. In this case, he was uncharacteristically brief.

To the sixth graders, who'd be making their first appearance as members of a Trottier band: "You are a performer. You are not an 11-year-old."

To them all: "When you walk through those doors," he pointed to the double doors leading to the band room, "the performance has started."

Without a doubt, the main event of the night was the premiere performance of the elite Big Band. Though the seventh- and eighth-grade band dwarfed them with numbers—eighty students—the Big Band had the most songs, four. Their faces reflected their angst. The normally confident-seeming Jesse was uneasily tuning his guitar and the sound that was coming from his instrument was just terrible. Mr. Clark looked bemused, cocked his head to the side and said, "Nope."

I wondered how they'd fare given that their last rehearsal was a disaster. Mr. Clark had been very hard on them, called them arrogant, insinuated that their elite status had gone to their heads, that they hadn't earned anything. That was a lot of pressure to press down onto the shoulders of a 12- or 13-year-old. I hadn't spoken with Mr.

Clark since that practice so I couldn't get a bead on where he was in his head, or where the students were for that matter. My Big Band son and I agreed I wouldn't attempt to question him until we sat down for a "formal" interview, so I didn't know where he was emotionally, either. This would be the group's first big test.

The first selection, "Back to the Basement," opened with a burst of sound and likely caused some auditory discomfort to those sitting in the front rows. Reader, they were outstanding. Mr. Clark radiated pleasure and danced, despite his earlier pronouncement to the audience that there would be none of that. From top to bottom, they sparkled. Richie's bass solo grooved. Ethan's sax solo was like melted caramel. *Go! Go! Go! Go!* Mr. Clark thundered, slamming his hand onto an imaginary drum with his right hand so hard that it looked like he might pull a muscle. The group concluded the piece with a musical fusillade followed immediately by applause and whistles from the crowd ,which by now packed the auditorium to the point where people were standing in the back. Former members of the Big Band, now high schoolers, rose from their seats and hooted appreciatively. This Big Band did not sound like a bunch of middle schoolers who were still shedding baby teeth. They had soul. They were playing beyond themselves. And they didn't even know it.

Mr. Clark introduced the funky "Dat Dere" by saying that it resembled a groovy theme from a 1970s TV show. Plus, he said, "It features the best big band flute section." From beginning to end, the wry song was smooth, rising like a rollercoaster and plunging excitedly into notes and melodies. The shout chorus, the most provocative part of this chart, revved like a sports car, with Mr. Clark at the wheel, steering, making his own sharp turns and fluid motions.

The same cannot be said for "Fly Me to the Moon." Perhaps buoyed by the success of the first two pieces, Mr. Clark raised audience expectations. "Now we're going to channel our inner Sinatra," he said. He overpromised. Facing the ensemble, he breathed onto the back of his hand as a signal to the kids to breathe easy, delicately, like warm fog. This was a lilting love song but the students were still in high gear, still revved up to a level where they couldn't restrain the tempo or their breath of fire. "Fly Me to the Moon" suffered, coming on the heels of their top-notch rendition of "Dat Dere."

"Groovin' Hard" was the sticky, sweet cherry on top of their performance. Upon hearing the name of the last tune, the Big Band alums in the audience cheered approvingly. It was a student favorite. The smile that curled around Mr. Clark's face was enormous. The sax soli, when the seven boys rose from their seats in unison, went off brilliantly. I could feel their power, passion, life and, most important, the fun these kids were having, something not in evidence during "Fly Me to the Moon." Still, Mr. Clark pushed, yelling, *Go! Go! Go!* prodding them to kick up their playing one more, impossible notch. By the end of "Groovin' Hard," I was surprised that the kids had any air left in them, that they didn't just flop down on the floor from the emotional energy they'd just laid bare. The crowd celebrated their achievement with a well-deserved standing ovation.

Afterward, there was an abundance of hugs, sweaty children and the blinding flashes of smartphone cameras as the students dispersed in the band room and the congested lobby area. Mr. Clark's triumphant arrival into the band room was delayed because members of the seventh- and eighth-grade band, mostly girls, were throwing their arms around him, hugs which he reciprocated in papa bear-like fashion. Trottier alums came rushing into the room to embrace him, even if they already hugged him before the show began. As Mr. Clark tried to make his way from the band room to the lobby— some of the alums were arm-wrestling current band members—he was similarly swarmed like a celebrity. And here at Trottier, he was.

Now for something entirely different: New pieces. Duke Ellington's "In a Mellow Tone" and Erik Morales' affecting "Finding You Here."

Upon hearing the ballad "Finding You Here," a testament to love and longing, over the auditorium speakers—all the band equipment was still in the auditorium from the concert so rehearsal was in here—Mr. Clark told them that this piece was about long notes. It was very, very slow and soft.

"Yes?" he said with a big question mark at the end, seeking their approval for his selection.

"That was just chill," Danny said softly.

"Can you hear that these two tunes are different in tone and style than the previous four?" Mr. Clark asked, referring to both "Finding You Here" and "In a Mellow Tone." "That's no accident." Musical variety was a key factor for their upcoming musical competitions where demonstrating a mastery of an array of genres was necessary in order to be considered for top honors.

Mr. Clark had them sing notes from the first several measures aloud in order to get a handle on the timing and tone. They sounded like an angelic choir. It wasn't as smooth-going when they started to play the piece from the beginning on their instruments, but it wasn't that bad considering they'd never seen the music before.

Mr. Curtis, their elementary school band director with a reputation for being dedicated and a little off-beat, appeared in the auditorium shadows. He was the one who ushered these students into the world of jazz at the Neary Elementary School, where many of these kids were part of the Neary Blues Band or the concert band for fourth and fifth graders. Mr. Clark, eager to show off his band, had them play "In a Mellow Tone," bragging that they *just* got the music.

"It already sounds good!" Mr. Curtis enthused.

Delighted by how quickly the kids were getting to know the new piece, Mr. Clark asked them, "You want to play 'Dat Dere' for him?"

"Yeah!" the majority of the kids shouted.

Mr. Clark told them to stand as they played. "Mr. Curtis is in the house, you should be standing anyway," he added, as he high-fived his colleague from the nearby Neary Elementary School. Their "Dat Dere" was as strong today as it had been during the concert.

Mr. Curtis clapped heartily. "That was great! That was a great Christmas gift!"

"Finding You Here" was a difficult song for these middle schoolers to fully grasp. In the introduction to the 2005 piece, composer Erik Morales said this is a ballad which "pays homage to the great work of Neal Hefti, specifically, to a piece he wrote for the Count Basie orchestra entitled 'Li'l Darlin','" describing it as having "a slow and easy tempo." A music website referred to it as a "laid-back … slow cooker." However, the Big Band's early rendition of it was uneven, loud in the wrong places, not tender enough in others. Mr. Clark asked them to start and stop several times, trying to guide them to the right frame of mind, describing the piece as "warm, gentle and lovely." None of that worked to his satisfaction. He laid his head on the music stand, face down.

His comedic act seemed to break the tension, a cue to the class to loosen up. Bari sax player Danny took the opportunity to make a crack about the possibility of a constipation plague. Plagues were a big thing in the band room, all kinds of plagues, the grosser the better. It was a running joke that cropped up in conversation from time to time, usually prompted by Danny or Ethan. This current plague discussion was sparked by Danny noticing that Mr. Clark had been straining and red-faced while conducting, hence a plague of constipation popped into his head. This led to Mr. Clark's recollection of how, during Health Week, he mercilessly mocked a former Big Band member, who was now in ninth grade, after the boy had been asked to make a school-wide announcement about constipation and eating a high-fiber diet. Since several kids in the room knew the boy and one had a brother who was also a freshman, Mr. Clark encouraged them to immediately text the ninth grader about regularity and constipation. They gleefully whipped out their phones.

It took quite an effort to rein the class in and direct them back to "Finding You Here," which Mr. Clark described as, "Love made audible, like chocolate is love made edible." This piece had something Mr. Clark called "forward-falling momentum that needs to be contained."

"Practice so that you can get your instruments to express your emotions," Mr. Clark added before he played the tune on his iPod. "Let this piece speak to you." The looks on their faces belied boredom, spacing out, or perhaps, they really were concentrating. It was unclear. "You're dancing with someone and you never want it to end," Mr. Clark said, closing his eyes, putting his arms up in the air, pretending to sway with an imaginary partner. As the recording came to an end, he raised his hands and said, "From the beginning…"

♪

The guitarist and both bari sax players were still out sick. Adding to the tally of the missing: a clarinet and flute player. Bassist/drummer Richie arrived a half hour late. Mr. Clark didn't call attention to it.

That was also the day when, according to the 5,125-year-old Mayan calendar, the world was supposed to end. The story was sucking up all the oxygen on the Internet and on cable news. It wound its way into the band room, hitching a ride on the back of one of many references saxophonist Ethan liked to make about some kind of killer plague. Making note of the multiple absences this morning, coupled with the fact that several kids had been coughing, Ethan declared it eerily ominous. Even Danny was out with a fever. After hearing that, Mr. Clark quipped, "Danny *is* a fever."

"We have about twelve hours to live," added sax player Harry, who, like he had been the day before, looked exhausted and could not stop yawning. He didn't look like someone who was all that worried about the demise of humanity.

Mr. Clark decided that, if the world was going to end, the students should "spend it making music. If we're going to go down, let's go down swinging."

The students did not agree. They appeared to want to go down gabbing, mostly nonsense, amongst themselves. It was as if a funnel cloud of chatter had dipped down in the middle of the ensemble. Anisha, a diligent student and precise clarinet player, got into an argument with Farah, another A-student and flute player, with Anisha loudly insisting, with a panic threaded through her voice, "The world is *not* going to end!" Later, Anisha, who was standing behind Farah, started kicking Farah, as though kicking the flutist who said humankind was on its way out, would somehow make Anisha feel better. Mr. Clark, who rarely reprimanded these two, said if they kept fighting it *would* be the end of the world.

Despite the talk of doom and destruction, the Christmas spirit was able to float above the fear like pine-scented air freshener. Rebecca, a mostly mum clarinet player, was wearing a red Santa hat and a festive green dress that spoke loudly on her behalf. Mr. Clark tried to elevate the mood by telling a story about how, during a recent trip to the Solomon Pond Mall in the neighboring community of Marlborough, he was sassed by the mall Santa. "You're getting there," Saint Nick said rubbing his own white beard and portly belly, eyeing Mr. Clark's protruding pooch. The forty-something Mr. Clark, with his whitish-gray hair, mostly white beard and wire-rimmed glasses, did bear a striking resemblance to Santa. His father had been a mall Santa for years, and when Mr. Clark worked at McDonald's in high school, he, too, was a Santa for two seasons. His mother, Maureen, even gave him a handmade Santa suit, something which he stuffed into his closet only to be discovered years later by his two daughters who seriously speculated about whether their dad could possibly be St. Nick, complete with his deep and contagious chuckle.

Music did not seem to appear anywhere on the students' agenda this morning, even though Mr. Clark tried to redirect their attention to Ellington's "In a Mellow Tone," a tune with notes that, when played well, sound like how drawn butter tastes. However, the way the Big Band was playing it, it didn't sound smooth and rich. It sounded mangled. The song's overall rhythm was faulty. The sax section was awkward. "I think the word that best described this section is 'pathetic,'" Mr. Clark told them unsympathetically, something one could not imagine a benevolent Santa saying.

Instead of fighting the ennui hanging over the ensemble like a fog, Mr. Clark shifted to Morales' lovely "Finding You Here," which slowly unfolds itself like a languid kiss. With a slow ballad like "Finding You Here," Mr. Clark said mistakes are much more obvious. To place an accent on a note, they needed to do so like they were giving it a firm but gentle push, not a slap like they'd done with other, more up-tempo pieces.

To maneuver them into the right mental space, he drew more analogies, applying the light touch of Monet's paintbrush to his portrait of the piece. "You need to find something that you don't want to end, and it *can't* be the world," he said, raising an eyebrow in Ethan's direction. He suggested that they think of items like a book, a movie, a meal, a nap, even a slow dance with the love of your life. That last one seemed to be the image he hoped they'd hold in their minds, although asking 11-, 12- and 13-year-olds to consider dancing with a soul mate seemed a tall order. "It's gotta have something that you don't want to end. … For you eighth graders, it could be that you don't want to leave Trottier." Now it was that last analogy that I think clicked with the kids because their second rendition of "Finding You Here" sounded eminently better. Carol, a dual flutist/pianist, played the opening piano measures exquisitely. About a minute into the piece, Ethan delivered a lush sax solo that had no business coming out of the bell of a 13-year-old boy's wind instrument.

"Whatever you just did," Mr. Clark said, a Cheshire cat smile creeping across his lips, "was so much better."

CHAPTER ELEVEN

Tiny Capers

‖: Upon walking into the band room on the first Friday in January, I spotted this written in green ink on the white board in the front of the room: "Gangnam Style should NOT have been Teen Nick Top 10 #1 video of 2012." The declaration about the odd one-hit wonder by South Korea's Psy and the wave of yawns overtaking the students notwithstanding, Mr. Clark used this rehearsal to introduce new pieces of music, four more of them, hoping to spark the kids' interest. Two compositions were upbeat and playful, the others were polite and very, very low-key.

The first, "Cute," a classic 1950s Count Basie tune written by Neal Hefti, a composer who had written a lot of music for Basie's band as well as the theme songs for the *Batman* and *The Odd Couple* TV shows. It was a soothing piece that shined the spotlight on the rhythm section as the drummer, in this case, my son Noah, would use metal brushes instead of harsh sticks. Normally, he preferred the loud, aggressive pieces, but in this case, he relished the challenge of playing with the brushes. The rest of the students smirked upon hearing the song's name, but as Mr. Clark played it from his iPod through the speakers, only one of the sax players seemed to be bopping along with the music. Most were motionless. Some kids were expressionless, mouths open. His Big Band did not look jazzed.

The other mellow piece, "Tiny Capers," by Clifford Brown from 1953, reminded me of a restrained-yet-perky game show theme. In the sheet music for the Carl Strommen arrangement, Strommen referred to this as a bebop tune, an early modern jazz, post-World War II style that utilized improvisation and complex melodies, not the type of tune to which one dances. There was no reaction from the students as they heard this for the first time, unless you call looking bored a reaction. They looked like they'd been asked to demonstrate the box step in front of the class with an elderly teacher. Bari sax player Danny, usually brimming with energy, sighed.

However, "Tiger of San Pedro," a classic Latin jazz 1970s piece by John LaBarbera, brought them alive with its excitement and the undeniable force of forward motion, starting off with lively plunks of the piano keys, authoritative trumpet blasts and precise, fast-paced drumming. Hearing this pulled some smiles out of the kids, injected some fresh air into them. As the piece came to an end, I thought that if I had been a member of the Big Band's trumpet section, I would have been freaking out because this piece was very trumpet-heavy.

The tune that was like a Molotov cocktail of energy tossed into the middle of the room? "Play That Funky Music." The 70s ditty, made famous by the group Wild Cherry, slid into the band room on a slick of cheesiness, funk beat, a cowbell and sick guitar chords. Smiles all around, tapping feet, happiness, anticipation. Danny enthusiastically lip-synched as he grooved his head back and forth. Jesse, upon hearing the booming guitar solo, broke out into a giant grin. This was something they really wanted to play. Ditto for "Tiger of San Pedro."

The pieces were dangled in front of them, chum in the water, as Mr. Clark pulled a little bait-and-switch, asking them to pull out the original pieces on which they'd been working for the past few months.

"Back to the Basement" sounded great. The trumpet players seemed unusually confident. I could hear it in their strong notes and see it in their solid, bells-up stances, except for Brad who was still crouched behind his music stand, his chest caving in as he looked like he'd rather be elsewhere.

"Groovin' Hard" was filled with noticeable pleasure. The kids really got into it, even as Richie strolled in twenty minutes late and no one remarked upon it.

"Nice!" Mr. Clark said. "Nice, nice, nice, nice!"

On "Dat Dere," the playing was much shakier, not including the sensational shout chorus which the band had now mastered. The uncertainty, the hesitation hung over this composition. "We lost a lot of ground on this one," the band director observed. This was one of three pieces that they would definitely be playing at the University of New Hampshire jazz festival in March, he said, so they needed to get really comfortable with it.

They bounced back with their version of "In a Mellow Tone," which was surprisingly sharp. As I was growing impressed with their sage performance, about three-quarters of the way through, it crumbled. "You've got to practice," said the master of understatements.

♪

It was the start of a week of mourning and rubber bracelets by the boxful. Not too far into that morning's rehearsal, Ethan, Brandon and Noah left with two other non-Big Band eighth graders to distribute bracelets, which Eric Green's mother Suzy had ordered, to fellow Trottier students as they arrived. The thick, green rubber accessories said, "Eric" bookended by hearts on either side of his name, and "Trottier-Southborough" on the other. One was handed to each member of the Big Band, a group in which Eric would have been playing his silver-colored trumpet had he not passed, as the students were reminded that Friday was the one year anniversary of his death. Kids encouraged one another to wear green.

"Go! Do good things," Mr. Clark said to the boys as they left to hand out the bracelets.

It had already been a somber time for Mr. Clark, whose mood had been darkened by the recent string of terrible news all occurring within a few weeks of one another: the murderous rampage at Newtown's Sandy Hook Elementary School, the death of a former student in a bicycle accident, the suicide of another former student, and now the anniversary of Eric's passing. His eyes watery, he told me that he had been "very heartbroken" as of late. His wife, Colleen, said he hates it when he cannot help his students or friends when they're in pain or having trouble. He likes to go into action hero mode, wants to help, to rally the troops, to give the kids what they need. "He worries about all of his students," Colleen said. "He sits there and stews on how he can help." Longtime friend Matt Newton, who Mr. Clark called "Fig," observed, "Jamie is one of those people who gives and gives and gives until there's nothing left."

Years prior, one of Mr. Clark's seventh-grade Big Band members, Danielle Doherty, lost her father, leaving her mother Julie to raise four children including a baby. Mr. Clark, who'd also been giving Danielle private music lessons, swooped in to help, offering to drive her to and from school to ease the burden on her overwhelmed mother. He allowed her to seek solace in the band room during the school day whenever she needed it. He also made sure she had lunch every day. "He kind of took care of her when I was struggling to keep my head above water," Julie said. On Danielle's birthday, Mr. Clark bought a fast food buffet of fries, burgers and chicken tenders for Danielle and her friends to enjoy in the band room. "He would reach out to me and reach out to me," Julie said. "I always knew he was right there, taking care of her." The Dohertys grew quite tight with the Clark family as Mr. Clark's daughters befriended Danielle and the two families went on a vacation together. One evening, Mr. Clark surprised Julie and Danielle by getting them tickets to a Bruce Springsteen concert in Boston for Julie's birthday because a Springsteen tune had been Julie and her deceased husband's wedding song. Mr. Clark drove the mother-daughter duo to the concert, watched a ball game on TV in a restaurant near the Boston Garden until the concert ended, then drove them home. "He just makes life easier," Julie said.

When Dennis Wrenn, the music director at the Algonquin Regional High School, died in Greece before heading home from a school jazz group trip, Mr. Clark and the band director from the Northborough middle school met the airplane carrying the grieving students at Logan Airport in Boston, so the kids would have familiar, comforting faces there to comfort them. "My high school jazz band had arrived home from Greece twelve hours after our teacher and friend Mr. Dennis Wrenn had collapsed in Athens and passed away before our eyes," wrote Jacqueline Cole, a former student of Mr. Clark's, in a letter. "It was without a doubt the worst thing that has ever happened to me. When we reached the airport we met our parents and Mr. Wrenn's family and we hugged them and cried. There was very little that could be said to make us feel better. But there in the crowd of parents, I saw that same man who had lifted my spirits so many times before. And though I was by no means better, I knew that I was being supported, and that someone who knew how to care with all his heart, cared. And for that evening, that was enough."

Jacqueline's classmate, Kelsey O'Hare, agreed. "I'm not entirely sure why, but it was such a relief to see him there," said Kelsey, who followed in her mentor's footsteps to become a music teacher. "The music teachers knew the situation better than the parents did."

Although she was initially afraid of Mr. Clark when she met him when she was a sixth grader, Kelsey said he was the type of big-hearted teacher who noticed when she was struggling with her parents' divorce and the death of her grandmother. He gave her the space and opportunity to vent. "He's so supportive," she said. "He makes everyone feel like they're important." Kelsey even became the Clark family's babysitter for a while, watching Mr. Clark's two young daughters, uniting his home life with his working one.

Count college music student Channing Moreland, a former Big Band member and student who took private lessons with Mr. Clark, as another member of the Mr. Clark fan club. "I had a hard time in eighth grade and he would talk to me about everything," she said, relating how, when she would attempt to mask her angst, he would draw it out of her, insisting that she tell him what was going on because he knew things weren't quite right. Channing started keeping a notebook into which she'd jot questions about religion, politics and life, which would constitute the "topics of the week" she'd discuss when she sat down with Mr. Clark for her private music lessons. Bonding with him "changed my life," she said. When Channing graduated from high school, he gave her "the most thoughtful thing I've ever received," a letter about how she had been a "true joy" to teach, along with a series of books about music, Shakespearean sonnets, a music journal and an actual journal. Channing says she still remembers the emotions that playing in the Big Band drew out of her. "I have never cried so much playing an instrument as I did in eighth grade."

When Steph Bacon, who went on to attend NYU and study vocal performance, was a member of the Big Band, he said Mr. Clark made him feel supported and safe. "He was like my first mentor that I idolized," Steph said, saying that his band director attended all of his theater productions when Steph entered high school. "I really looked up to Mr. Clark. ... He made me feel comfortable with whom I am."

Another boy, only one year removed from the Big Band, wept when he tried to articulate how much he missed making music with Mr. Clark. Like many of his peers, he partook of Band Lunch multiple times a week when he was in middle school. Why? "Because we wanted to be with Mr. Clark," he said. "He's a friend."

"My hero is Jamie Clark," wrote former student Torie Shakespeare in an essay for middle school that was shared with Mr. Clark. "... [A] hero is someone who makes a difference, changes your life for the better, and who can constantly make you smile. Mr. Clark: a common, yet perfectly special hero."

"Rarely will you find a middle school teacher who has students who are in high school and college still coming back to visit him regularly," Jacqueline wrote in a letter about her former band director. "I know that I personally will always keep in touch with him and I am not far out of the ordinary. His effect is that monumental."

It was Green Day at Trottier. Especially in the band room. There was green of every description. Moss. Kelly. Mint. Forest. Sea green. Lime. It came in the form of scarves, golf shirts, Celtics jerseys, a Champion T-shirt, a Summer Youth Music School tee, a Nike shirt, a Life is Good pullover, hair ribbons, a green and black plaid shirt, a headband. Nearly every member of the Big Band was in green of some kind. I joined in, wearing a green blouse and donning the green rubber bracelet Mr. Clark had given me.

It was baby-faced Brandon and his earnest trombone playing during "In a Mellow Tone" who broke the mood open with joy, despite the green. "You've got a big, fat, gorgeous jazz sound," Mr. Clark told him, praising him as the best trombonist in middle school.

"'cept for you!" Danny said.

"But he's not in middle school," Ethan replied. "He's 800 years old!"

The tension was starting to ease, like roiling waters had been sprung from behind the dam wall.

"I knew Abe Lincoln," Mr. Clark said, noting that although the sixteenth president was kind of a dark dude, attitude-wise, he had a "wicked sense of humor."

"How many vampires did he kill?" Ethan asked, referencing the horror flick from the prior year, *Abraham Lincoln: Vampire Hunter*.

I was concerned about how they would handle the fragile "Finding You Here," given the day, given their mental states. This piece was rich with longing and demanded that they be extremely vulnerable. "Think about your sounds as being three-dimensional. I want it deeper. ... I want a giant mass of sound. It needs to be thicker and deeper, warmer. ..." Mr. Clark's appeal for them to patiently stoke the embers of the sound was shattered by his piercing shriek. Mr. Clark had knocked over his travel mug of coffee. It was a false alarm. Not a single drop of his precious, caffeinated liquid gold had spilled.

♪

It was nearly epidemic. The not practicing business. The not knowing the piece business. The befuddled or self-conscious looks on the students' faces, some of whom were confused by parts of the pieces. Surveying the situation, Mr. Clark didn't seem to be inclined to make things easier for them. They had to show him that they wanted to play these pieces better, or, at the very least, appear to be making an effort.

Right from the outset, Mr. Clark seemed like he was in a difficult mood, peppering the students with questions. Did they tune? Did they have pencils? Were they ready to play?

Guitarist Jesse said he couldn't find the sheet music for "Cute," the first tune for which Mr. Clark called. Instead of directing the eighth grader to the front of the room where he knew there was a large wooden shelving unit filled with music for all the pieces the Big Band played—something that Jesse should have already known to do since he'd been playing for Mr. Clark for two years—his band director shook his head and didn't respond to Jesse's feigned help-lessness.

"I'm a little annoyed with some of you and we'll talk about that in a minute." He charged ahead, cued them to start "Cute" and pretended not to see that Jesse was just standing there, not playing, actively blushing a plum red. After listening to his bandmates play for several measures, Jesse reluctantly put down his guitar and pushed past the other members of the percussion section in order to fetch more sheet music.

In the meantime, "Cute" proceeded a tad unevenly as some of the students weren't articulating their notes clearly enough during this paragon of musical restraint. Singling out Noah, the drummer, whose application of his brushes to the drums during this song was as smooth as an icy milkshake in a chilled metal cup, Mr. Clark said, "Awesome! Awesome! Awesome!" encouraging the rest of the band to applaud the eighth grader. The compliment was quickly followed by the criticism. He critiqued the trumpet section, saying they played with their bells down and many in the brass section clearly hadn't familiarized themselves with the piece. "Sorry brass, I am not gonna teach you that," he said, indicating that a particular measure on which they were fumbling "wasn't very challenging," especially for them. As a listener, I shared his frustrations with their lack of preparedness. The situation reminded me of a parent who asks a child to put away his backpack instead of dumping it in the middle of the kitchen floor. But the kid keeps leaving it there anyway. At some point, the parent is going to lose patience.

When they played "In a Mellow Tone," the Big Band sounded first-rate until about three-quarters of the way through where there was supposed to be a dynamic shift from irreverent bleats being punched out staccato-like, balanced alongside smooth brass lines, to a softer mode of playing. After playing loudly and joyfully, the band was supposed to yoke the volume in order to build it back up into a swelling of sound, sprinkled with whimsical piano playing at its conclusion. "No, no, no, no, no! You've gotta be soft!" Mr. Clark shouted.

At this point, the fact that students hadn't practiced or showed up late or didn't have their music faded into the background, replaced with thoughts of Eric and the memorial mass that had been held for him over the weekend. Patrick had played "Taps" on his trumpet during the mass at St. Matthew's, which several of the band members had attended, bunched together in the front pews in their pull-over sweaters and bulky winter coats. For the second time during this rehearsal, Mr. Clark asked the band to celebrate a fellow band member, this time for Patrick for representing the Big Band with great poise.

Now he turned the spotlight on himself, on his error of omission from the prior rehearsal. He said a member of the Big Band, who he declined to name, had told him it was wrong not to have had a Big Band moment of silence for Eric on the one-year anniversary. "Eric is never far from my thoughts. *Ever*," Mr. Clark said, his eyes filling with salty tears. "I apologize for that."

For a long-seeming sixty seconds, the usually noisy room fell silent. The students looked down, as if saying a prayer in their heads. Lauren—who was standing in what was once Eric's spot in the trumpet section, the only eighth grader in the section—reddened. Others appeared to be trying to contain emotions within their growing bodies. "I hope you accept my apology," Mr. Clark said, breaking the quiet. "Thank you to the person who spoke with me." He continued, almost as though trying to make restitution for earlier crankiness, "I give you a hard time because I want you to do well. ... You are a remarkable group of people and individuals. What's important are the people in this room, the music, not the competitions or awards." The students met his gaze, nodded in silent agreement and, when he dismissed them, the children softly filed out of the room, lacking their usual loud bustling.

CHAPTER TWELVE

Chicken-in-a-Can

𝄆 There were three drummers in the Big Band, two of them eighth graders, Noah and Richie, the third a seventh grader, Martin. Noah and Richie typically divvied up most of the songs, with Noah taking the up-tempo pieces and Richie the ballads. Martin took a smaller mix of the two. But all three were expected to know every Big Band composition because if someone was absent, the remaining drummers were expected to fill the gap. These three were reserved boys who infrequently spoke out during rehearsals.

On this particular morning, both Noah and Richie were late to rehearsal. Noah, who'd overslept, despite my prodding and hollering from the bottom of our stairs, breezed in at 7:15 after his father drove him in. (I left the house without him because I didn't want to be late.) Richie, whose frequent tardiness had not been explained, at least not to the band, walked in at 7:37. That threw the spotlight onto Martin, who was unaccustomed to and distinctly uncomfortable with it. It was Martin's bad luck that the opening piece for this rehearsal was "Back to the Basement." The thoroughly chill Martin did not maintain the rapid tempo. Even when Mr. Clark stood in front of the boy and clapped out the rhythm loudly, Martin didn't alter his relaxed playing. "Martin! You've got to get to the tempo!

You're slower than me," Mr. Clark said, huffing a bit. "I'm winded from clapping."

To further demonstrate what he wanted, Mr. Clark picked up mallets and pounded the beat on a nearby timpani drum that he wanted Martin to replicate. Then he banged the wooden ends of the mallets together. During the band's second attempt at "Back to the Basement," the students seemed at ease even though they hadn't played this piece in a while. Maybe a bit too comfortable, like a warm, cozy blanket and fuzzy slippers that make you feel ready-for-a-nap comfortable. "Wow! Talk about boring!" Mr. Clark said. "No life, no anything." Again, they started the shuffle, and again, Martin's tempo wasn't right, which was a problem because a band follows the tempo set by the drummer.

"Tiny Capers," which had a much different vibe, was no better for Martin. "Martin, buddy, do you drink coffee?" the band director asked the seventh grader. "I'm not telling you to drink coffee, but you're playing like," he yawned and then pretended to tap on imaginary drums with molasses-like speed while continuing, "We need a bit more energy and life," he added, telling the typically strong sax section that they, too, were playing "lifelessly." "Martin, you're affecting people."

Sometimes, when Mr. Clark was trying to inspire his students, it seemed as if I could see him thinking, trying to find the right approach, the right anecdote, the right move. Here, his clapping, pounding and stick banging wasn't working. *Maybe, a ridiculous story would do the trick*, I imagined him saying to himself. There was a new trailer for a zombie movie, he said, in which the scary zombie's still heart burst to life upon seeing a pretty girl, an instant reaction.

He looked directly at Martin now. "We are going to go a little *faster*! We are going to go faster when the rhythm section goes faster, electro-shock therapy."

"Maybe we could all bring in our own tasers," Danny suggested, as a few snickered.

Mr. Clark asked Noah, who'd just arrived and taken his place behind his usual drum set (Martin used a different drum set arranged for lefties), to demonstrate the "Back to the Basement" tempo. There was an obvious difference as Noah ruthlessly pounded away at a Mr. Clark-approved clip.

The rehearsal ended with the leisurely "Finding You Here," with a tempo almost the polar opposite of something like "Back to the Basement." In fact, Ethan, who played a prominent solo in the piece, was playing his sax so icily that Mr. Clark joked afterward, "Check him for a heartbeat."

♪

The rehearsal seemed all over the place as the band covered familiar terrain—Martin not playing the right tempo, the trumpets not knowing their parts, Danny cracking wise and being told to be quiet, Mr. Clark poking fun at his own weight. It had so many ups and down it seemed bipolar.

It started with the Patriots fan-in-chief's disgust that he was the only one in the room wearing New England Patriots merchandise, given that, in two days, the Patriots would be playing the Ravens for a chance to go to the Super Bowl. "Nice to see all the Patriots' gear. Nice spirit," Mr. Clark sniped.

For the second consecutive rehearsal, a great deal of time was devoted to trying to press Martin to modify his drum playing. During "In a Mellow Tone," Mr. Clark began clapping hard and fast in front of the seventh grader. "You're behind them. You've got to lead."

Later: "Martin, you are very laid back and mellow, except when you're eating lunch in my room. ... If you aren't, naturally, a spaz, music will make you be a spaz." This seemed like more of a wish than a statement of fact from the band leader. Urging the boy to adopt a stronger, more aggressive drumming style, Mr. Clark said he was playing "extraordinarily well" but needed to get out of his comfort zone. As he had during the previous rehearsal, Mr. Clark asked Noah to show Martin what he wanted. That's when Mr. Clark honed in on the way Martin was holding his drumsticks, with the back of his hands downward toward the drums. This, Mr. Clark said, might be part of the problem with Martin's lack of volume. Judging by the determined look on Martin's face, I didn't believe he was going to change his grip or his style. Indeed, when they played "In a

Mellow Tone," Mr. Clark did his hand-clapping routine in front of Martin just before roaring, *More!* at the entire band and there wasn't much of a change.

The trumpets found themselves in Mr. Clark's line of fire too when, during their work on "In a Mellow Tone," he remarked, "Trumpets, I can't really hear you today. I'm missing my great wall of sound, my Lords and Lady of Sonic Death." Keeping with the Patriots theme, he likened the trumpets' failure to provide that layer of sound to a lineman missing a blocking assignment and allowing quarterback Tom Brady to be turned into "a pretzel." "Tom Brady will yell at you. ... You can be mad at me, that's kind of the point."

Surprisingly, the flute section was corrected on its playing during "In a Mellow Tone," being told, "You have to hit stuff louder and harder. ... Every note matters. The audience won't know why it sounds bad, but it does."

Danny provided ample moments of levity amidst the shouting. Echoing Mr. Clark's sentiments about moving from "In a Mellow Tone" to the more romantic "Finding You Here," Danny sang a line from *The Lion King,* "Can, you feel the *looove,* tonight." He joked about large hamburgers, which was like kindling for Mr. Clark's own comedy routine about his penchant for buying "a heart attack in a sack," and requiring quadruple bypasses because he ate too many cheeseburgers. When Mr. Clark's joke fell flat, largely because the students didn't know what a quadruple bypass was, Danny started laughing, sarcastically, almost maniacally. Following the faux laughing jag, Danny started teasing Ethan, who sat in front of him, by repeatedly putting his hands on Ethan's impeccably coiffed hair until Mr. Clark told Danny to knock it off.

Danny looked like he was about to speak again, like he was going to explode if he didn't speak, but Mr. Clark preemptively cut him off: "Danny, shut up!"

Seeing the pleading look in the boy's eyes as he went to open his mouth, Mr. Clark added, "What? Stop!"

Danny asked, "How do you know what I was going to say?"

"How do I know? Because thirty years ago, I *was* you!"

Chicken-in-a-can. This is what dominated the rehearsal, not the fact that their work would be showcased in two weeks in front of a local orchestra's annual fundraising dinner.   The road to the subject of boneless chicken-in-a-can was a winding one. It was so noisy in the band room before rehearsal started that I couldn't even tell what song Mr. Clark was playing over the speakers. A large number of students seemed to be in a chippy mood. Ethan grumpily plopped himself down on his front row seat after arriving ten minutes late but, lucky for him, the rehearsal hadn't begun yet. Picking up on Ethan's mood, Danny decided to tease him. "Ethan! How was your breakfast?" Danny shouted in a cheery, sarcastic tone.

"I didn't have breakfast this morning," Ethan said, sounding defeated. And a little hungry.

Why this exchange led to Mr. Clark revealing to the group that his sister-in-law K.C. hated eating chicken meat off the bone, I will never understand. He further shared that one night a friend had told him there was such a thing as canned boneless chicken. After learning this, he said he looked up chicken-in-a-can when he got home. The images Mr. Clark found showed slick-looking chicken covered with a grayish, gelatinous jelly. He emailed the links to K.C. who he said, was unamused. "So for her March 13th birthday, I'm going to send her a case of chicken-in-a-can!" he vowed.

This was exciting material to ponder, particularly for middle schoolers who were eager to avoid playing "In a Mellow Tone" again. Talking about chicken-in-a can, obviously, called to mind the notion of digestive unrest, diarrhea specifically, a favorite topic of Mr. Clark's.

It was at this point in the conversation that Danny introduced the notion of gas station sushi, which, one might reasonably conclude, could also lead to diarrhea, although the question of which would be worse, chicken-in-a-can or gas station sushi was still up for debate. As my delicate stomach churned, I was relieved when Mr. Clark changed the subject and called for them to play "Cute," reminding the trumpet section not to play angry. Jesse, who wasn't as absorbed by the gross food discussion as the rest of his brethren, was obliviously strumming on his guitar in the back of the room. While the students took out their music, Jesse continued playing a song I couldn't discern, although I knew it wasn't "Cute." Mr. Clark glared at the guitarist, prompting Jesse to turn red for the 1,897th time this year and stop strumming.

But chicken-in-a-can would not be denied. Mr. Clark himself kept the subject going when he said, "They should write a tune called 'Chicken-in-a-Can.'" This declaration was akin to a verbal flashbang device being dropped in the band room. After everyone reoriented themselves, after the ringing in their ears stopped and their vision readjusted, they exploded with the possibilities of setting an ode to de-boned canned chicken in jelly to music. Students shouted out suggestions at the same time, talking over one another like pundits on a political cable TV program. There was a jumble of words that brimmed with excitement bouncing off the walls, accented by laughter and gaiety. When the conversation showed no sign of ending, Mr. Clark tried to pull back the animal he'd unleashed. "Stop working on 'Chicken-in-a-Can!'" he half-shouted, half-laughed, eyes alight.

Not long after he attempted to guide Martin in the proper tempo for "Tiny Capers"—he stood behind the boy and gently tapped on his shoulder to the beat he wanted—Danny mentioned the topic du jour again. He said he was going to open up a restaurant called D.Sheff's (for Danny Sheffield) and that he'd serve chicken-in-a-can, gas station sushi and have a catapult on hand. (No, I didn't get the catapult reference either.)

Although Mr. Clark asked them to pull out "Finding You Here," he continued to contribute to the madness by pulling up an image of chicken-in-a-can on his iPhone and walking around the band room showing it to everyone. The photo reminded me of the Passover food gefilte fish, a pickled fish meatloaf of sorts that is sold in glass jars filled with a gelatinous substance that resembles mucus. That gelatinous mucus image was on my brain when they played a sloppy, uneven rendition of "Finding You Here." "It's like pulling back the covers and finding a chicken-in-a-can in here," he said, a reference to *The Godfather's* horse-head-in-the-bed-scene which likely went over all the kids' heads, although I chuckled aloud.

The following day, the last Friday in January, upon entering the band room and finding it only slightly warmer than the sub-zero temperature outside, the white board on the front of the room had the beginnings of a score for "Chicken-in-a-Can" written on it in black, dry erase marker. I prayed silently that there would be no more talk of that culinary oddity, the idea of which had torpedoed my appetite the day before. Thankfully, there was no talk of chicken-in-a-can or gas station sushi on this morning. Today, Mr. Clark discussed their upcoming forty-minute performance at the Portuguese Club in Milford for his colleagues in the Claflin Hill Symphony Orchestra. It was their annual fundraising dinner. The more he talked about it, the more anxious he became. "I have bragged about you to many, many of my professional musician friends. These aren't people who will clap because they're related to you," he warned. "You need to be able to play eight songs in a row without having your lips on the floor." Although he concluded his opening remarks with an upbeat, "It's gonna be awesome," his nerves were showing, as subtle as a forehead tattoo. There were six rehearsals left before the performance to ace the eight tunes. "Get up. Get out. Jump on your parents to get here on time," he said.

Lil' nubbin' and tiny capers. These two phrases dominated this rehearsal at the end of January. Lil' nubbin' was ushered into the room by Danny when he started muttering, "lil' nubbin'" in a squeaky-high voice before shifting to what was supposed to be a scary tone after Mr. Clark had asked the students to pull out the music for "In a Mellow Tone." "Do you have anything better to do, like, looking at your music so you don't screw up?" Mr. Clark asked Danny.

Seemingly thrilled by the attention, Danny persisted in making weird noises as his bandmates and his band director laughed. "Danny," Mr. Clark said, pausing for a long time. I couldn't get a read on his mood or how he was going to handle the pre-performance prep. "Let's get started before we screw around."

Although they were able to get through the entirety of "In a

Mellow Tone"—including Mr. Clark giving Brandon a high-five for his trombone solo—Danny started muttering, "Lil' nubbin'" again after Mr. Clark made the mistake of using the phrase "lil' bit" when saying that it would help the dynamics of the piece if they read their music.

"Danny, *lil' nubbin'* is creepy."

"My sister says it all the time."

"Stop!" Mr. Clark responded despite his smirk. "Everybody, play!"

At the end of the rehearsal, after playing "Cute" and "Dat Dere," Mr. Clark sent me this text, "They have no idea how good they are."

Was Mr. Clark really worried about whether the Big Band was ready for an eight-song show in front of a musically-savvy audience or was his increasing crankiness, his cavalcades of warnings part of a calculated effort? I wondered this as I watched him hammer away at the Big Band on a Tuesday morning rehearsal, the performance at the Claflin Hill Symphony Orchestra fundraiser now four days away. As he had them play the eight selections, he repeatedly appeared annoyed and accused them of failing to work on their music over the weekend because there were errors littered throughout their playing. Three songs in, he said, aggravation coloring his voice, "Guys, it really sounds like you haven't done anything since Friday."

"Fix it!" he complained after hearing a passage in "Fly Me to the Moon" where the trumpet section was supposed to issue a gentle invitation to listeners but instead offered an angry-sounding shout.

He roamed around in front of the group, shook his head and repeated his bit about not wanting to get pity-applause. "You have to understand that on Saturday, we're going to be performing for people who have no reason to clap for you. If you suck, they won't clap. ... You've got to show up. And you're not *here* today. You've got to show up. It's not just going to happen."

Thinking on the matter a bit, a prickly pause hanging in the air as no one, not even Danny, said anything, Mr. Clark pressed forward. "Can you feel that we've backtracked since Friday?" he continued in a quieter tone. "You really don't want that polite applause from strangers. Step up your game right now. Don't accept mediocrity. Top. Play."

At that, the middle schoolers delivered their boldest tune, "Groovin' Hard," with a gusto I could feel in my chest. They did exactly what their band leader asked: play this piece like a slap in the face, like something that had a burn and ended with an electric jolt of sound. If they played like this, they would be golden.

CHAPTER THIRTEEN

Snow Apocalypse

𝄆 It was going to be a snow apocalypse, according to the weather forecasters. More than two feet of snow was supposed to blanket, and subsequently paralyze, eastern Massachusetts during on Friday. It was all but a certainty that school would be canceled, robbing them of their last chance to tweak and polish before Mr. Clark put his and his band's reputation on the line in front of his peers.

What did that mean for the Big Band? They had to squeeze two days of practice into this fifty-minute rehearsal on Thursday morning. Mr. Clark seemed as though he was making plans for an invasion, coordinating who and what would go where and when in the event that snow dared to interfere with his plans. They all needed to take their sheet music and instruments home today after school so they would have them if school was canceled. The only way the Saturday night gig would be rescheduled, he said, was if Governor Deval Patrick declared a snow emergency and closed the roads. That almost never happened. Mr .Clark added a caveat. However, if their parents balked at making the fifteen-plus-mile trek from Southborough to Milford on Saturday night because of the weather, he said, "I don't want you to argue with your parents about going to the gig. If your parents say you're not going, don't be a middle schooler!"

Jesse arrived late to rehearsal, per usual, and bassist/drummer Richie had yet to show; both had missed Tuesday's rehearsal. Mr. Clark handed the ill-prepared guitarist yet another copy of sheet music because the boy again left his several copies at home. Mr. Clark ordered the redheaded eighth grader to tune. "Here's your music, Jesse. Anything else you need? Do you want me to play for you too?"

"Everything's not going to be a perfect set-up when we get there ... Every note matters. Every dynamic counts," he said as he walked around in front of the children while they tuned. Were they listening? It was hard to tell.

Noah raised his hand. He never raised his hand. "Mr. Clark, is Richie going to be at the performance?"

Mr. Clark took a long draw of cold coffee out of his travel mug, looked around and noticed that, at 7:20, Richie hadn't arrived. Not that Richie being late was unusual. "That's the theory," he said. Five minutes later, Richie arrived, but he was too late to play the Sinatra tune, which Noah wound up playing.

When it was time for "Tiny Capers," Richie finally got his chance to sit down behind the tan and black Pearl drum set for the first time during the rehearsal. But he didn't have his sheet music and he didn't know the order of the playlist for the gig because he'd been late to or entirely missed several recent practices. The boy said nothing as he slouched on the stool with his sad brown eyes and looked lost. Feeling badly, Noah handed Richie his sheet music and the Big Band waited for Richie to get settled. A third of the way through "Tiny Capers," Mr. Clark stopped them and told Richie he was playing the wrong tempo. It didn't take long for the boy to pick up the right tempo and fall into place with the rest of his bandmates.

"Dat Dere" followed. It was another piece for which Richie was supposed to play drums. It was another piece for which Richie didn't have his music ready. He frantically flipped through his tattered music folder while Mr. Clark stood silently. Waiting. No reason had ever been given, at least not to the larger group, for Richie's absences and frequent tardiness, and unlike with Jesse, who was apt to get verbally blasted for being late and unprepared, Mr. Clark held his tongue with Richie. Once Richie got "Dat Dere" arranged on the music stand, the Big Band began. They played with increased confidence and even a little swagger, adroitly conveying the mysterious playful nature of the arrangement. "Very, very good! Very, very good!" Mr. Clark boomed, quickly advising the sax section and the brass players to withhold their full volume at one particular point. To the flutes, he said they needed "a little more direction" on a measure.

♪

As it turned out, the meteorologists were right. Winter Storm Nemo, as the Nor'easter was dubbed by The Weather Channel, was the Boston area's fifth biggest snowstorm to date, bringing with it, hurricane-force winds. Southborough received 25.5 inches of snow on Friday. School was canceled and, for the first time since the infamous Blizzard of '78, the governor ordered all cars off of the roads for twenty-four hours as the storm reached its climax on Friday. The Saturday night gig had to be rescheduled due to the street closures but not before Mr. Clark inundated Big Band parents with emails throughout the day. When the performance was rescheduled for Sunday at 4 p.m., the parents whose kids played town basketball games or were participating in the school play *The Little Mermaid* had to scramble to make arrangements.

By Sunday afternoon, the roads between Southborough to Milford were plowed. Kind of. The driving remained somewhat treacherous. My car, a sturdy SUV with four-wheel drive, skidded numerous times on the way there. The parking lot surrounding the Portuguese Club was slippery, snowy and rutted when members of the Big Band arrived. The conditions proved to be a struggle as all the musical equipment had to be transferred from parents' cars to the building, including an entire drum set. The kids, their parents and Mr. Clark attempted to stomp the snow off their shoes on the saturated rug in the entryway before trudging across the white linoleum floor in the main event room. As they scaled the twin sets of narrow stairs to access the sides of the tight space of the stage, they discovered that there were no music stands. Mr. Clark—looking spiffy in a black tux, crisp white shirt, black bow tie and vest, emerald Eric ribbon on his lapel—sighed emphatically.

The band members exuded a jumpy vibe. Their faces grew wan as they eyed the thirty-three round tables—with ten place settings each—decorated with winter-themed centerpieces composed of square glass vases with stalks of pine, pinecones, silver peacock feathers and twisted, sparkly silver sticks with hearts made out of sheets of music dangling from them standing upright in the inch-thick layer of decorative salt on the bottom. Multi-colored votive candles surrounded the centerpieces atop thin black tablecloths inside the facility, frozen in a late-1980s style of floral patterns and heavy drapery.

Luckily, the tuxedoed professional musicians who would be playing later in the evening began to show up, their own music stands in tow. With a quick smile and plea for help, Mr. Clark commandeered their stands and toted them up to the now-crowded stage which offered precious little space in front for the conductor before a precipitous drop down to the linoleum floor. As the children arranged the chairs, warmed up their instruments and ran through measures of pieces, the audio coming out of the speakers made it sound as if the Big Band was performing inside a teeny, tiny tin can someplace far, far away. The trumpets were especially tinny-sounding. Ethan's solo on "Finding You Here" was barely audible. Mr. Clark's voice sounded echo-y and when he pounded, flat-palmed, on his chest to set the tempo, it sounded like his hand was slapping a hollow wall. These were all things Mr. Clark had to fix during the brief rehearsal before the fundraiser attendees started arriving in earnest. Mr. Clark did the best he could with the audio equipment on hand, along with the few microphones that were stationed around the stage. He shouted directions, in rapid-fire fashion: "Rhythm! Listen to each other! You're not listening to each other!" "Bells up!"

A red-faced Lauren, the trumpet player, rushed into the room. Her parents had driven her to the wrong Portuguese Club. In Hudson. Some twenty-two-plus miles north of Milford. Mr. Clark didn't make a big deal out of her tardiness. He was focused on the sound quality which improved tremendously once more musicians handed over their music stands and Mr. Clark was able to put more microphones in place. Between glad-handing colleagues—some of whom belonged to his quintet, Brass Venture—and friends, Mr. Clark drew a smile tightly across his face. He couldn't fully camouflage his unease as the heels of his shiny black dress shoes grazed the edge of the carpeted stage in front of the sax section. He stood on the very edge of the stage. Some of the Big Band parents with whom I was sitting discussed the possibility of him falling backward during an exuberant move, which he was apt to make. He'd already planned for this. During earlier rehearsals, he'd told his students in the event he were to keel over or fall off stage, they were supposed to continue playing. No matter what. The kids laughed at the time, but as I watched Mr. Clark stomp his feet and pinwheel his arms around, I speculated about whether his directive would be put to the test today.

Slowly, the crowd filed in, ranging from middle-aged folks to seasoned citizens, some dressed for cocktail hour in sports coats and ties or dresses, others more casual in festive sweaters and pressed khakis. Their chatting initially sounded like a low buzz, an off-key accompaniment to the Big Band's music. More people arrived and the bar was bustling. The audience's conversations—many about driving in the snow—grew louder, peppered by jagged bursts of laughter, an occasional, *Woo-hoo,* at the conclusion of a song. This was the first time the 2012-13 Big Band had performed in front of a distracted audience, one that wasn't riveted to their every note. Unlike their normal concerts, there weren't dozens of parents, who knew everything these kids had gone through, holding up iPads and iPhones above people's heads to record every gesture, every note. How would this atmosphere affect their playing, performing in the uninsulated real world? Despite his experience as a performer himself, sometimes in front of sparse audiences, Mr. Clark was all business.

How did they fare? Overall, they did well with some spotty weaknesses.

On the normally thunderous "Back to the Basement," it was evident that the trumpets needed to be miked better. It was tough to hear the five students who performed solos. All but one of the kids delivered a good-to-excellent solo; a couple boys blushed as they stood, alone in front of a group of strangers who didn't understand the significance of the green ribbons and green bracelets that adorned their instruments and wrists. The drum solo at the one-minute mark was fierce, but was followed by a slightly discordant rush of sound which sullied the impression of the piece overall.

During the second number, "Fly Me to the Moon"—played as though it was a reluctant child being dragged by the hand through a grocery store—it was clear that the piano wasn't miked well, either, as its notes could barely be heard over the percussion section. Near the end, the band's playing grew in power. Its tempo—finally—pulsed with life rather than listed along like a protracted yawn, that is, if you chose to overlook the intermittent metallic-sounding bleats of the wrong notes coming from the trumpet section.

It was only as they played the sprightly "In a Mellow Tone" when the children seemed to settle down; their playing was smoother, more self-assured. They maintained the vacillating tempo well and Brandon delivered a strong trombone solo which sparked a gust of applause from those waiting in line at the bar.

"Cute's" light-as-a-feather drumming balanced with some silken sax lines, was even smoother, however, it didn't elicit the electric response to which the Big Band was accustomed when they played well, and that seemed to disappoint them. There was one stray hoot and a smattering of applause, but it wasn't comparable to the level of their playing. The Big Band parents tried to make up for the lack of applause by over-exaggerating our clapping.

In response to the delicate "Finding You Here"—a caviar-topped hors-d'oeuvre in a fragile egg shell—the audience response was still polite, but lacked genuine enthusiasm, which was a shame because the sax solo Ethan offered was heartbreakingly vulnerable as the drumsticks tinkled gently on the cymbals in the background. Mr. Clark gave Ethan a fist-bump and, at the conclusion of the piece, and prodded the boy to rise and take a bow. The applause seemed to be coming mostly from the Big Band parents in attendance.

The good-humored "Tiny Capers" was fleet of foot and quickly coasted along until a few horn players missed their notes which created small pockets of noise amidst the call-and-response section of the piece.

The sly "Dat Dere" is what finally got people's attention. It's a song that creeps up on the listeners, intriguing them with its looping notes that gently crisscross one another like lines on a Spirograph drawing, its receding then advancing sections, its reducing then amplifying volume, its deft waterfall of notes gushing forward at a rapid clip, its killer shout chorus—prefaced by bellowing from their band director, *Gooooo!* like a man falling to his death off the edge of a cliff—all demanded to be listened to. The further the band got into the song, the quieter the audience got. The applause for Ethan's solo in this chart was loud as was the response at the end of the piece.

"Groovin' Hard," their most robust number, capped the performance, but not before Mr. Clark told the audience, "I can assure you that jazz is alive and well in these kids behind me." Their musical strength didn't really shine through until they reached the sax soli section, where they stood and played as though they were one instrument delivering a complex, layered sound. From there on out, they blazed through the piece, a hot knife through butter, horns blasting melodically, eliciting the strongest applause of the evening.

When I saw Danny in the lobby after the show, his black bari sax case heavily dragging his arm toward the earth, he was still so red that I asked him if he was feeling okay. He didn't look it. "After all that playing, I feel lightheaded," he said.

A few days after the Portuguese Club performance, the roads hadn't improved. This morning, it was very icy. Very icy. Inside the band room, however, things were feeling cozy. It was Pajama Day. About half the band members had donned fleece and faux-fur-lined flannel pajama tops. Two girls sported footie pajamas—one featuring cartoons of cupcakes, the other with snowflakes and snowmen—with shoes crammed over the feet. The boys were mostly in primary-colored lounge pants similar to the ones worn by their band director who sported navy and green plaid pants and a heavy navy fleece top.

Warmth also exuded from Mr. Clark's lips. "On Sunday, you guys did an awesome, awesome job. You have no idea how many people told me how good you were."

Mr. Clark's verbal confections were interrupted when he couldn't find Ethan. "Hey, Ethan Scarpetti? Wait. Where did you go? What … [*sighs*] get over here!" Ethan was rifling through the shelving in the front of the room searching for sheet music.

"How can you not have your music again? You do this too much."

Ethan countered that he'd left his music at home because he had been practicing. And at least he was doing that.

There was little more talk of their accomplishment in Milford as Mr. Clark had his eye on March 9, the day of the University of New Hampshire jazz festival. The prior year, just weeks after Eric's death, the Big Band performed with what Mr. Clark called "a desperate passion that matched their anguish and grief" which nabbed them an honorable mention award. Mr. Clark had pulled the laid-back, horn-heavy swing piece, "Swing Shift" from their planned playlist that year because of its connection to Eric. The removal of "Swing Shift" left the band's 2012 three-piece set list lacking diversity, specifically something in the ballad genre. A judge later told Mr. Clark that the decision not to play a ballad prevented the band from winning a top prize. When Mr. Clark explained the situation with "Swing Shift" and how the kids weren't ready to play it given that Eric's final solo was still bouncing around inside the grieving corners of their hearts and minds, the judge said he wished someone had given them a heads-up beforehand because they would've taken that into consideration. But Mr. Clark was unwilling to make excuses for his band.

For this year's 2013 set list, Mr. Clark was going to do it differently. They'd be playing "Back to the Basement," "Finding You Here" and "Dat Dere," a good representation of the genres.

"March 9," he repeated. "I don't want to hear anything about soccer games."

The invocation of the jazz festival seemed to awaken Mr. Clark's competitive juices. The warm and the cozy sentiments were gone. It was drill time. Take those pieces and lock down every bolt and screw, he said. Make everything sharp or rounded or full or restrained or whatever other quality Mr. Clark called for. *Precision, people! Articulations! Emotion! Tempo! Take cues from fellow band members!*

On the stellar "Dat Dere," it was as though Mr. Clark was performing microsurgery. He had them play the chorus really, really slowly. A forty-five record being played at 33 rpm. While it was a fine way of discerning if they were hitting all their notes at the proper times and with the right strength and volume, it sounded quite strange to me, this slow-mo playing. He dissected their music, pulled it apart, and in doing so, he discovered that there were problems with a few of the trumpet players and that Josh's bari sax wasn't tuned properly as it burped the wrong notes, like a belch in the middle of dinner. Josh blamed his instrument.

A storm front of band director irritation gathered strength. Mr. Clark snapped at Jesse for sitting around plucking guitar strings while he had been giving instructions to other band members. He snapped at Martin for continuing to drum for several beats after he'd asked the band to stop. "Dat Dere's" ending—a mixture of sass and intrigue—had to be *perfect* because he said, "That's going to be the last thing they're gonna hear us play." Over and over he had them repeat the final measures. He remained frustrated. "You're not taking the time that I'm giving you!" he said to Martin who wasn't adhering to Mr. Clark's beat. The fourth trumpets were ordered to deliver "a much fatter sound" and "three times the power." For that matter, the third trumpets weren't playing "fat" either, he noted.

He stood up, pushing the metal stool away from him, and again said, "Fat. Sound." Uncertain if his point was sinking in, he added, "Am I not inspiring you, all fat in my jammies?" He paused to allow for the expected laughter. "You're playing it fine, but you're not doing what you need to do."

CHAPTER FOURTEEN

UNH

‖: The Big Band was slated to perform right before the Newtown, Connecticut middle school jazz band at the UNH jazz festival. The Newtown kids were just weeks removed from the tragedy at the Sandy Hook Elementary School where twenty-six people, including 6- and 7-year-olds and six adults, were gunned down by a local 20-year-old who then took his own life. And although the Newtown Middle School was not the site of the massacre, the horror of the violence had reverberated throughout not just the small Connecticut town, but the country. During Newtown's performance, it was expected that the students would be sporting green and black, the same colors the Trottier Big Band would be wearing to honor Eric.

After he learned this, Mr. Clark asked me whether I thought he should contact the director of the Newtown jazz band director to see if he could do anything to assist the band in any way. "Why not?" I asked, guessing that he'd already made up his mind to send an email and was just looking for affirmation.

When he told the Big Band members the order of the performances, a handful of them approached Mr. Clark in private, suggesting that Trottier should withdraw from the competition. "They wanted Newtown to win and they knew that we were in the mix to win.

They wanted the Newtown kids to have something to smile about," Mr. Clark told me. Last year at this time, they were the ones who were fresh with loss. Each time a student asked him if the Big Band should drop out of UNH to give Newtown a better shot, he cried and told each child the suggestion was generous and selfless, but not a good idea. "They don't want to win that way."

"I don't care if we win UNH. At all. Honestly! I don't care what anyone else thinks of us."

Six rehearsals until the jazz festival.

"Do I think we can win?" Mr. Clark asked the band during their first practice since winter vacation ended. "Yeahyeahyeahyeahyeah." He said the five words like they were one big word mashed together. "We're going to have to set the bar. We need to make an impression that lasts by 6 p.m. I want the judges to go, 'Oh, holy crap,' when they hear us."

All of this talk, on the first rehearsal after February vacation, was it meant to rouse the troops, to build their confidence, even though he'd warned them, pretty recently, about the dangers of complacency? That question popped into my head after the Big Band took a stab at "Finding You Here" and it was, in a word, dreadful. Kids didn't seem to know when to come in. It was as though they'd completely forgotten how to play it.

"That can never happen," Mr. Clark said grimly. "That was so pathetically bad. No, I'm not accepting that. That's garbage."

They tried again and fared no better. Mr. Clark turned on Richie, who had arrived twenty minutes late. The eighth grader was not responding to his directive about the drum tempo. "You didn't practice? Over ten days, you didn't have time to listen to something on iTunes?"

"I didn't have any time to practice or listen," Richie said.

Frustrated, he told Noah to take over the drums for this piece.

They made another attempt. It was somewhat better, but only somewhat. The piece seemed to present a challenge to some of the kids. It had an adultness to it that some couldn't access. The yearning it expressed was a mature one. Mr. Clark tried to explain it, the withholding nature of the song. The element of holding back and then permitting longing to leak out slowly, like air out of a balloon, was nuanced, subtle. What struck me most about "Finding You Here" was its gorgeous vulnerability, something only sax player Ethan seemed to have an innate comprehension of at age 13.

Mr. Clark extended his arm out and pointed to Gabe in the trombone section without saying a word. Redness crept up the boy's neck. When he asked Cassidy to fine-tune her bass playing, it was hard to tell if she was blushing because all I could see of her were her eyes above the music stand. "Some of you have not practiced," he concluded. "Vacation is *over* people!"

Less than an hour later, Mr. Clark emailed Mark Mahoney, the Newtown, Connecticut band director:

> *Hi Mr. Mahoney,*
>
> *My name is Jamie Clark and my band is performing right before you at the UNH Jazz Festival on March 9.*
>
> *I wanted your guidance on something. Would it be better for your kids if my kids acknowledged your town and the tragedy that you have all endured or would you prefer that nothing be said or done? I assure you, that if we were to do something, it would simple and subtle. I certainly understand if it would be best for the kids if nothing were done.*
>
> *Also, if there is anything I can do to help out with the festival please don't hesitate to ask. (Or help out with anything actually.)*
>
> *I'm sure that you have been offered condolences more times than you can count but please know that I and everyone I know is heartbroken and wishes you and your community only the best.*
>
> *Please let me know your thoughts when you get a moment. I look forward to hearing from you.*
>
> *Sincerely,*
>
> *Jamie Clark*

Twenty-six minutes later, Mr. Mahoney emailed a reply:

Hi Jamie,

Thank you for the kind thought!

I just had a talk with my kids yesterday and explained that they have a serious responsibility upon them at UNH. I reminded them that Newtown is now world renown; for reasons we could have never imagined. It was emphasized that it was their job to show those in attendance, not only are we carrying on but, have risen above and are proud to perform at (what hopes to be) a high level of achievement.

With all the well wishes and generous donations that have been coming to Newtown, we are well aware that everyone 'Is with us.'

As such, I'd rather they just focus on playing their best; it would be best that we forego your offer of acknowledgement.

But thank you for the offer.

There is one thing that you (and other directors on site) could do. Once you are packed up, come in the theater and catch part of our set. My kids thrive on an audience.

Please introduce yourself when you get the chance. You won't be able to miss us. We'll be in all black with bright green ties.

Regards,

Mark Mahoney

A few minutes later, Mr. Clark, a compulsive iPhone checker, replied and told Mahoney:

Just to let you know we will be wearing all black and green as well. Last year one of the students in the band passed away suddenly. His last name was Green which is why we will be wearing green as well. Didn't want you to think we were copying you.

None of the girls wanted to solo in "Back to the Basement,"

their opening number for UNH. None. The entirety of the alto sax section—Chris, Owen, David and Aaron, Ethan on the tenor sax, Patrick on the trumpet, Jesse on the guitar and Noah on the drums, all eagerly raised their hands for the chance to solo. But no female musicians volunteered. Some of the kids tried to persuade Danny to do one, but he just shook his head, "No." "Danny doesn't need the attention," Mr. Clark said. Ironically, Noah, who rarely called attention to himself, asked if his drum solo could be extended to a "double solo." It was like looking in a funhouse mirror. Danny waved away the spotlight while Noah wanted it. But a double solo? The kid didn't just pull that phrase out of the ether. Mr. Clark had just finished telling them about the time he ordered a double cheeseburger at Five Guys and was told that two hamburger patties normally came on a Five Guys cheeseburger. Ordering a double cheeseburger was actually ordering a quadruple burger, something the always-hungry Mr. Clark declined. Noah came up with his double solo idea, which led him to be christened with the short-lived nickname "Double Cheese."

They tried out the improvised solos (judges at music competitions like to see students afforded the chance to improvise) as they ran through "Back to the Basement." Noah missed Mr. Clark's signal—rotating his index fingers forward over one another—to double his solo, per the boy's request. Mr. Clark stopped the band and told Noah he'd missed the cue to which Noah responded with a soft, "Oh."

As Richie arrived at 7:35, he tried to make himself invisible by hewing to the instrument cages. The rest of the band was surprisingly relaxed and joking around. Some real gaiety seemed to be in the air as opposed to tension and admonitions about succumbing to complacency. I realized that frivolity and playfulness had been absent for a while, a casualty of pre-UNH jitters.

The University of New Hampshire Jazz Festival, which started in 1974, was named after Clark Terry, a famous jazz trumpeter—called a "master improviser" and "effervescent, irreplaceable" by

The New Yorker—who believed in promoting jazz music education. The festival drew upwards of 60 high school and middle school bands from New England and the New York area to their Durham, New Hampshire campus, according to the university. In the middle school category this year, there were 18 middle schools competing. Mr. Clark thought his Big Band could make a serious bid for the top honor.

The main roads were clear but the secondary roads were not great when I arrived at Trottier at 6:45 on the morning of the festival. It was in the 30s and the sky was a cerulean blue and cloudless. Mr. Clark was carrying his second large Dunkin' Donuts coffee of the morning, with a turbo shot of espresso. He was stoked. Bleary-eyed parents who would be chaperoning the trip stepped over patches of ice and large swaths of snow to load the instruments, the Pearl drum set, Zildjian cymbals and the drum mascot, the demented stuffed leprechaun-like creature "Fill" (as in a drum fill, a section of improvised drum playing) into their cars and onto school bus number twelve. Mr. Clark looked like a game show host in his black striped suit, black shirt, green striped tie, hair slick with gel and a caffeinated bounce in his step. I alerted him to the fact that the back of his pants were covered in some kind of white dust. Perhaps he had brushed up against a salt-covered vehicle. He quickly brushed it off. I wasn't the first or the last parent to point out dust, lint or stray threads on Mr. Clark's clothing before he conducted the band. Big Band parents, myself included, seemed to be quite comfortable pointing out such things before Mr. Clark mounted the conductor's riser to serve as the public front man for Southborough. Meanwhile, students filed onto the bus, oblivious to the crankiness of their parents. Flute player Ashley, wearing a black skirt with no hose and high-heeled slide sandals which showed off her green nail polish, stood out amid the parents who were clad in heavy boots, sweaters and winter parkas. I felt cold just looking at her. The earthy emerald color was present in the ribbon around bassist Cassidy's waist and the ribbons in her hair, as well as in the green ribbons pinned to boys' black shirts and represented on the neckties.

By 7 o'clock, when the bus was slated to leave, Mr. Clark realized that Richie was the only one who wasn't there. (Lauren and

Danny had given him advance warning that they'd be missing the event, which displeased the maestro.) Not one for patience, Mr. Clark kept looking at his iPhone, watching the minutes pile up on top of one another. He was looking up the number for Richie's parents in his contacts list when a vehicle pulled in. Mr. Clark's clenched shoulders lowered away from his ears when he saw Richie. He breathed a little easier. The color on his face returned to its normal tone.

As the bus chugged out of the Trottier driveway, onto Route 9 and then onto Interstate 495 heading north, snow was flying off the back and sides of the bus. I pitied any poor motorists who were driving near the bus because the snow was likely blinding. The sound of the snow sliding off the vehicle and whooshing into the air entertained the kids for a while, until they settled into their deep bus seats. I couldn't see many of their heads above the thin, brown seat backs. A lot of kids slouched in their seats and played with their phones. Occasionally, Martin's squeaky-high voice carried from the back of the bus even though, when I turned around, I couldn't see him, as if he'd been swallowed by the seat. Martin chimed in when a group of seventh-grade girls started belting out lines from Sia's "Titanium." It struck me as an odd combination, listening to them sing a song about being bulletproof as the Big Band was preparing to take the stage right before the Newtown Middle School band, weeks removed from the Sandy Hook Elementary School shooting. But maybe that was just me, an adult who had been unable to stop thinking about it. Days before the festival, Mr. Clark told me he was planning to have his students hastily leave their instruments behind after they performed at UNH so they could race into the audience and cheer for Newtown. The Sandy Hook events were still in the forefront of the adults' minds.

After being dropped off in front of the Johnson Theater on Academic Way, there was some temporary confusion about where the band was supposed to check in. The Paul Creative Arts Center, which housed the Johnson Theater, was labyrinthine. While college student volunteers from the 147-year-old university with over 12,500 undergraduates at the southern New Hampshire coastal town tried to help, they seemed as lost as we did. We were shuffled from room to room, lugging all the equipment—a drum set, a guitar, an amp and other assorted instruments—down narrow halls with our snow- and salt-covered shoes and boots until the students were finally told that they could tune their instruments in a large, empty holding room with instrument cages, chimes, gongs, drums and racks of chairs shoved into one corner. Natural sunlight was pouring in through the large bank of windows on one wall, giving the students a postcard-perfect view of a 2,600-acre, rural, New England campus, dotted by red brick buildings and coated with a blanket of fresh snow. The room—which felt dated, somewhere in the late 1970s, with chalk boards featuring musical scales on one wall—was populated by gray and red plastic music stands that couldn't have been more than two feet tall. They reminded me of panels you'd see on the inside of an airplane. Even when sitting in chairs behind the music stands, the students had to hunch over in order to read their music. Brandon, who stood at six feet, had to hunch over the most, which was no easy task while holding his trombone.

Though it threw the kids off to be in an unfamiliar location, to be dragging their equipment around and not having their usual room in which to warm up, Mr. Clark tried to keep to his usual pre-perfor-mance patter: "You need to own the tempo." "This first note is huge, huge, *huge*!" "All you have to do is to do what we've always done." He reviewed who was going to do solos and in what order. He had them play a few measures of "Back to the Basement," stopped them and said, "That's going to do *juuuussttt* fine."

Some twenty minutes later, the Trottier Big Band took to the stage in the 688-seat Johnson Theater, filled with parents, fans and jazz aficionados. About thirty Southborough parents made the trek north to see their children play. If the middle schoolers were nervous, they didn't look it, as they set up their instruments in front of the judges who sat at a long table set quite a way back from the stage. Each man had a microphone in front of him and was scribbling notes as he listened to the children play. One, a bald man with glasses who was sitting in the middle of the table, was smiling broadly after the Big Band wrapped "Back to the Basement," during which Ethan played a rocking solo while wearing a blank look on his reddened face, staring out into nothingness as he played.

"Back to the Basement" was a homerun. After the last earth-shaking notes of the slick, wise-guy shuffle finished echoing throughout the theater, the audience cheered, I wondered if these young kids could deliver a delicate ballad without stepping all over it with nerves? "Finding You Here" was rendered like a finely-made pastry, with a buttery crust and warm, delicate inner layers. No bite. No crunch. Just smooth restraint that, when it was over, made me want more. The children delivered, Ethan in particular with a soulful sax solo. Moving from the delectable dessert to "Dat Dere" was akin to polishing off some crème brulee illuminated by the warmth of candlelight, and then heading to a cool bar afterward for gin martinis and a cigar. The musicians in Mr. Clark's Big Band pulled it off, though the trumpets still needed to be a lot louder, a problem that continued to plague them. Their shout chorus at the end, building up, level by level with sax notes, increasing in volume and power until the entire band sounded as if it had suddenly become sassy and turbo-charged—like Mr. Clark's two coffees that morning—was their closing argument.

The Big Band members cleared the stage of their gear, dropped it just out of sight, then quickly slid into seats in order to cheer on the Newtown Middle School band whose members were sporting similar bright green ties, black pants and shirts. Twenty-six Newtown Middle School musicians played their three-piece set, highlighted by their final selection, Rich Woolworth's "Café Caliente," a fast-moving samba featuring their aggressive drummer—whose drum set was placed in front of the band, unlike in Trottier's which was in the back of the formation—and solos by their guitarist, pianist and a sax player. The moment the Newtown band finished, the audience leapt to its feet, howling, cheering and whistling its approval. The standing ovation went only for nearly a full minute, as Mr. Mahoney led his students off stage. Trottier's Big Band students were among the last to stop clapping.

On the bus ride home, Mr. Clark stood in the middle of the aisle and told the kids, "We did everything we could do. I could not be happier with how you played and how you behaved." Upon noticing that some kids were sharing candy with one another, he walked a little further toward the back of the bus with his hand out. "Help a fat guy out." He returned to the front of the bus with a handful of gum drops. Two years prior, the Big Band earned an Outstanding Performance award, the festival's top designation given to two bands in each age group. A year ago, weeks after Eric had passed away, they won an Honorable Mention.

The following day, Mr. Clark texted me. He sent 36 smiley faces followed by nine exclamation points. "We won!" The Trottier Big Band and Northborough's Melican Middle School jazz band were the only two middle school bands to receive Outstanding Performance awards out of a field of 18. The Newtown Middle School received an Honorable Mention, one of four in the category.

CHAPTER FIFTEEN

Funk & Blues

𝄆 Every time he coughed, he curled forward and winced as he whispered, "Ouch!" And he was coughing. A lot. It had been four days since the Trottier Big Band's win at UNH. It was only the third day since daylight saving time started, which meant lots of kids were late to rehearsal. It was also the start of Health Week at the middle school, which meant smoothies and other goodies like whole wheat waffles and fresh fruit were available in the cafeteria before school. And Mr. Clark was sick, so sick that, mere minutes after the Tuesday morning rehearsal concluded, the school nurse sent him home after hearing his deep, hacking cough that racked his entire body.

But he wanted to dole out compliments.

"First of all, congratulations! That's pretty awesome!" *Cough.* "All your hard work, starting back in September paid off." *Cough.* "Your playing was phenomenal. And I was so proud of the respect you showed the Newtown band." *Cough, cough, cough.* He had reviewed the recordings the UNH judges had made and given to him, however one CD was blank, the second was incomprehensible and the third, he said, included a lot of nitpicky observations. "The judges are really, really nitpicky. But they *LOVED* the rhythm section!"

More coughing. More "ouch"-ing.

"There's a lot of excitement and buzz from the town because we won," he said, clearly thrilled, adding that they displayed just the right amount of control and excitement up in Durham.

With UNH behind them, Mr. Clark decided now was the time to start working on their new music, to mix up their set list. He distributed the sheet music for "Tiger of San Pedro," which he had first played for them during their initial 2013 rehearsal several weeks ago. He again played a recording of the fast-moving samba which featured a rousing trumpet chorus that would require the trumpet section to step it up. They initially tackled it by playing it at half its normal speed. Not many measures in, he stopped them to tinker and adjust. He asked the rhythm section—drums, bass, guitar, piano— to tackle the lively beast of a song. Without much commentary, he had them quiet down and asked the bari saxes to play, eventually adding the rhythm to the baris, then throwing the saxophone section. The trumpets played alone, then everyone played together. Listening closely to the evolving sound, he asked seventh-grade drummer Martin to join in on the pellet-filled metal shaker, which looked like a shiny cocktail shaker. Mr. Clark began wheezing and coughed in three long bouts. "How many of you would like to get a smoothie?" he said, panting slightly to catch his breath. "It *is* Health Week."

Another violent coughing fit overtook him as his face reddened up.

"Mr. Clark," Danny said, his eyes widening with alarm, "are you all right?"

He looked up at the clock. Seven-forty. "Go get some smoothies."

After the students left, he said to me, "This band is funny. I expected a wildly cheering response, a celebration of the UNH win, but they were pretty cool about it. I wonder whether they've become used to this high level of achievement." Mr. Clark seemed to want to bask in the win and was a little disappointed the kids didn't. However, the congratulatory emails and texts and Facebook posts from Big Band parents—who have been referred to as "disciples of Mr. Clark"—did please him.

♪

It was a never-before turn of events for the Trottier Big Band. On the heels of their UNH win, their first rehearsal back was cut short because Mr. Clark was sick. The second rehearsal of the week was canceled because Mr. Clark's cough was still bone-deep and insistent. The third and final rehearsal of the week was also canceled because Mr. Clark's silver 2004 Hyundai Sonata had a flat tire. I received a text message from Mr. Clark at 6:24 a.m.: "Flat tire!!!! Grrr." Ten minutes later: "Won't make it for BB. It's been a lovely week." When he finally got to school, after missing the Big Band rehearsal, he found handwritten notes left on his chair in the front of the band room from students telling him to get better and saying that they missed him. The very next rehearsal, on Tuesday, March 19, there was yet another snow day, thus the Big Band rehearsal was canceled, for the third time in a row. At least it gave Mr. Clark time to get a chest X-ray—his cough had not subsided—so he could learn that he didn't have pneumonia. He was prescribed powerful antibiotics. "I don't think I've ever been sick three days in a row before."

♪

Vibra-slap.

For the first time this year, a trumpet player would be performing with this handheld, L-shaped instrument with a maple colored wooden ball at one end connected by a silver colored metal rod to a hollow, triangular wooden block that makes a rattling kind of sound when the ball is struck by the palm in a downward motion. This instrument is the manmade version of the donkey jawbone—*quijada* in Spanish—that musicians sometimes still use when playing Latin-infused pieces and some concert pieces. As the story goes, Mexican musicians would take a foot-plus-long donkey jawbone, with many teeth still in their sockets, and strike it on the side, causing the teeth to rattle in place. I've never seen a quijada in person, but in photos and online videos, it looked fairly grisly to me so it made sense that someone came up with a less skeletal-looking version.

Mr. Clark explained the history of playing the donkey jawbone and how it evolved into the vibra-slap, which he held aloft in front of the band members. "I can see if I can get an actual donkey jawbone … not!" He handed it to quiet Jeffrey in the back row of the trumpet section. The boy would be tasked with hitting the vibra-slap a handful of times during "Tiger of San Pedro" to add its unique, arresting, rattling sound to the mix. The painfully shy trumpet player took it, eyed the odd instrument closely and solemnly nodded.

They had stepped up their game on "Tiger of San Pedro." Today's version was far superior to the one they'd played during the previous rehearsal. The students seemed happy to be tackling new material, particularly their first Latin piece all year. Although he was still coughing very often and remained severely congested, Mr. Clark's mood had lifted. He even overlooked the fact that Jesse and Richie arrived twenty minutes late. Mr. Clark did not explode when Richie said he couldn't get his bass out of his case because the case had rusted closed. Mr. Clark just brushed past it all and proceeded to tweak their playing. "There's a swoopy kind of *da-da-da-da-da-dah-DAH* part of this where the trumpets come in like a ton of bricks," he said. The crashing trumpets weren't the only things Mr. Clark wanted to be dramatic. He stood up, pretended he had a trumpet in his hands, arched backward, rocked on his heels and aimed the pretend trumpet at a 45-degree angle toward the ceiling. On the final *dah* of the *da-da-da-da-da-dah-DAH*, Mr. Clark wanted the trumpet players to not only hit that last note hard, but he wanted them to forcefully and exaggeratedly point the trumpets upward and outward, punctuating the note with a physical embellishment. When they began again, only a few of them lifted their trumpets toward the ceiling on that note. All the band members were asked to clap out the beat of the song as they sang, *Da-da-da-da-da-dah-DAH*. Having the trumpet players shift their instruments upward would add an exciting spark plug, he said, a visual element to their performance, provided all the trumpets cooperated.

The school copier was broken, something Mr. Clark discovered in the 6 o'clock hour Tuesday morning before the Big Band rehearsal which meant there would be no new sheet music today.

Oh, and there was a concert in a week.

"Nice to tell us *now*," snapped Ethan, who had a point. It was the first time Mr. Clark had mentioned an early April concert in the midst of all the other events they had coming up including the Massachusetts Jazz Educators (MAJE) junior jazz festival, the Eric Green Memorial service in early June, another concert for all the bands and a final Jazz Night with guest artist Walter Beasley at the end of school.

Light-hearted, unfocused chatter swallowed the room. Mr. Clark appeared to be adapting a rather laissez-faire attitude, at least this morning. He wasn't riding them, which was unexpected given the upcoming show. Or maybe his normal, pre-show jitters just hadn't manifested themselves yet. Maybe Mr. Clark was simply delaying hammering them. I was still trying to discern if he was playing everything by the seat of his pants or whether he had some kind of meta-plan. I leaned toward the former.

"Tiny Capers," Mr. Clark declared. Danny, whose fondness for the piece was well known in the band room, smirked. They didn't get far into the chart before Mr. Clark signaled for them to stop. To Martin, who was on the drums, he asked, "Do you normally play this song?"

"Richie does," Martin responded.

But Richie wasn't there. Noah, the lead drummer who was fond of compositions with driving beats, had ceded the piece to Martin.

The band didn't spend much time with "Tiny Capers," and quickly moved on over to "Cute." "You getting the tempo from me is pretty much the most critical thing for this piece," Mr. Clark said as he hit his flat-palmed right hand over his heart for about fifteen seconds, demonstrating the "right" tempo. Noah, the drummer on "Cute," liked overly-complicated drumming. In this case, on this piece, Mr. Clark suggested that Noah start out simple "so you can get more complex later. It's like if you ever lie, start out simple. But, I didn't really just tell you that."

One run-through was sufficient for this morning, at least by the band director's account. "Good! 'Mellow Tone!'" Despite Ethan's moaning, he and the rest of the band did well with this Ellington classic. The towering Brandon, looking embarrassed, played intensely during his solo, stretching his long arms out alongside the long trombone like a young giraffe learning how to move its limbs. As the band was nearing the end of the piece, Mr. Clark started getting excited by how it was all coming together. He jumped up and down in front of them to the beat. "Wow! That was really nice! Good stuff! Good stuff! Good stuff!"

Jeffrey had the vibra-slap ready for their next tune, "Tiger of San Pedro." As much theater as Mr. Clark wanted to see from the trumpet players when they thrust their instruments up in the air during the punchy chorus, he wanted Jeffrey, one of the least theatrical of all the Big Band members, to do the same with the vibra-slap the two times he was supposed to hit it. "You've got to make a show of it, dude!"

Mr. Clark checked in with Martin to see if he had the long, rusty-looking cowbell ready. He'd decided to throw the cowbell into the mix, along with the metal shaker Martin was manning. When they launched into the samba, they launched it into the stratosphere.

Jesse didn't believe Mr. Clark would cede large swaths of any one piece to him and his blue 1993 Fender Stratocaster guitar. Many weeks before Mr. Clark handed out the sheet music for "Play That Funky Music"—sheet music Jesse lost and didn't replace until the first time the Big Band played it live—the eighth grader wanted to bet me there was no way that, when the Big Band played the piece, there would be a blasting guitar solo or even close to the amount of guitar playing featured in Wild Cherry's 1976 jam.

For Jesse, playing the guitar had become everything. It was all he wanted to do since Mr. Clark suggested he take it up. Jesse was now the lead guitarist and raspy-voiced singer in a rock band he'd created, Indignous, with Noah on drums, Josh on keyboard and another eighth grader, Ryan on bass guitar. A few of their pieces included cameos from Ethan on the sax and Brandon on the trombone. Jesse wrote original pieces for the band—some with angsty, melancholy lyrics—which the band performed along with covers of Red Hot Chili Peppers', Black Crows' and Kinks' tunes. The group published its music on iTunes, performed at the YMCA and at the Trottier talent show. When it came to music, Jesse was all in. "I knew Jesse loved music by the way he played, by the way he talked about it," Mr. Clark said. When he watched Jesse play, Mr. Clark said the boy's passion for music was obvious.

Halfway through the year, Jesse approached Mr. Clark and told him he didn't want to play in the seventh- and eighth-grade concert band any more. He just wanted to play guitar, nothing else. But Mr. Clark didn't want him to quit the concert band. If he dropped out of the concert band, Jesse would attend a study instead of a band rehearsal and that boy needed to keep playing music, Mr. Clark thought, rather than fooling around in a study. The two struck a deal: Jesse would nominally "stay" in the concert band, but during class time, when the concert band was working, Jesse would sit in the back of the band room and play guitar with his headphones on. "He acted like he was losing sleep over me being in the band," Jesse told me, a note of bewilderment in his voice.

"It was healthy and helpful for Jesse to stay connected to the Music Department," Mr. Clark said firmly.

Ultimately, Jesse was glad he decided to stay. "Mr. Clark is a good mentor," Jesse said. "He taught me a lot of stuff. He taught me about playing. He taught me about inflection and emotion. Without him, I'd still be able to play fast on the guitar but without him I wouldn't be able to put emotion into it."

On the subject of "Play That Funky Music," however, Jesse was right. I'm glad I didn't take his bet. The sheet music for the jazz band's arrangement of "Funky Music" did not prominently feature the guitar, unlike in the pop song where the guitar dominates. However, Jesse was given a solo, which, if he handled Mr. Clark in just the right way, he could possibly stretch out to a double solo like Noah had done with "Back to the Basement." When Mr. Clark played a recording of this arrangement that was available via an online educational music site, it sounded significantly slower and more subdued than Wild Cherry's. "This arrangement is taken from the original full-length version of the song rather than only the single version," wrote Victor Lopez in the "Notes to the Conductor" section on the sheet music. "The tempo is a bit slower than the original, but the feel remains intact. As with most funk charts, the focus is on the rhythmic feel." In the list of instruments needed to play this song, the guitar is listed as optional. Jesse wasn't there that day to read his sheet music and be disappointed in person that "Play That Funky Music" had no designated, elongated guitar solo. But I was confident Mr. Clark would give him all the time he wanted.

"Did you hear that was kind of boring and dull?" Mr. Clark said of the recording on the music website. He sang a line from the pop song, *Play that funky music 'til you die.*

"We won't do it that way," he said. Ultimately, he would have them speed up the tempo and add a cowbell. But before they commenced with their first sight-reading, Mr. Clark warned them, "The first two measures have to be huge. *Everybody's* got to do it. Mark it in!" The first run-through wasn't so much of a run-through as a play-some-measures-then-come-to-a-screeching-halt kind of deal. The trumpets weren't feeling it this morning. "Really?!" Mr. Clark shouted, directing his annoyed glance to the back row. "Bells up! Hit it hard!" Alas, halfway through, the trumpets lost steam and their way through the funk.

The first rehearsal after their April concert was more celebration than practice. One of the Big Band parents, Josh and Brad's mother, decided to organize a before-rehearsal brunch in the band room. She set up folding tables by the front window, covered them with tablecloths and loaded them with food she brought, as well as with food contributed by the other families: coffee and Munchkins from Dunkin' Donuts. Bagels and cream cheese. A huge bowl of fruit salad. Cookies and icing-laden Danish. Twenty-five people, not including the Big Band members, attended, from Big Band parents to the Northborough-Southborough School Superintendent Gobron, Principal Lavoie and Vice Principal Gary Hreschuk. The band room had more empty space than usual because the bulk of the blue plastic chairs were still in the auditorium on stage, leaving plenty of room for visitors to sit in a ring around the front of the classroom as they watched the group work.

Mr. Clark, a little more stylish than normal in his olive-tan sports jacket worn over a black polo shirt and blue jeans, began the rehearsal in much the same way he did with performances. He thanked the parents for getting up so early and for providing all the sugary goodies, items that most definitely didn't adhere to the state public health department's recommendations for healthy food. "I think we should do this every Friday!" Mr. Clark said before telling the parents they'd be hearing pieces the band hadn't yet played publicly, including two brand new compositions he'd recently distributed and planned for them to sight-read.

Before unveiling "Play That Funky Music," Mr. Clark gave the band members the same advice he'd offered the first time they played it: "Those first two measures have to be *huge!*" Once the music started, the parents became energized. Much to the mortification of their children, some of the parents began dancing in their seats. (Keeping my promise to my son not to make a spectacle of myself while I shadowed the Big Band, I was not among the seat-dancers.) When Mr. Clark caught sight of what the parents were doing, he lifted his hands, stretched his arms up on either side of his head and swayed them, back and forth. He said something was missing and raced, as fast as Mr. Clark can race, over to the cardboard box inside one of the instrument bins and pulled out the cowbell. He held it aloft, like a prize fish he'd just caught, and handed it to Noah. "You've got to make a show with that cowbell!" Before he cued the band to start again, Mr. Clark sang a portion of Wild Cherry's lyrics, *Lay down that boogie and play that funky music till you die.*

"Late Night Diner," a 2009 piece by Doug Beach, is a song that evokes smoke-filled rooms, hard liquor and bawdiness. It has been described as having a strong "'down 'n dirty' blues groove." In the note to the conductor on the sheet music, it refers to the song as "a slow, greasy blues—the greasier, the better." When Mr. Clark introduced it to the parents, he didn't choose those adjectives. "This piece is all about attitude," he said, adding, "There is nothing as good as eating late-night diner food." Previous Big Band students were quite fond of this piece, as the handmade "Clarks Late Night

Diner Coffee & Café" sign on the side of the room reminded every-one. The first time through, they just didn't capture its boozy, bluesy feel.

"You're playing like you're from the 'boros. … You need to be hip," he told the band. They tried it again but the results were a bit messy, and not in a good way. "First forty measures of this. By Tuesday."

♪

Dark Ray-Ban sunglasses. Black suits. Skinny black ties. Black fedoras. Wardrobe staples for the Blues Brothers, Jake and Elwood. The duo—John Belushi and Dan Aykroyd—were the lead characters, musical siblings in *The Blues Brothers*, a film which featured cameos from jazz and blues legends, and was filmed 33 years prior in Chicago. Belushi and Aykroyd, who created their characters for *Saturday Night Live* back in the 1970s, released a hybrid rock/blues double-platinum blues album along the way. One of the pair's famous tunes was a rendition of Robert Johnson's 1936 blues tune "Sweet Home Chicago."

It was a long way from the *SNL* soundstage circa the 1970s and Chicago blues clubs on a Tuesday morning during the second week of April when Mr. Clark handed out the music for Andy Clark's arrangement of "Sweet Home Chicago" to the members of the Big Band, most of whom were born at the end of the 1990s or the first few years of the 21st century. "This is kind of a blues standard," he said. "How many of you have ever seen *Saturday Night Live*?" No hands went up, which really wasn't a surprise given that it aired at 11:30 p.m. and these kids were in middle school, although a few of them could have seen old episodes online. As Mr. Clark provided an explanation of the Blues Brothers characters, there were not many flickers of recognition when he mentioned the names Belushi and Aykroyd either, or when he played their version of "Sweet Home Chicago" on his iPod, a song he told them wasn't "overly challeng-ing"—a "hard-hitting blues classic" one website said—but required attitude and fearlessness.

The students weren't quite ready to rock out like Jake and

Elwood today. Noah was still slowly putting the drum set together. It had been taken apart and transported over the weekend for a music competition. A tune like this one couldn't really start without the drums. And it certainly wasn't going anywhere without the guitar. Jesse started beaming after he looked at his sheet music. "Am I gonna get a solo?" he asked, still smarting from the fact that his part in "Play That Funky Music" wasn't as prominent as he had hoped it would be.

"Yes!" Mr. Clark said encouragingly. "Lots of sections get high-lighted in this piece, piano, guitar, sax, trumpets."

Jesse told me later he was shocked. "I don't know if I got the solo because I improved on my instrument or because Mr. Clark wanted to get rid of me. I don't know, I guess it was my first solo."

Their sight-reading of this piece was thoroughly expressive, and not just musically, but visually. It was so satisfying to see the trumpet players point their instruments aloft without having to be told. The band's driving notes rocketed to the other side of the room. Jesse was in a zone inside himself, his face flushed, his mouth open, lips barely parted while he stared blankly at the sheet music and played whatever felt right. His solo roared. Chris, a confident but restrained seventh-grade sax player, was a reddish-purple when his precise solo ended. Seventh-grade Patrick's sheet-white skin bright-ened as well as he started and finished his trumpet solo. Ethan, however, rose smoothly for his sax solo—decidedly not blushing—and channeled a blend of icy-hot notes delivered as if it was as easy as ordering a pizza. Mr. Clark almost allowed them to go all the way through the piece, which, overall, was a little messy in parts but still a fun, bluesy romp, but stopped them near the end. "Oh! *Soooo* close to landing the plane," he said, as Richie walked in the door, a half hour late. Mr. Clark focused on a handful of corrections, mostly for the trombone section which he said should "come in like a ton of bricks" and should, on a number of measures, "hit it hard."

After a lackluster "Late Night," Mr. Clark did more fine-tuning. "Saxophones, this is like the baddest song ever, and you're like," he used a chipper tone that sounded like he was skipping along, "*Dah-dah-dah-dah* Do *not* rush. Find your soul."

To Richie, who was playing drums: "I need more nastiness."

To the third and fourth trumpets: "Everything you play in this piece, you need to honk it out."

If their first version was vanilla ice cream, the second time through was a chock-full, gritty bowl of Rocky Road. They had embraced the nasty and spat it back out with swagger. However, because they were children, the energy they'd created in the room led to sax players Ethan and Aaron, in their excitement, to start whipping things, including pencils, at one another. The pencil hurling aside, Mr. Clark was not satisfied with how the sax section—a pivotal section for "Late Night Diner"—performed.

"You guys in the sax section randomly stopped playing," he said. When one sax player heard that another stopped playing, he stopped, and that behavior was repeated down the line in the section, like lemmings following one another off a cliff, Mr. Clark said. *"Oh, he stopped playing. And he stopped playing. I'll stop playing.* Why is NO ONE playing?" He commanded Richie to play the drum line and for the sax section to play along. He was still dissatisfied. "For Thursday. This *whole* piece."

When clarinet-playing Anisha got to her little corner of the band room on Thursday morning, she noticed something unsettling on the band room floor. It was brown and hairy and kind of large, about the size of a soccer ball. She was concerned it was some kind of dead animal, which wouldn't be all that outlandish given that the room did have an external door and the kids liked to have snacks and lunch here. On most days, the band room floor was covered with crumbs, papers and other middle school detris. Calmly, she alerted Mr. Clark to the mouse-brown heap near the window. Appearing curious, Mr. Clark picked it up with the tips of his right index finger and his thumb and held it up for inspection in front of the band while he raised his eyebrows. It was a curly brown wig. Flutist Ashley had planted it there as a prank, going off Mr. Clark's comment during the Big Band party about wearing a curly, 70s-inspired wig during "Play That Funky Music." Mr. Clark smirked and placed the wig on top of a blue plastic chair, refusing to be derailed from his to-do list today which included tightening up "Late Night Diner." The wig would have to wait.

The room was tense. The five-minute "Late Night Diner" felt much longer. The rehearsal came to a halt when he not only signaled for them to stop, but angrily pointed at eighth-grade Noah, who was sitting on a stool behind the percussion section while seventh-grade Martin played the drums for "Late Night Diner." "Play!" he commanded Noah. Looking at Martin, he said, "Listen to how loud he's gonna play!" Undaunted, Noah played at a noticeably stronger volume. When it came to the percussion section, the drums specifically, Mr. Clark's favorite saying was that the drummer drove the bus that was the band. Without the drummer's direction, the band wouldn't know where to go. However, Martin wasn't really driving. He was kind of spacing out behind the wheel, unaware that he was allowing the bus to hit the rumble strip on the side of the highway. "Martin, you got it? If you're angry, you can pretend my face is on the drums."

Again, he cued them to start "Late Night" with Martin at the drums. Again, Mr. Clark ferociously air-drummed, trying to persuade Martin to step up his playing. "Stop! You all are totally mailing it in! You are totally mailing it in! It's like," he copped a sing-song tone, "*We are the Trottier Big Band and we're awesome!* Come on guys! You're better than this!"

They started once more and were quickly stopped by the dour-looking bearded man. Silently, he walked over to the flute players, smiled and fist-bumped each one of them. That smile disappeared when he turned to face the row of trumpet players who were sinking behind their music stands. "Three flute players and seven trumpet players. And they are wiping the floor with you, outplaying you volume-wise, with articulation. Wow!" A pause filled the room, expanding like a balloon the longer it went on. "Some of you have not practiced. Didn't I ask for the first forty measures of this song on Tuesday? You haven't done this in a long time. I'm very much getting the sense from the band that, *We got this.* You're resting on your laurels." He held up the "Late Night Diner" sheet music in front of them. "By tomorrow people. Tomorrow!"

♪

It was the last rehearsal before spring vacation. One minute fist-bumps and compliments were being dispensed like glazed dough-nuts on *The Simpsons*. The next minute, the students were being chastised for not practicing their individual parts and for letting down the team. On the plus side, Richie was relatively on time—at 7:13—quickly followed by Jesse at 7:15, and both had their instruments in hand. The pieces they played this morning, "Tiger of San Pedro," "Sweet Home Chicago" and "Late Night Diner" were all fast-moving, get-your-blood-pumping compositions.

After the first rendition of "Tiger," the band was stopped early because they weren't playing together, and the sax section in particular was way off. "Yeah, guys," Mr. Clark said matter-of-factly, "this piece needs to be taken out to the woodshed and beaten." This necessitated an explanation of what the phrase "taken out to the woodshed" meant. They tried "Tiger" again. The results marked an excitedly pulsating improvement. Patrick's prominent, challenging trumpet solo, was strong, considering the slender boy from whom it came. "Patrick, that is naughty hiney baby. That's naughty hiney. That is going to get everyone to say, 'Shut the front door!'" Just as the compliment slipped out of Mr. Clark's mouth, a loud, unpleasant blast of staticky sound came out of the bass amp, causing some students to shudder in their seats.

"Dude, do you even *know* what you're doing?" Jesse snapped at Richie who was adjusting the amp. Lauren, who was standing next to Jesse at the end of the line of trumpet players, scowled and kicked Jesse in an attempt to silence him.

Ignoring the amp snafu, Mr. Clark said, "I offended the trumpet section yesterday and I'm glad that I did because you're playing loudly and better than you were."

Could they channel that volume and quality to "Sweet Home Chicago," which hauled a tractor-trailer full of attitude and serious horn power along with it? If the students were feeling pressure, they weren't showing it. Violinist Natalie and clarinet player Rebecca danced in the back row of their section while the band played. The trumpet section didn't deliver at first, but, after Mr. Clark put his arms out to his sides as if to say, "Come on!," they transformed into the Sonic Lords (and Lady) of Death the second time, sending loud, cheeky bursts of sound outward. The sound of Josh's bari sax was sorely needed in this piece, but he wasn't providing it at the right time or tone. "Do you need a new reed? You sound like a giant goose," Mr. Clark observed. Ironically, as Mr. Clark said that, his voice cracked like an adolescent's. "Old, fat, losing my hair *and* my voice cracks. Epic."

CHAPTER SIXTEEN

Kaleidoscope

The first day of spring vacation, April 15—Patriots' Day in Massachusetts commemorating the start of the Revolutionary War—was a gorgeous one. Sun. Warmth. Blue skies. The Associated Press called it "perfect weather" for the running of the 117th Boston Marathon with its 24,662 participants. The Red Sox completed a three-game sweep of the Rays, winning 3-2 in their 11 a.m. contest. A good chunk of the tens of thousands of baseball fans flooded out of Fenway Park after the game ended at 2 p.m. to visit the marathon's finish line in Copley Square, less than a mile away. My husband and youngest son, who'd attended the Sox game, toyed with the idea of walking over to cheer on the runners—the quotidian runners, the non-elite ones, people we knew—who were crossing the finish line. But they decided against it and headed home. For making that decision, they were lucky.

Meanwhile, twenty-five Southborough residents were running the race, while folks from town were watching from the sidewalks of Boylston Street. Guitarist Jesse's mother Jen was running her second Boston Marathon. Jesse, his little brother Jack, a sixth-grade band and Stage Band member at Trottier, their sister and stepfather were sitting in the grandstands. She finished the race and her family left the finish line area five minutes before twin bombs went off, killing three marathon spectators, including an 8-year-old boy, and seriously wounding hundreds.

Shortly after 2:49 p.m. that day, Jen's Facebook page featured pleas from her friends who had seen the news reports and knew she was running the marathon. "Please tell me you are okay?" one South-borough friend wrote. "Ru ok???" another asked. I too reached out to her that afternoon via text message, as I watched the carnage unfold on a local Boston TV station.

Big Band pianist and clarinet player Olivia's father also was fortunate enough to have finished his marathon before the bombs exploded. Olivia's mother posted on Facebook, "Thank you to our friends for checking in. We are all okay – Jim finished with a time of 3:20 and we were on our way home when we saw all of the emergency vehicles. Praying...." After expressing her gratefulness that Olivia's dad was okay, a fellow Big Band mom commented online, "What an unreal experience and day. I am having 9/11 flashbacks."

Another Southborough friend, the mother of two Trottier students—one member of the sixth-grade band, the other a member of the seventh- and eighth-grade band—also took to Facebook shortly after the bombs planted by the Tsarnaev brothers detonated. She was in Boston with her three children, waiting for her husband who had been running the race but hadn't yet crossed the finish line. Her status updates, in chronological order read:

"Explosion at Copley ... Not sure what's going on are runners stopped?"

"Need to hear from my husband please..."

"My family is all fine in Boston and safe just heard from Jim he is fine!"

"I have never been so scared – was waiting for Jim in the [Boston] Common while people were telling us to leave right away – kids were terrified. I'm still crying – could not get out quickly enough."

Word eventually spread, mostly through social media, that the spectators and runners from Southborough were safe, shaken, but safe. However, on Friday April 19, the last day of spring vacation—hours after an MIT police officer was fatally shot and there was a

gun battle with the Tsarnaev brothers in the streets of Watertown—
those Southborough parents who commuted into the city for work
were, essentially, grounded after Governor Patrick closed the public
transportation system and asked residents in the Boston metro area
to "shelter in place." Officials had released the names of the two
suspects in the bombing and were hunting them down. Although
Southborough wasn't directly included in the lockdown area, busi-
nesses in the immediate vicinity of Boston were expected to excuse
their employees from venturing into the city. The Associated Press
put it this way: "… [T]he population of greater Boston overwhelmingly agreed to shelter in place—it was not mandatory—and that
there was little second-guessing despite the inconvenience and dis-
ruption of commerce it caused, was viewed as a reflection of the
anxiety gripping the region."

My three children asked me not to go to work at a local university that day, while I learned that commuter students living in the
Boston area had been told by university officials not to come to
campus because of the manhunt. Red Sox and Bruins games were
canceled. People living in Boston, Watertown, Newton, Belmont,
Waltham, Brookline and Cambridge were told to stay in their locked
homes and to avoid windows. Mr. Clark, who was on vacation with
his family, texted me, "Massachusetts has never seemed unsafe to
me until now."

Around 6 p.m., the governor rescinded the stay-in-your-homes
request and said he'd reopen public transportation even though the
suspects hadn't been found. Dzhokhar Tsarnaev was apprehended
from his hiding space inside a boat next to a Watertown home by
8:45 p.m.

Over spring vacation, there was a first for the Big Band. A student abruptly quit the ensemble. Via email. Or, rather, his parents
sent Mr. Clark an email saying that seventh-grade drummer Martin
wanted to quit not just the Big Band, but the seventh- and eighth-
grade band as well. Effective immediately. Mr. Clark didn't
understand. This had never happened. Kids *never* quit the Big Band.

What had gone wrong? I was surprised to learn that Martin—whose drum enthusiast father had shown me many iPhone photos of his extensive drum collection and who had brought a left-handed set of drums to the band room for Martin's use—was leaving. "I was blindsided that it happened," said Mr. Clark, someone who prided himself on being able to read students' body language and figure out when they are unhappy. There had been several small moments throughout the year where Martin had seemed distinctly uncomfortable, moments when Martin didn't seem as though he was having any fun, but then again, there were several Big Band members who, as their faces twisted in concentration, didn't look like they were enjoying themselves either but I didn't think they were about to drop the Big Band. There was something in Martin's eyes though, when Mr. Clark would, as he was attempting to encourage him, make jokes, a "why are you picking on me?" kind of look. The smallest and frailest of the Big Band members had also seemed insulted by Mr. Clark's advice and never seemed to capitulate. When the band director wanted a faster pace, more volume, Martin played in a laid-back fashion. When the director wanted light, concentrated drumming that was subtle, Martin played in a laid-back fashion. When the director had Noah play a section in order to show Martin the desired tone and tempo and then asked Martin to play again, Martin would play in the same, laid-back fashion. I was never able to speak with Martin's parents or with Martin after spring vacation despite attempts to do so. They did not volunteer for Martin to participate in a mid-year or end-of-year interview like most Big Band families. Because I did not hear back from Martin's family, I was unable to learn the exact reason or reasons for his sudden departure. Now there were thirty-three students left.

Also over spring vacation, Mr. Clark told me that he'd received the conductor's score for the Big Band piece he'd commissioned in Eric Green's honor. Mr. Clark had been eager for the kids to get to work on it because he knew they'd inevitably place a great deal of pressure on themselves to ace it, while, at the same time, they would struggle with their own feelings of loss. Now he finally had the music by Erik Morales in his hands, but not the music for the individual instruments, something he hoped to have by Thursday's rehearsal. Coming on the heels of a stressful vacation week filled with local news of bombings and violence, the departure of a band-mate and the introduction of a song for Eric, Mr. Clark wasn't sure what to expect from the Big Band.

He looked at the assembled students. There was no Martin. Richie was missing; was he just late? Was he going to show? Would he be the next Martin? Richie, who told me during a mid-year inter-view that he didn't trust Mr. Clark because he said the director didn't do what he promised in terms of who got to play what instrument and what pieces, had already threatened to leave once, but Mr. Clark talked him into staying.

Although Mr. Clark would have preferred that they spend the beginning of the rehearsal working on "Tiger of San Pedro," a good selection to get their blood pumping and to wake them up, he was instead talking about tuning and reeds. After hearing them play "Tiger," he scoffed at the bari sax players, "That's disgustingly out of tune!" Everyone was ordered to tune. Tuning led to the discovery that Danny and Josh were using old reeds in their bari saxes, some-thing Mr. Clark said they should've realized without him having to tell them. This provided a launching pad for a discussion about the sludge, slime and mold that can accumulate on and under reeds in the instruments, including a rather vile tale about a green, gelatinous blob that Mr. Clark once saw removed from a brass instrument's mouthpiece. Almost as stomach churning as Brad's projectile vom-iting earlier in the year. Mr. Clark swiveled toward the clarinet section and asked Angelina when in the past two weeks she'd changed her reed. There was no response.

"Your reed should *never* taste like *anything!*" he warned, as the conversation swerved, like a car skidding out of control on a patch of ice, to Mr. Clark's affinity for Greek yogurt—which struck me as odd, given that he didn't seem drawn to anything in the healthy food category—to bacon-flavored gum and Bertie Bott's Every Flavor jelly beans. Despite all the talk about moldy reeds, yogurt and Harry Potter jelly beans that come in flavors like booger, earwax and vomit, Danny and Josh didn't get up from their seats to take care of their reed issues. Like the children they were, they had to be prodded to do so by a man who seemed like a scolding father. "Reeds! Now!" Mr. Clark said, his eyes flashing.

"Okay, let's run through this again."

♪

The conductor's score for most of the pieces the Big Band would play throughout the year were between ten to fifteen pages long, which equals about three or four minutes of music depending on the tempo. "Kaleidoscope" stood apart from the rest for many reasons, chief among them that its score was twenty-three pages long and counted one hundred eighty-three measures. The next-longest piece they would play, another Morales tune, "In the Doghouse," was seventeen pages long and had one hundred thirty-six measures. When played, "Kaleidoscope" was approximately six minutes long, not including time for solos. But there were other reasons why "Kaleidoscope" was different. First of all, it didn't sound like a garden variety jazz piece, at least not like any I had ever heard. Its tempo and tone changed radically throughout. It required tremendous precision and concentration from the trumpet section. It was much more complex and layered than anything the Big Band had played. It was at once serious, vulnerable and haunting, then three minutes in, it was playful, light and bluesy, before reverting back to its urgent seriousness, with its waterfall of notes, six-plus minutes into the piece. Initially, Mr. Clark didn't like it because it wasn't what he was expecting when he asked composer Morales—whose "Finding You Here," "In the Doghouse" and arrangement of "Dat Dere" are Trottier Big Band favorites, part of their institutional canon—to write a jazz piece in Eric Green's honor. *Eric Green.* Those two words added another level, another dimension to the playing of this intricate song. It was supposed to honor Eric, the unobtrusive, dark-haired 12-year-old who played his trumpet atop the black riser in the last row, the boy whose spot and music stand his bandmates wanted to leave empty, the boy whose presence was still felt.

In the performance notes accompanying the conductor's notes, Morales wrote:

"The Kaleidoscope is much more than a child's toy.
It's like a scope that peers into one's innermost creativity.
Its characteristics include a constant symmetry, angularity

and an infinite array of colors. These are the traits that I instill in this composition. 'Kaleidoscope' features many instruments but focuses on the trumpet section. Additionally, the piece is dedicated in the memory of Eric Green, a trumpet player in the Trottier Middle School Band who recently passed away. The sound the trumpets convey the bright, angular characteristics I was striving for. The idea of angles and symmetry are evident from the very first notes played and resonate different times throughout the piece."

A trumpet player himself who also had a 14-year-old daughter, Morales wrote this piece hoping to feature "the bright sound of trumpets." "I wanted it to be an uplifting kind of a piece," he told me. Calling it a modern jazz composition with a "smorgasbord of influences," Morales structured it around the notion of images one sees inside a kaleidoscope as one puts it into motion, reflecting the crisp sounds of the trumpets. "I didn't want the music to be sad. I wrote it like I would like to think [Eric's] life was, bright and happy." After the song was published and made available for purchase, a music web-site described it this way: "Sporting a diverse set of styles, this incredibly unique swing chart features a flugelhorn solo and the trumpet section with angular themes that invoke images of light, color and symmetry."

The Eric Green Committee—the twenty-eight-member group of students, parents and teachers organized to memorialize him—used funds from the Eric Green Fund to pay Morales $1,500 for the commission, as well as the $3,000 commission to composer James Swearingen, who wrote the heartbreaking "A Kind and Gentle Soul," also in Eric's honor, to be played by the Trottier seventh- and eighth-grade band. The Eric Green Fund originally had around $9,000, money that the Green family decided to donate to the Trottier Music Department. "We tried to think of organizations that Eric would like," Eric's mother Suzy told me. "Kaleidoscope" and "A Kind and Gentle Soul"—the latter's title was taken from Suzy's description of her son—would be premiered on June 8, 2013, at the Eric Green celebratory event. The committee, which met about once a month, decided to schedule the event for a Saturday morning in the Trottier auditorium. The seventh- and eighth-grade band would play "A Kind and Gentle Soul." His friends and family would speak, followed by the Big Band's rendition of "Kaleidoscope." Attendees would then proceed to the front of the grassy area in front of the school, where a tree would be dedicated—the committee hadn't yet determined what type of tree.

The first few meetings of the committee served as an ad hoc support group for grieving students, rather than as solely an event-planning body. However, as time went on, the students began pressing Mr. Lavoie to do something concrete, something tangible. As he shared a pizza with some of Eric's friends three months after Eric's death, the principal said he learned, "They were mad at me because I hadn't done anything to commemorate Eric." The question was, what to do. There were students who wanted to paint the front of Eric's locker green and keep it permanently unassigned. There were some who wanted a statue made of him and placed in the lobby. Mr. Lavoie was in a tough spot. He feared setting a precedent by doing something official because, what if, in the future, another student passed away who wasn't as popular or as beloved as Eric and who had two older siblings pass through the school? Would the family of that child be offended that the death wasn't treated equitably? Mr. Lavoie didn't want to put himself in a situation where he'd be fielding angry calls from bereaved parents whose child's passing wasn't given the same attention as Eric's. But the students in Eric's class were adamant. They wanted something done.

Eric was one of those kids who didn't hang with one specific crowd. He transcended cliques. He was an athlete, a scholar, a musician and a smiling boy who seemed to be liked by everybody. The emotional outpouring after his passing was significant. At the one-year anniversary of Eric's death, students were given the chance to write their thoughts and feelings on a large green paper hung up in the eighth-grade hallway.

Mr. Lavoie, Trottier teachers and parents on the Eric Green Committee gently guided Eric's peers toward the idea of planting a tree as opposed to hanging a photo in the lobby or erecting a statue. But when it came to the Eric Green event, Mr. Lavoie was tentative, as Eric's friends pushed for a year-end event, a capstone to their

Trottier careers, a way to say, "Goodbye" to their friend. "I didn't want it to become another funeral," Mr. Lavoie said, noting that some of the students wanted a slideshow, an idea to which he gave "a big, fat, 'No'" because of how emotional that might become. Suzy—a deceivingly frail-looking woman with a soft voice and an iron spine—said she liked the idea of a concert, a celebration of his life. "In that way, it wouldn't be a memorial service," she said.

For Mr. Lavoie, planning the event was "one of the biggest herding events I've ever had." But he believed, given the makeup of the eighth-grade class, this was something that would help them achieve some degree of closure. "We did this because that's what the students wanted to do and what they needed. You can't go wrong if you take care of the kids in your school."

But first, the Big Band had to master "Kaleidoscope," no small feat when the limelight was going to shine on the fledgling trumpet section. And, Mr. Clark himself had to warm up to the composition, adjust his expectations. "It's a cool piece," he told me after first hearing it, "but, okay, holy crap, what are we going to do with it? I had to kind of think of it in a different way. It's just, *different*. That opening ... I had to step back from the piece."

One person on whom the pressure was almost crushing was Lauren, the eighth-grade trumpet player, the only trumpet player who had played alongside Eric. Though she projected an aloof, cool girl vibe, she was extremely unsure about her playing in the Big Band. She also didn't like other kids in school seeing her toting her trumpet around, Mr. Clark said, because it jeopardized her reputation. Despite that, she decided she needed to play the first solo in "Kaleidoscope" because she owed it to Eric. "Mr. Clark told me there was a solo up for grabs and he wanted me to have it, if I felt I should take it," she said. "I never thought I was good at it, though."

The rest of the band felt the pressure too, exuding a loud and kind of stunned, *Whoa*, when Mr. Clark distributed the sheet music and they saw how long the piece was. Throw in complexity and the demand for precise timing and the band had a lot of work to do before June 8.

"Do you guys know what a kaleidoscope is?" Mr. Clark asked as the students arranged the music on their stands.

"You look through it and there are eight of you!" Danny blurted.

"Eight! That's a lot of *you*! ... The whole thing is based on this opening thing with the trumpets." He played the electronic version of the piece that Morales had sent him—not the best rendition of the piece—and told the trumpet players that they needed to practice their introductory cascade of notes slowly at home. "You need to create muscle memories for this. And you need to listen past the cheesy piano on this recording. It's all patterns." The electronic version made this unusual song sound otherworldly. The first time I listened to it, alongside the Big Band students, I couldn't get a read on the piece, couldn't get inside it because it was so different, particularly its moody intro. The students had no reaction as they listened and followed along on their sheet music. Many told me later that when they first heard it, they hated it, which was going to be a problem, since it was supposed to be played to celebrate their friend. "I didn't think it represented anything about Eric," Lauren said of her first listen to the song. So not only was it their longest piece, most complex piece and most genre-bending piece, it was their most emotionally-loaded piece. And they hated it.

Mr. Clark asked the trumpet section to try the beginning. He had pairs of trumpet players play the repetitive notes that sound like trumpets urgently heralding some important news. Tentatively, slowly, the trumpet players waded into the music. But once the duos were asked to play their disparate parts simultaneously, with the sets of trumpet players' music overlapping one another, it was chaos. The timing was complicated, like a domino-effect sound with one set of trumpet players, kicking off another set at a rapid clip, then playing the notes all over again in a round. Given that it was April 25, I thought the likelihood that the young, shaky trumpet section would ace this piece in time for the performance was poor. Mr. Clark was privately skeptical too, but he didn't share his fear with the students.

Mr. Clark was in a Latin kind of mood this morning, so he started the rehearsal with "Dance Like No One's Watching" and

"Tiger of San Pedro." Uplifting, danceable, fun pieces. By this point in the year, the Big Band had enough experience playing together that they were be able to quickly pick up new charts—"Kaleidoscope" being the exception—and play them well. When they remembered their music and set up their instruments properly, that is.

Guitarist Jesse didn't have his music. Mr. Clark demanded that Jesse do that walk of shame up to the front of the room and fetch a fresh copy of "Dance Like No One's Watching." In addition to not having his music, Jesse was taking a rather long time setting up his guitar and amp. It took him until 7:15 to get himself situated and ready to play, something which Mr. Clark also pointed out to him, despite the fact that the rest of the band played solidly. The on-time trumpet players, however, were playing their instruments in a way that made them sound like they were "whining quietly" instead of "pushing it" like the rest of the band, their director said.

Sax player Ethan missed the cue for his incredibly rapid sax solo and blushed a deep red as he stood alone and motionless in the front row of sax players, as though stunned. Mr. Clark didn't remark on Ethan's error and instead cued the band to start at a measure just prior to Ethan's solo. Mr. Clark gestured energetically as if he was trying to pull the music out of Ethan while simultaneously injecting energy into the sleepy band. "Really, really, really great stuff," he said genuinely.

Before they commenced "Tiger of San Pedro," Mr. Clark said he expected them to "play the crap out of this." The results were mixed. It sounded good, but there were several missteps which marred the overall effect. Bari sax-playing Josh, who was spacing out, missed his cue to allow the drummer to solo. "Watch that you don't ever go on autopilot!" Mr. Clark said lightly. And the trumpets, whose grand theatrical gestures are required multiple times in this piece, weren't elevating their game. Or their instruments. "Somebody bring me a trumpet!" Mr. Clark said. As soon as one was placed in his hands, he dramatically arched his shoulders and backward toward the floor. His elbows pointed outward and the trumpet bell was pointing at a 45-degree angle. This is what he wanted the trumpet players to look like when playing. When they played again, I was surprised to see that only about half of the kids pointed their trumpets in the air with flourish, like Mr. Clark had shown them. Were they just too shy? Too afraid? *Why didn't they just do what he asked*, I wondered. *It's not that hard to lift your trumpet up during one note.*

This didn't make for a great segue into "Kaleidoscope," which relies heavily on the trumpet players. Only a few measures into the piece it was evident that the students hadn't practiced in the twenty-four hours since they'd received their music. Gently, Mr. Clark told them to work on the beginning over the weekend. Then, he went to work, guiding them, note by note, section by section, giving suggestions to smooth out the transitions. He did so gingerly, more so than he had done with any other piece. Because this wasn't any other piece. Both the students and the band director's behavior affirmed that fact. But now, Mr. Clark felt as though he had to bring it up, remark on the obvious, the fear that no one wanted to discuss.

"Guys, you're treating this as if it's a different kind of piece, different than the 15 or so other songs. You're playing hesitantly, like you're afraid to make a mistake. You know what happens when you're afraid to make a mistake? You make a mistake."

Just as he was starting to dive into their feelings about this piece and Eric, his classroom phone rang. It never rang. "I can't help you right now with the Middle East, Mr. President. I have my Big Band rehearsal," Mr. Clark joked as he walked over to the phone. He informed whoever was on the other end of the call—he didn't share—that he was in the middle of a rehearsal and would call back. But instead of plunging into the subject of Eric, he tried a different tact: "If you break this down, to the notes, the individual ones, it's not so daunting." He placed his hands into prayer position. "Please, please, please practice the first one hundred measures for Tuesday."

CHAPTER SEVENTEEN

Seizing the Stage

It was unusually bright in the band room. Almost blinding. The shades on the windows behind the trumpet section were only drawn a third of the way down. Bright streaks of sunlight reached through the branches of the bushes that were unfurling their bright green leaves, through the tall, double-hung windows and beamed, laser-like onto the salmon-colored linoleum floor. It was too bright for me to look at, especially when the light bounced off the brass instruments. I had to look away. Not Mr. Clark, though. It didn't seem to bother him, even when he glanced over to the side of the room where Martin's personal white drum set, set up for lefties, had been. It had been removed from the room without so much as a comment or remark, almost like Martin had never been there at all.

Mr. Clark was too busy trying to figure out how to get the Big Band past their emotions on "Kaleidoscope," to just play it, particularly since the feedback he'd received from some of the band kids had been negative. Disappointment was a more accurate description.

"I think some people really, really like this, and I think some people really, really don't like it, and feel bad about it. 'Kaleidoscope,' is very, very different from what is usually written for middle school bands," Mr. Clark, who would grow to love this piece, said. "Just come at it from, *Okay, it's not Count Basie. It's not 'Groovin' Hard.* I think the audience is going to be blown away by all the effects Morales has in it."

With the students, Mr. Clark tried making an analogy to the premiere of Igor Stravinsky's "Rite of Spring" ballet in 1913. "When this was played a hundred years ago, audiences rioted and threw things at the orchestra because it was so different."

PBS' WGBH website said of "Rite of Spring:" "The intensely rhythmic score and primitive scenario—a setting of scenes from pagan Russia—shocked audiences more accustomed to the demure conventions of classical ballet. The complex music and violent dance steps depicting fertility rites first drew catcalls and whistles from the crowd, and are soon followed by shouts and fistfights in the aisles. The unrest in the audience escalates into a riot."

Shifting back to "Kaleidoscope," Mr. Clark asked, "Can you hear that this is a different kind of piece, not whether you like it? If you go at it from hating it right away, you'll likely grow to hate it more." Mr. Clark had told me on a number of occasions that he would not have his bands play music he disliked. One year, after listening to the Big Band play a piece he personally had grown to hate, he had them rip up the sheet music and toss it. No point wasting time on music that irritated. But this was different. This was a piece that he had commissioned. He *had* to like it and the kids had to play it.

The band room sounded like a nightclub. The 2006 Gia Farrell song "Hit Me Up"—which was featured on the *Happy Feet* soundtrack—was booming out of the speakers. But sounding like a nightclub and feeling like one are two different things.

People were trickling in late. At a nightclub, that's completely expected. It would be uncool to be the first one to arrive. Not so in the Trottier band room. "Rehearsals need to start at 7! They're getting later and later." Mr. Clark was able to, even this far into the school year, get that out without gnashing his teeth or getting red in the face.

When they finally did arrive, the students didn't automatically tune their instruments, something that became evident once they started playing. When the band director heard Josh play a few notes on the bari sax, he threw his hands up, slapped his thighs and yelled, "Tune! This is like the beginning of school!"

After hearing a handful of notes come out of Ethan's sax, Mr. Clark's eyes bulged. "You didn't tune, either!"

"What, do you want, an invitation? Tune! You people better have pencils!"

This was the angry Mr. Clark, someone I hadn't seen in a while. The mood in the room, initially set by the pop song, shifted.

Mr. Clark spent several minutes ripping the band for lackluster playing in "Tiger of San Pedro." At 7:20, Lauren arrived. She received no admonishment. Instead, Mr. Clark asked the sax section to play section 89 again. After they were done, he declared it "boring and dull."

Mr. Clark redirected the band to "Back to the Basement" just as Richie arrived. Mr. Clark shook his head. A quick run-through of that upbeat piece was followed by Mr. Clark announcing their set list for the central district's Massachusetts Association for Jazz Education (MAJE) festival, to be held at Trottier in two weeks: "Late Night Diner," "Tiger of San Pedro" and "Back to the Basement," although the students seemed too preoccupied with nailing "Kaleidoscope," on which they spent a great deal of time reviewing, instrument section by instrument section.

"Kaleidoscope" was starting, ever so hesitantly, to unfurl itself within the students' instruments, within their heads, but not yet their hearts. "That opening is starting to sound really good. Do you hear the difference when you warm up the sound?" the band leader asked.

After months of observing Mr. Clark and his students, it had become clear that he didn't handle his students' mishaps (being late, not having sheet music, not practicing, not having a pencil) the same way. Some kids he verbally clobbered. Some he let slide. Why? Mr. Clark told me he tailored his approach to the student, based on each student's personality. He pushed those who he thought needed pushing, backed off those who were sensitive souls, and spoke in private with those who he believed were having difficulties, in conversations to which I was not privy. Jesse and Ethan, for example, could handle being called out for being late or ill-prepared. Jesse, in fact, needed it, Mr. Clark said. However, when it came to students like Lauren and Richie—who were quiet, routinely tardy—Mr. Clark backed off and chose to deal with them one-on-one in exchanges I never witnessed. After Martin quit the Big Band, Mr. Clark did some soul searching, wondering if he'd chosen the wrong tactic with the seventh grader, trying to goad him into playing louder by joking with him in the middle of rehearsal then later, privately telling him to step it up. Maybe Mr. Clark's public ribbing had been too much for the boy who, the next time I saw him at school, sported a radically shorter haircut, closely trimmed on the sides instead of the Justin Bieber-like shag he had worn earlier in the year.

As Mr. Clark was giving them some pointers for "Back to the Basement" during a rehearsal, Richie arrived at 7:43, clutching his bass guitar. The following day Richie walked into Big Band rehearsal at 7:53, essentially having missed the entire practice. I emailed Richie's father near the end of the school year to request a second interview, but the interview never happened. I was left to worry and hope that Richie was okay and that the constant tardiness and absenteeism was simply a result of a child sleeping late. As with Martin, Mr. Clark would later question how he handled Richie's difficulties throughout the year, uncertain as to whether his talks with the boy helped or hurt. "I have been inconsistent with him because I don't know what's happening. I have no gut feeling," Mr. Clark lamented. "I don't have an intuitive read on him." By June, he said he felt terrible about never having "reached" Richie.

Rehearsal started fifteen minutes late, irritating Mr. Clark. The MAJE competition was days away. The students hadn't yet played all three charts on their set list, consecutively, all that well. Without their chief bassist there, with Jesse arriving fifteen minutes late and

Lauren walking in twenty-five minutes late, Mr. Clark did a good job of hiding his frustration. He had them start "Back to the Basement" twice in a row, stopping them early, emphasizing articulation. This opening piece was intended to make a strong statement to the other competitors. Mr. Clark said, "'It's *our* stage.' Take it if you can. Then we're going to follow up with 'Late Night.'"

The hard-charging piece provided sax-player Ethan with a showcase solo, his opportunity to seize the musical leader position in the Big Band, if he wanted it. At times it was hard to tell if Ethan really wanted to be a leader or just wanted to make music on his own groovy time. Mr. Clark clearly needed him to step up to grab his leadership role and make it his own. As the band waded into "Back to the Basement," Ethan got to his feet to solo but awkwardly squeaked out his notes. Startled, he responded like the 14-year-old he was. He giggled. Then he composed himself and delivered a powerful bit of jazz, eliciting a fist-bump from his band director. Three more students soloed, including one whose playing was significantly weaker than the others. Why would Mr. Clark allow students whose playing wasn't particularly strong to solo, especially during a jazz competition? Because the band is about and for the kids. Anyone who asked for a solo would get one. End of story.

"Does anyone else want to solo?" Mr. Clark asked. No one else raised a hand, which meant that only boys would have solos on "Back to the Basement." In this particular Big Band, boys dominated the solo scene, by the students' own choices, with the exception of Lauren in "Kaleidoscope."

They moved into the smoky maturity of "Late Night Diner," in which Ethan had an extended solo during which he could improvise. Mr. Clark was very pleased. "Let's throw down on 'San Pedro.'" Prior to the throw-down, he said, "It's been a while since we haven't gotten gold at MAJE, so let's not start now."

"Is there something we can get that's better than gold?" someone shouted out from the band.

"Don't get cocky."

The choice boiled down to two: a kwanza cherry or a yellow-wood tree. The kids on the Eric Green Committee spent a lot of time researching tree varieties. After weeks of debating they pared the selections down to two. One student initially suggested a type of tree that could grow as tall as 200 feet. But that variety wasn't native to New England, and as the parents in the group Googled it on their smartphones, they realized that wouldn't be the best option for the Trottier Middle School grounds. God forbid they choose a tree that would not thrive or worse, would die. Though the adults were trying to give the students latitude, they wanted to guide them toward a choice that would work, a choice that would live.

That was the problem with the kwanza cherry tree. It blossoms vibrantly, but like a brilliant firework display, fades away. This type of cherry tree that a few of the kids on the Eric Green Committee coveted "is the most popular cultivar of all the double-flowering cherries, thanks to its stunning pink blossoms, good fall color, lack of fruit and upright, vase-shaped form," the Arbor Day Foundation's web-site said. "... While it has a limited life span that typically doesn't exceed 15-25 years, the beauty of this tree makes it well worth planting." The short lifespan was a turnoff to the Trottier parents. No one wanted to say out loud that it would be a bad choice to honor a 12-year-old boy whose own lifespan was abruptly cut short.

The last of the final two options was a yellowwood tree, described as hardy and low-maintenance with a showy, fragrant flower that appears in the spring, the Missouri Botanical Garden reported. "Yellowwood is a medium growing, deciduous tree of the legume family which features a broad, rounded crown and typically grows 30-50' tall," said the Botanical Garden web-site. "Yellow-woods are native to the Smoky Mountains region in Tennessee, from which some of Eric's father's family members hailed," said Gretchen Hartnett, one of the parent members of the Eric Green Committee and mother of a Big Band member and a member of the sixth-grade band. "They have flowers that hang like bunches of grapes. They are unusual trees. Conservationists love them." One of the boys on the committee likened the clump of flowers the yellowwood produced to a tightly-knit group of friends. A bonus: the blooms were expected to appear around Eric's birthday in May. However, there were some who didn't think the yellowwood was flashy enough. Those children thought the cherry tree would really stand apart.

The children on the committee went back and forth. Finally, they got Suzy Green to weigh in. While she said she liked both choices, she preferred the strong, understated and rare yellowwood tree. That was more like Eric. She told the group she really wanted a tree that, decades from now, when these students had children of their own, they could visit it and remember. A yellowwood it would be.

As a consolation to the children who desired the brilliant cherry trees, Mike Hartnett, Gretchen's husband, ordered kwanza cherry trees for the families of the kids on the committee who wanted them. Seven opted to buy them, including mine. A mother of one of the boys—a boy who still had music from Eric's last song, "Swing Shift" tacked up in his bedroom with the words "For Eric" written in pencil across the sheet music, with the mass card from Eric's funeral tacked just below the 78th measure, beneath the trumpet solo—said she couldn't take the risk that a cherry tree they might plant in their yard in Eric's memory would die. She didn't want to even contemplate how her son would react.

Once the decision had been made to go with the yellowwood, Mike coordinated with a local nursery, which donated the tree and its staff's time to get the 6-year-old yellowwood planted at Trottier. The students on the committee wanted to plant the tree themselves, but the adults insisted that they needed the folks from the nursery to unload the heavy tree off the truck and deposit it into the hole that the all-boy group would dig.

The night before the tree was to be planted, it poured, saturating the grassy area just off the Trottier front drive. The rain let up just before the team arrived. Eight eighth-grade boys, Eric's friends, including three members of the Big Band, and Eric's older brother—who shared a birthday with Eric—showed up bearing shovels and work gloves. It took two hours for the boys to dig the 6-foot-wide and 3-foot-deep hole. "They muscled through it. They dug it out," Mike said. Once the hole was deep enough, the five guys from the nursery gently placed the tree in the middle.

Before covering its roots with enriched topsoil, there was a solemn pause. For the letters. Forty of them. Days earlier, half-sheets of white paper had been distributed in the eighth-grade homerooms. At the top of the biodegradable paper it said, "A note to Eric" across the top. If students wanted to write notes to their friend and have them be nestled among the roots of his tree, they could deposit them in a designated box in the lobby. Suzy Green kept custody of the box until the tree planting. What did the children say in those letters? What did the 13- and 14-year-old children want to share with Eric? Did they mourn that he couldn't come along with them to high school? That he wasn't there to finish out that basketball season? That he wouldn't be going to the eighth-grade banquet in a few weeks? That they would have rather had him play "Swing Shift" again instead of the band playing "Kaleidoscope" in his memory? My son wrote one of those letters and didn't care to discuss its contents. None of the kids did. The letters were private. Between them and their friend.

"Words are kind of nurturing the roots of that tree," Suzy Green said to me a year later during a conversation at a Southborough coffee shop. "That's one of the reasons the tree bloomed."

There was a photo taken just after the boys deposited the folded letters around the tree's 3-feet-wide ball of roots before they covered it with soil. The papers looked crisply white against the chocolate brownness of the fresh earth. The boys, the guys from the nursery and Mike stood in a semi-circle atop the mounds of dirt around the fragile-looking tree. Some of the boys were leaning on shovels. Some were slouching in a bashful sort of way or had their hands in their pockets. A shovel was laying upside-down in the foreground. Minutes later, they took those shovels and buried the roots of the tree along with the letters. Unfortunately, Trottier's exterior water spigot wasn't working that morning. But as they were burying the roots, it began to rain.

Once the tree was safely situated, the boys burst out of their somberness. "I feel like the whole time, they were focused but they were still goofy 13- or 14-year-olds," Gretchen said. "At any given moment, there was somebody giving someone a ride in the wheelbarrow. Brandon was in the wheelbarrow and everybody was trying to move him."

Unlike the small Christmas tree that had been placed on Eric's grave in Southborough's Rural Cemetery—onto which his friends placed tokens like Patriots and Red Sox ornaments, musically-themed ornaments and a sports medal a boy had won but wanted to share—this tree, everyone hoped, would signify life, Eric's life, bursting forth in vivid color and in the hearts of the boys who were being silly and playing next to their middle school, next to their pal's tree.

CHAPTER EIGHTEEN

Seizing the Stage

||: "He was not happy," Jesse told me of Mr. Clark. "Put lightly, he was not happy, just the fact that I couldn't be there. I don't think he was mad at what I really did. He was mad because I let the band down."

Here's what I was able to piece together after speaking with several students, Mr. Clark and guitarist Jesse on a mid-May afternoon, the afternoon of the MAJE Junior Jazz Festival at Trottier: Jesse had been in gym class. Another student allegedly slapped Jesse on his bad back. Jesse, according to students who were there, retaliated by extending his right arm out, sharply clearing his arm toward the other boy away in one swift motion, knocking the student in the head. The boy fell to the floor and sustained a concussion, Mr. Clark said. Jesse was suspended from school for a day-and-a-half, starting just hours before the MAJE performance. That meant the band was going to have to play jazz and blues-infused pieces, which included guitar solos, without its sole guitarist.

"I'm really angry with him," Mr. Clark muttered to me under his breath when I entered the band room an hour before the Big Band was set to take the stage as the first act of the MAJE festival. "I thought he might be able to win an outstanding musician award tonight for guitar."

It was as if a stink bomb had gone off in the band room as the students entered, having already donned their concert black attire and affixed their green neckties, ribbons and bows to their outfits, added their green Eric bracelets to their wrists. Everyone seemed frenzied. Several students were chewing over the details of "the fight" the way bad actors chew up scenes. Suzy Green was spotted manning the ticket table at the auditorium door. Seeing her there, on a performance day, was surprising for some of the kids, who looked at her with woeful eyes wishing there was something they could do to purge her of her grief. The Big Band parents hugged and welcomed her, placing their arms around her as though she was a crystal vase instead of the strong, sturdy elm she actually was. Between the buzz about Suzy being there and Jesse's absence, the students were distracted. While everything and everyone seemed to be humming with energy, I noticed that drummer/bassist Richie was sitting in the middle of the last row of seats in the front of the band room alone. He wore white socks with his black sneakers. He wasn't talking to anyone.

Angelina sat down at the piano and played "Stay" by Rihanna. *Round and around and around and around we go,* the lyrics say. A few bandmates milled around, listening. She played "Viva la Vida" by Coldplay as one student—I couldn't see who it was or tell if it was a boy or a girl—sang the lyrics out loud. *I used to rule the world/Seas would rise when I gave the word.*

Kay, who wasn't a Big Band member but was an orchestra and seventh- and eighth-grade band member, was hanging around the band room. She took over for Angelina and started playing a soft, classical piano composition I didn't immediately recognize. When someone pronounced, "Wow! You're a professional!" she changed over to pop songs.

Mr. Clark, clad in a dark green dress shirt and a black suit, ushered the students onto the stage to warm up. Most of the bands who'd been bussed in from other central Massachusetts communities to perform for the MAJE judges wouldn't have as much time to set up as the Trottier students did since the Southborough musicians were the first act of the day. Adjusting the acoustics and balancing the sounds was going to be tricky this afternoon, particularly without a guitarist. "The dynamics will be tricky without Jesse and without Jeffrey." Trumpet player Jeffrey was out sick.

Big Band parents and supporters filed into the auditorium. Several members of trumpet player Patrick's immediate and extended family took seats in the middle row of the auditorium. Ms. Murdock, the fellow musician who hired Mr. Clark and who was now the principal of the Neary Elementary School, was also in the house.

Finally, they got the signal to begin.

"Back to the Basement." The first thing I heard was the sharp snapping of Mr. Clark's preferred tempo, a brisk walk on a chilly day. They slayed the first notes. The piece rolled along with attitude, the frosty cymbal crashes and the warm sax tones were complemented by Ethan's sax solo, which he delivered as if he were standing up on stage wearing a pork pie hat and Blues Brothers shades. The drum solo, Noah's double solo, tore through the measures. Some of the other solos were shaky, didn't sound as though the students had enough air or sufficient confidence. Part of me wished I could go up on stage, pat the struggling soloists on the back and tell him it was okay, *Just let loose. Don't be afraid.* But I've never stood on stage like that and played, alone, while people were recording me and literally judging me. Once the students were back safely playing under cover of the whole band's sound, their confidence appeared to return and they closed strongly.

"Late Night Diner." Here it was. That bad assery Mr. Clark had been practically begging them to put on display … but minus the guitar. They didn't sound like kids who, minutes earlier, were having their teacher tie their neckties for them. If—once they got past the intro, which wasn't perfect but was solid—you closed your eyes, you wouldn't guess that there were young kids who had yet to hit puberty pumping out that jazz club music. Ethan started his solo out slowly. At first, I wondered if something was wrong with the volume until I caught on that he was building power and complexity incrementally. After the solo sections wrapped and the band braced for its sassy ending, Mr. Clark signaled for them to kick up the volume, although he, himself, was not shouting at them.

"Tiger of San Pedro." What fun this chart was to listen to, both as an audience member and as someone who had watched them struggle with it for weeks. It was an explosion of trumpet and percussive energy whose only faltering points were the lack of the vibra-slap at the beginning of the piece—Jeffrey wasn't there and no one thought to fill in for him on the vibra-slap. Patrick missed a few notes, but he recovered and pushed out the rest of his solo all the way to the back of the room so everyone could hear him.

"They sounded off," Mr. Clark confided in me. "And I think they were thrown off by Jesse's absence."

What did the MAJE judges ultimately want from the band's performance? They assess each group by five criteria: Improvisation, ensemble, rhythm section, music analysis and overall presentation. Within each of those categories, they look for: time, feel, tone, phrasing, dynamics, articulations, creativity, intensity, emotional content, precision, clarity of sound, balance and blend between sections, drum fills, difficulty and variety of materials and stage presence. Groups receive one of four designations: merit, bronze, silver or gold. Hours later, once all the seven central Massachusetts elementary and middle school jazz bands had played for the day—students from Boylston Elementary, Tahanto Regional Middle School from Boylston and Berlin, Dudley Middle School, Berlin Elementary, Hale Middle School from Stow and the Gibbons Middle School from Westborough—the judges made their decision. The Trottier Big Band was awarded a gold medal for an outstanding performance, three students won outstanding musician awards (Ethan on sax, Patrick on trumpet and Noah on the drums) and Ethan was deemed an MVP for the Central District. In the judges' commentary that Mr. Clark received, they said the rhythm section, which was missing its guitarist, needed more balance.

Less than twenty-four hours after their MAJE performance, the members of the Big Band—except for Jesse—were back in the band room and were blasé when they learned that they'd won a gold medal and that Ethan received the district MVP. Mr. Clark applauded their achievements. They were just like, *meh*. "Really, it's so old hat?" Mr. Clark asked, sounding disappointed. He stood there for a moment before he shook his head, shook off what seemed like indifference and moved quickly to "Dance Like No One's Watching." It sounded as if there was more give-and-take between the trumpet and sax sections, almost as if they were trying to engage in a musical conversation, but Mr. Clark stopped them abruptly. "It's all loud and it's not supposed to be! Pull it back!"

He looked around at the kids, specifically Cassidy, the bass player on this piece. "Cassidy, you *love* this, right?"

She smiled shyly. "Yes."

"Have fun with it! You're too tense."

To shatter the tension on this May morning, Mr. Clark asked the band to take out the sheet music for "Play That Funky Music." "This piece is not subtle or nuanced. This is clearly, obviously, a rock tune."

As they dove into the musical world of Wild Cherry and the 1970s, Mr. Clark again abruptly stopped them and asked Danny to play a loud note on his bari sax. "That sounds like a goose honk!" The students were laughing as Richie arrived at 7:25. "Richie, do the cowbell!" Mr. Clark slapped a smile on his face as he cued them to start again, this time with the accompaniment of a low-spirited cowbell player.

"Richie! You've got to have more fun with that cowbell!" Mr. Clark declared.

"I don't know where to hit it," Richie replied.

"Who cares? Just wale on it!"

Although he was calling for the kids to have fun with their music, tension remained in the room like a nagging cough, increasing when Mr. Clark requested that they take out the "Kaleidoscope" sheet music and he discovered that many of the students hadn't practiced it. He kept asking for a nice round quality of sound, wanted the rhythm section to back off more, the trumpets to blend but not play uniformly. He was unhappy with how the trombones and saxophones sounded because he thought "that's not the character of this song at all!" Mr. Clark imitated them and made a loud, livid honking sound. "It sounds like some kind of angry people."

The trumpets—minus Lauren who never showed—were asked to play individually, by first trumpet, second trumpet, and so on, something he hadn't done in months. I'd almost forgotten how painful it was to witness. "*This* has got to be, now, top priority. I know you've been practicing for MAJE, but *this* is our top priority."

♪

Mr. Clark wanted Lauren to solo in "Kaleidoscope."

"I asked her about the solo, specifically because it was a written one. She wouldn't have to improvise. It was written for an eighth-grade trumpet. I told her she could do it. She *could* do it. I would work with her endlessly. She viewed it as her responsibility to do. I think she used me to put pressure on her to do it." Mr. Clark paused for a moment. "Maybe I did, but that was not my intent. I knew she could do it. I honestly believe there was a no-fail solution."

Lauren said her decision to play a solo in "Kaleidoscope" was a direct result of Mr. Clark, "I had never done a solo. I never thought I was good at it."

After the two spoke, Mr. Clark sent her a link to a computerized excerpt of "Kaleidoscope" and told her to listen to it. Although she didn't initially like the piece, she said, "When Mr. C explained it and we started playing it and it grew on me." For weeks after receiving the music, Lauren played the trumpet solo over and over again in her basement, trying to nail it, to buff it to a brilliant shine to match the brightness Eric's smile friends said they saw in the back of their minds when they thought about him. The burden Lauren felt to solo was significant. The anxiety she felt about doing it was of equal power. It was only the help of Mr. Clark that helped this otherwise confident-looking girl muster the courage to allow the spotlight to fall on her during the Big Band's most emotional performance of the year. "I think Mr. Clark has always seen in me things that I didn't think I had in me, that I didn't believe were in me," Lauren said. "He's not gonna judge you."

In sixth grade, Lauren had wanted to quit the sixth grade band after having played the trumpet since the fourth grade, but "Mr. Clark wouldn't let me quit," she said. When Lauren was in seventh grade and a member of the seventh and eighth grade band, she wasn't planning on trying out for the Big Band. "I actually didn't try out, but the next day, my name was on the list." Why did Mr. Clark just put her on the Big Band? "I knew that she had the ability. I knew that she had a love of music. I knew that where she was as a teenage girl, as a person, as a popular girl, she wasn't going to audition. Lauren is such a musical soul, an old soul. She needed to be in the Big Band," Mr. Clark said. He would watch her play and see her just fall into the music. "The kids forget when I'm conducting music, they're watching me, but I'm watching them," he said. There was precedent for putting a student on the Big Band without a tryout, although just barely. On three other occasions, Mr. Clark said he put kids who hadn't auditioned onto the Big Band because he knew they could play and would benefit by participating. But in none of those cases, he added, did the additional student ever bump a student who auditioned and who could play out of the group. If there had been another talented trumpet player who auditioned, he would have just expanded the trumpet section, he said.

In most school years, a handful of students tend to bond tightly with Mr. Clark, either because they hang out in the band room looking for conversations, regularly eat their lunches in the band room, directly seek out his counsel, or all three. "I like to think I offer to all the students the opportunity to do so, to get whatever the kids want and need from me," Mr. Clark said. "I feel it's they who communicate more with me. I try to treat kids as the best possible versions of themselves, and that's why I think they respond to me."

When it came to coaxing Lauren to stay in concert band, to giving her a Big Band spot in seventh grade that she didn't seek, Mr. Clark said, "Some kids I can just read. ... I think that all people need is for someone to believe in them, particularly someone they respect." When a student says she wants to quit, his first response is to tell the student she can't. During this school year, Richie said he wanted to quit Big Band, and Jesse said he wanted to quit seventh- and eighth-grade band. He told them, "No." If a student really wants out, he will quit, like Martin did.

"He doesn't only teach music," Lauren said. "He's definitely taught me about family, respect, bravery. As down as his downs can get, his ups are so happy. When he gets that way, he's that way to do the best for you, for your best interest."

Lauren was planning to practice her solo for the first time in the band room. Mr. Clark looked nervous for her. At 7:09, he had already drained his first travel mug of coffee and was on his second. It was highly likely that he'd had more java at his house before heading to school. He had spent the previous day at part two of the MAJE competition during which his Trottier Stage Band won gold, a double-gold week for his bands. "It's been a very long week and if I wasn't psychotic I would've cancelled practiced," he said.

They were short on some people this morning. Jeffrey was still out sick. Emily, an eighth-grade clarinet player, was out because she had sustained a serious concussion during a soccer game and the noise in the band room was too much for her. Richie and bari sax player Josh were not there, either. Jesse, however, was back from his suspension, about which nobody said a word. Lauren arrived fifteen minutes late and looked uncomfortably tentative, her complexion florid. Mr. Clark whistled to get the students' attention, to draw it to "Kaleidoscope." They plunged right into the piece and into her solo, which seemed to surprise the rest of the band. The solo came a minute and twenty seconds into the composition, after the moody introduction with the butterfly fluttering of the trumpet notes and the somber sax line. Lauren's single trumpet called out high, then low, lingering on long notes as the sparse drums, bass guitar, and other accompanying instruments provided a supportive backdrop, one which told her, "We got you." It started out timid but grew in strength during its one-plus-minute duration. When she finished, her face flushed, her eyes watery, her left hand was raised to her mouth, the sleeve of her boat-necked tan sweater was pulled down nearly covering her hands. Mr. Clark entered the trumpet section where he gave her a 10-second hug as the members of her band clapped. She held back tears.

She had passed the first hurdle, playing the solo publicly. Mr. Clark returned to his spot in front of the band and asked her to go again, to try to normalize it. Part of his advice to her was to practice it repeatedly so that the solo would become second nature. The second time wasn't as successful. Her face contorted as the air she blew into the trumpet sounded as scared as she looked, yet she got to the end. When she finished, she started nibbling the fingernails on her left hand and biting her lower lip. Harry, a close Big Band friend who ran with the same crowd as she did, gave a big smile and nod from his spot in the front row of sax players.

"It was one of the best moments of my teaching career for her to realize what she could do," Mr. Clark told me later. In the event that Lauren was unable to play the solo, if she became overwhelmed with fear or broke down, Mr. Clark had a Plan B. He had asked two other students to learn the solo and have it ready. Just in case. Throughout the rest of the rehearsals, Lauren said a lot of bandmates, Kyle in particular, "said stuff about my solo. It felt good."

CHAPTER NINETEEN

The Duck Analogy

||: The next week began with a building-wide lockdown after a
22-caliber bullet was found on the floor in a classroom in the
seventh-grade wing of the school. Trottier Middle School teachers
and Southborough police officers, along with a state police dog,
went through the building, classroom by classroom, asking students
to empty their pockets, to reveal that there was nothing in their
waistbands and to remove their jackets. Lockers were searched. In
an affluent, low-crime community such as this one, a lockdown and
a big police presence at school for anything other than a DARE
assembly was highly unusual.

"I was part of a group that searched about eight or nine rooms,"
Mr. Clark said. "Pockets were emptied and loose clothing was asked
to be removed, sweatshirts and jackets and such." The search process
not only prevented classes from proceeding for an hour, it also
wound up canceling the marching practice the seventh- and eighth-
grade band was going to do, something they hadn't done since
October. With Memorial Day coming up, Mr. Clark wanted to get
some practice in.

"We weren't told what was happening," one of the students
told me, adding that the children were unnerved to see uniformed

police and a police dog roaming the halls.

Before noon, Mr. Lavoie sent Trottier parents an email giving them the headlines, stressing that everyone was safe even though police were conducting a search. This resulted in the parents texting one another and posting questions on Facebook seeking information about what was happening since none of their children—who weren't supposed to be using cell phones while in school—were responding to their texts. Newtown was still pretty fresh in everyone's mind, and contributed more angst to the parents' questions until, an hour later, Mr. Lavoie sent a follow-up email saying everything was fine. There was no danger. Students were still chattering about the lockdown when they showed up for Big Band rehearsal the following day, on Tuesday, May 21. Chattering was all they were doing well that morning.

The band members hadn't practiced. Several of them were absent when the rehearsal started—Jesse, Emily, Richie and Lauren. From "Fly Me to the Moon" to "Kaleidoscope," the music they played this morning could be compared to a spent bullet, sharp, jagged pieces of metal, blown apart and lying on the floor. Nothing was magical. No dulcet tones were in evidence. *How would Mr. Clark deal with this? Would he berate them? Joke with them? Softly encourage them? Which teaching tactic would he pick, fresh off a school lockdown and weeks away from the memorial service?* After the year they'd had, I wasn't sure what technique would work with them. How would they perfect these pieces?

The students made it painfully easy for him to decide what they should do first: tune. Virtually none of them had done so upon entering the band room, something that was evident from the few notes of "Fly Me to the Moon." "Oh my gosh! Do you know how out of tune you are? Did you tune? Did you? *Did* you tune?" Mr. Clark waited a few seconds but no one said anything. "If you don't start tuning before rehearsals, I'm going to start getting annoyed."

In addition to their lack of tuning, Mr. Clark had other worries. "You guys are getting a little bit of a big head, which will prevent us from doing what we want to do at the end of the year."

As he was speaking, Lauren walked in, twenty minutes late. "Lauren, go play some notes," he grumbled.

It probably wasn't the best time to play "Kaleidoscope" but they really had no choice. The piece had to be mastered. Mr. Clark asked them to start halfway through the piece, at an easier part of the score. They sounded fairly polished, until they didn't. Chris' sax solo was strong, at least at the beginning. "You need to be a little more free," the band director advised. Within a few measures, it became clear that several of the trumpet players had forgotten to bring their plungers. (Trumpet players use the rubber tops of plungers or plungers designed for the bells of trumpets—plunger mutes—in order to muffle and alter the trumpets' output to make a low, *wah-wah* kind of sound.) The kids who forgot the plungers attempted to cover the bells with their hands. Henry's and Brad's arms were too short. They couldn't reach around their trumpets to cover their bells. Their forgetfulness was a minor flub compared to how they sounded.

Mr. Clark was red-faced. "I don't think I need to say anything about that, do I trumpets? [*long pause*] That's just a lack of practice. I'm sensing a lot of, 'We got this.' Guess what people? We don't. We don't have this. We've taken multiple steps backward since Friday."

The only noise in the room was the metallic hum of the AC unit. Pressure, gentle pressure was moving them forward. Gradually. In an almost imperceptible fashion. I'm not even sure the kids understood or realized their forward progress.

The three strongest trumpet players were asked to flip their music back to the beginning and play the fluttery "Kaleidoscope" opening. "That is exactly the same as it was last week! It's not any better." Another weighty silence. Mr. Clark forcefully flipped through the "Kaleioscope" score, making a rustling noise that, if the band room was at its normal noise level, wouldn't have been audible. "Well ... [*a third long pause*] if the practice doesn't happen, if you don't tune like you're supposed to, we're not going to be able to do what we wanted to do. We're running out of rehearsals. The Trottier Big Band is awesome because you work your butts off. I have to tell you this is something that surprises me, having to have this conversation now. I would expect it in February, not now."

Referencing "Kaleidoscope," he said, "You can play the easy part of 'Kaleidoscope.' You can't play the hard parts."

In a low and restrained tone, Mr. Clark said, "I'm not listening to that. I'm *not* listening to *that*. You haven't practiced since Friday. I'm not listening to that." He exhaled loudly. More silence. This rehearsal was breaking records for its lingering silences. Mr. Clark's somber tone seemed to unnerve the kids. "That's the thing I hate the most," Lauren told me later, "when he doesn't get angry. He gets disappointed. When he doesn't say anything, that's worse than him yelling."

Four more concerts were scheduled before the end of the school year: The Eric Green ceremony, a spring school concert, a Big Band concert at the Southborough Senior Center and Jazz Night. That didn't include the performance at the Pawtucket Red Sox—the farm team for the Boston Red Sox which plays in Pawtucket, Rhode Island—at which the seventh- and eighth-grade band would perform "The Star-Spangled Banner" and "We Are Family." All the songs the Big Band learned up until this point, plus two new ones, would have to be mastered before then. If they didn't practice and build up their endurance, there's no way they'd be able to ace those performances, but endurance was something on which Mr. Clark had been working since day one.

Mr. Clark ran down the list of the pieces they'd learned as he continued shuffling through the scores on his music stand. "Any idea what happened to Jesse this morning?" he asked to no one in particular. His question was met by silence.

"Okay, get back to work. Start practicing again." Big pause. "Pack up. Go." It was 7:45. They usually practiced until 7:50 to 7:55. This was Mr. Clark making a point. At least once a year, he threw the Big Band out of the band room because he believed they weren't taking the music seriously enough. It generally scared the young students and made the eighth graders shrug their shoulders at typical Mr. Clark behavior. While most of the students were gloomy looking as they shoved their sheet music into their folders, seventh graders Natalie and Olivia, who were always ready and always practiced, were loudly cheerful. Ashley was also smiling. They knew they weren't the ones in trouble.

♪

Everyone in the room was in dire need of warmth, both emotional and musical. Harshness, loudness, and sharpness pervaded. Mr. Clark, whose tension about the Eric Green ceremony was slowly building, had lost his iPod and with it his Vienna playlist, the magical musical elixir that put him in an amiably supportive mindset when he drove to work in the morning. "I haven't been able to play it since MAJE," he complained to me shortly before snapping at students who were still arriving late. "If you're just getting here, rehearsal starts at 7. Get out and tune." Off the students went, banished to the hallway to tune, out of the eye line of the cranky director.

"Kaleidoscope" was the only order of business. They had a little more than two weeks before they would have to perform this piece. They were not even in the same time zone of being close to ready. The trumpets were just blasting out notes, with no accents, no feeling, no precision. The drummer was playing in-your-face forte when he should have been restrained. The trombones and baris were emitting harsh sounds. The flute and clarinet sections were moving too fast. ("If it was a race, you would have won.") He wanted everyone's dynamics, except the trumpets', dialed back. Lauren tried to slip in unnoticed at 7:15, but Mr. Clark called her on it. "Lauren! Go tune!" The clarinet section was the only one that was playing in a way Mr. Clark called "round and fat," "warm and round" that this piece required. The girls played a few mellifluous measures, at the director's behest, to demonstrate to the other students what he meant.

By the time Lauren had tuned her trumpet, she was asked to start her solo. It wasn't as strong as it had been the last time. She seemed to know this because her face grew very, very red. I wondered if she'd be able to summon enough oxygen to make it to the end of her one-minute interlude because the notes she blew out of the bell of her instrument sounded faint. Mr. Clark opted to not comment. Instead, he worked on a trombone section with Brandon in the part of the piece which transitions to swing. Mr. Clark asked Chris to play his sax solo, which was a bit stilted though technically correct. He checked in again with Ethan to see if he *really* wanted to take a pass on a "Kaleidoscope" solo. Ethan said he didn't want one. Patrick did, however, his trumpet solo was weak. The final solo, guitarist Jesse's, was the best of the lot: Powerful, smooth and loose, a perfect complement for the middle swath of the song that gets swingy and full of bounce. It was hard to believe he hadn't done a solo until recently. Jesse seemed like he was the only person in the room who was having fun with this song. He disappeared into the chords. He wasn't self-conscious or concerned about perfection. Right after his solo, the band came together so well in a cheerful portion of the piece that I could feel the music in my chest. I could feel its power. If only they could maintain that for the entirety of the long piece.

"Dance Like No One's Watching" was a palate cleanser, a back-door confidence booster. The Big Band had only possessed the sheet music for this piece for a little while, yet they were able to play the captivating composition well. It didn't present the same musical challenges as "Kaleidoscope." Performing this piece would set the stage for them to climb the mountain that was "Kaleidoscope."

Even though they were missing Lauren, Emily and Richie when they started "Dance," they were robust. After days of struggling, they finally sounded like the Big Band again. "Tiger of San Pedro" had the same bolstering effect. They demonstrated authority, even delight amid the playful, driving Latin beat. Except for the trumpet section. It's worth noting that all the trumpet players elevated their bells at just the right time. How did they get here? Practice. Nagging. Pride. Duty. All of which eventually led to joyous music. "Very good," their leader said. "Let's take that same energy, focus and concentration and apply it to 'Kaleidoscope.'"

Before they began, he broke the piece down into smaller parts, hoping to demystify it. "We have basically three different sections of this song." He waxed lyrically about playing vertically as opposed to horizontally, playing with a round sound that's open and full. Sometimes, Mr. Clark could get poetic like this, telling the students to imagine certain images or metaphors in their minds' eye, but I wasn't convinced that they fully comprehended what he was saying.

In the midst of the reverie, Richie, who hadn't attended a rehearsal in over a week, drew the attention of his bandmates away from Mr. Clark as he shuffled in at 7:32, his untied black sneakers flapping loudly against his feet.

The "Kaleidoscope" deconstruction went microscopic. Maybe at the microscopic level it wouldn't seem as difficult or as emotionally charged going measure by measure, note by note. Mr. Clark gently fine-tuned the trumpet section, helping them smooth out wrinkles. In the case of the third and fourth trumpets, Mr. Clark wagged his right index finger and said, "More practice!"

After every instrument section played a few measures, Mr. Clark complimented them. "Trombones, you're doing really well. Subtle nuances." During the swing section of the piece, he lauded the lot of them. "That sounds very good. There have been miles of improvement since yesterday."

Measure by measure. Note by note. Layering this atop a foundation they had built all year, a foundation of musical excellence, of can-do attitude and of trust built upon shared experiences.

The latter half of "Kaleidoscope" was much improved, so much so that my worries that they wouldn't be ready for the Eric Green event were starting to evaporate. Mr. Clark's advice on the lively section had transformed it and infused it with fun. By focusing on the swinging middle section, he'd given them a much-needed boost.

The students channeled that enthusiasm into their playing of "Sweet Home Chicago." But not at first. The jazz-club-esque Blues Brothers piece sounded phoned-in. It was as if Mr. Clark was a human barometer detecting what and why was off. He stopped them early and attempted to pull the bad ass out of them, the attitude they flashed during "Back to the Basement." They responded with vitality. Just as they were nearing the high point of the piece for the trumpet section, Mr. Clark turned to me, and in a loud stage whisper said, "Duck and cover!" The trumpets obliterated their section. He lifted his hands, pressed them together, cupped them to form a heart. But they hadn't reached the end of the piece yet. Mr. Clark thought they had more in the tank. Rising up on the balls of his feet, he puffed himself up, tilted his head up and circled his right arm around as he shouted, willing them to play louder. And they did.

♪

It was Memorial Day, 2013. It would have been Eric Green's fourteenth birthday. Members of the Trottier seventh- and eighth-grade band were standing in the thick shade of Southborough's lush Rural Cemetery next to the tranquil Sudbury Reservoir which wound alongside it and eventually paralleled Main Street. The old growth trees shielded them from the reach of the sun's blazing rays. After having marched several blocks down Main Street and hanging a left onto Route 85 South, the fifty-eight students who had marched in twenty rows stood silently as town officials, veterans and clergy spoke reverently of Southborough's war dead.

Mr. Clark leaned over to me. His whistle-on-a-string swung back and forth as he whispered: "Colleen asked me the other day where I wanted to be buried. I don't know why she asked me that. I said I want to be buried here, so I can keep track of the bands." It was an odd juxtaposition, Mr. Clark talking about his burial and watching over the future Trottier Middle School bands while the current members of his band were standing beside him, in the same cemetery where Eric was buried, just before the names of those who had served in war and had died in the past year were read aloud.

Then the lanky, dark-haired Brian Keefe—a freshman member of the Algonquin Regional High School marching band and a former Big Band trumpet player with Eric—stepped forward in front of the crowd. He was holding something silver in his hand. It was Eric's silver-colored trumpet on which he'd play "Taps." Eric had originally wanted a silver trumpet because Brian, who was a year ahead of him in school and someone Eric admired, had one, Suzy Green had told me. This was the boy who, during the Jazz Night performance months after Eric passed away, played Eric's solo in "Swing Shift" and was gripped with fear that he wouldn't be able to get through it. "During most rehearsals, I couldn't even play it without missing a note or getting mad at myself for tearing up," Brian said. "I felt honored to be the one to play it, but I was probably the most nervous I'd ever felt about playing. Ever." In the spring of 2013, Suzy Green called the Keefes' home and requested that Brian play "Taps" on

Eric's trumpet on Memorial Day, given that he had played Eric's trumpet at Eric's funeral mass. "When I first picked up his trumpet, I didn't know what to think because I played with Eric. Picking that up," Brian said as his eyes brimmed with tears recalling the funeral, "one of the last things he touched ... I remember he tried really hard. I kind of didn't want to play it because I didn't want to mess it up. When I opened the case, I just looked at it." Brian's feelings were still fresh when he was asked to play Eric's trumpet on Memorial Day. The hundreds of people in the crowd intimidated the freshman. "Right before playing, I just tried to relax, but my heart rate was through the roof. It was hard to play." The Trottier band members—who played "The Star-Spangled Banner," the "Indiana Jones" theme and "We Are Family" with precision and uneven enthusiasm throughout the parade— looked somber as they watched Brian play. When the 21-gun salute started, they looked like their young selves again, particularly Danny who ducked his head down and covered his ears like a preschooler to muffle the blasts.

The rehearsal on the Thursday after Memorial Day started off, frankly, disastrously, which was surprising, given that, two days earlier Mr. Clark had texted me, "They're back!" after they kicked the stuffing out of "In a Mellow Tone," "Dat Dere" and "Finding You Here." Even "Kaleidoscope" had improved, so much so that the prominently-featured trumpets were sounding almost confident in their playing. The middle swing portion was even outstanding, the best I'd heard from them on this piece. What happened between Tuesday and Thursday? I couldn't tell you.

For starters, rehearsal began late and with several students missing, including Lauren, Richie and Danny. Mr. Clark accused someone in the band of stealing his coffee. Eyeing the crowd, his gaze locked on Ashley, she of the staring contests and the creepy curly wig. She blushed deeply but denied taking it. After a bit of investigation, he determined his accusations were unfounded and impulsive when he recalled that he'd left his java in his Hyundai sedan in front of the school. He exited through the light blue external doors to retrieve it like the addict that he was.

Then there was the bickering. Between Mr. Clark and Jesse which started during, of all tunes, "Cute," the musical equivalent of skipping down the sidewalk.

"You don't have this piece, do you?" the director asked the guitarist.

"No, but I remember it."

"No you don't." Mr. Clark looked away from the guitarist and advised the rest of Jesse's bandmates to play soft, not angry. To drive home the point, he asked Noah to play the drums with the brushes while the rest of the students sang the notes.

The second tune, "Tiny Capers," another sprightly piece, yielded an additional sharp exchange.

"You don't have *this* music either," Mr. Clark snapped. "Jesse, you are killing us. You're playing the wrong chords and you're part of the rhythmic foundation for the band. What you're playing is garbage. That's nothing but arrogance and egotism, not getting up off your butt and getting the music from the front of the room."

"There are no copies."

"I would have given you the originals if you'd asked." Mr. Clark said. "Jesse, don't play!"

"I have the music at home."

"I don't care."

Mr. Clark directed yet another accusation at the students, suggesting that some of them were pretending to play in spots because they didn't know the music or were rusty with "Cute" and "Tiny Capers." "Tonight, look at 'Fly Me to the Moon.'" When he announced that he was going to hand out two new pieces—less than a month from the end of school—one of the band members whispered, "Yes!"

Erik Morales' 2006 firecracker "In the Doghouse" was an entirely different animal than his moodily haunting "Kaleidoscope," his achingly beautiful "Finding You Here" and his lively arrangement of "Dat Dere." "This phenomenal chart fuses boogie-woogie and shuffle into a chart with a unique style and attitude ... a huge shout chorus at the end makes sure your audience knows that this is one doghouse with an open invitation to all," a music website declared.

Mr. Clark sang "Doghouse's" praises. "This is one of the best swing tunes written for younger bands. It's a shuffle." When he played it on his iPod, the students seemed satisfied. Several listened with their whole bodies, swaying side-to-side or up-and-down, bobbing their heads, pretend-conducting with their hands and arms, jiggling their legs to the beat.

He played the other piece, the 2009 "Strollin' with Sammy" by Paul Baker, a laid-back tribute to Sammy Nestico, famed composer/arranger for the Count Basie Orchestra. In his notes to those conducting "Strollin' with Sammy," Baker wrote that this piece was a testament to Nestico's "signature style and sound … [which] has become a benchmark against which all other swing charts are measured."

The first playing of each song yielded some good music and some parts that needed work. With "Sammy," they liked it immediately. They didn't take to "Doghouse" quite so quickly. Mr. Clark stopped them fairly early during their first "Doghouse" sight-read and had them slow the tempo way down so they could get a handle on it. That tweak got instantaneous results. Confidence filled the room. There was so much less pressure to play these well than there was with "Kaleidoscope." As the smiling band members rose to leave, Richie crossed the band room threshold, arriving just as rehearsal ended.

♪

On the last rehearsal in May it was in the 90s, humid, the second of a three-day heat wave. Inside the band room, the kids didn't seem to be sweating. Neither did Mr. Clark. But just in case the students were sweating inside and hiding it, Mr. Clark wanted to prepare them.

"If something goes wrong during a piece, don't react," he said to them, after they delivered a much-improved rendition of "Kaleidoscope," almost tempting fate. (I wanted to knock on wood. Just in case.) He reassured them: "The audience will never know. No one knows this tune." He had a point here. This would be the first performance of the newborn composition so the listeners would not necessarily know if their playing went astray unless it was blatantly bad.

Mr. Clark spent a lot of this rehearsal smiling, a big, fat smile, like he knew something that everyone else didn't. This didn't seem like the same man who had just recently been telling the students that their successes had gone to their heads. Even his posture—leaning back on his stool, legs stretched out in front of him—was unusually relaxed considering what was coming up for the band, almost as if he was throttling back.

"This has come together," he admitted. Indeed, it was starting to sound like it. They played "Strollin' with Sammy" as though they'd been practicing it since October. When they performed "In the Doghouse," Mr. Clark turned to me with his knowing smile.

So, there was this duck analogy. And poop jokes involving Mr. Clark's goofy golden retriever Riley. Both were ways to lighten some of the weight of the service which was four days away. Mr. Clark used this week to soothe and push as much as he could. He would inject laughter back into the band room, something I hadn't realized was largely missing until it returned, that levity which had been eclipsed by MAJE and "Kaleidoscope" and Memorial Day. He even made sure that, even though Richie had missed or been dramatically late to most Big Band rehearsals in the past few weeks, the boy would have an opportunity to play the bass guitar on some pieces.

As he complimented their playing of their toughest piece, "Kaleidoscope," Mr. Clark prepared them for different possibilities. "Chances are very, very good that you will get a standing ovation," he said. "If the ceremony on Saturday is too short, if people run through their speeches too fast, the Big Band will fill the time. Bring all of your music."

The hardest obstacle to overcome was the students' nerves about "Kaleidoscope." "I want this to sound effortless, like the way a duck looks when it's swimming. From the top of a duck, while it's swimming, it looks calm, but if you look underneath, the duck is wildly moving his feet." A peculiar squawk came out of Mr. Clark's mouth just before he pretended to take a rifle and shoot a duck that was far off in the distance. "One time I went hunting but I didn't want to shoot anything. I wanted to go to Dunkin' Donuts for a doughnut."

The kids' eyes followed him as he grasped Josh's music stand, and emitted another, awkward duck noise to which Josh's bari sax playing bore, according to Mr. Clark, a striking resemblance. "You need to play rounder … like poop." Why did poop pop into his mind? The previous night, his dog Riley had relieved himself while walking down the carpeted staircase in the Clark home. "I'm still trying to figure out how he did that." This prompted Mr. Clark to suggest that someone should write a song, "Pooping on the Stairs." Bellies filled with laughter, which led right into a duck-like, effortless round of "Kaleidoscope."

♪

"Everybody get a good night's sleep last night?" asked Mr. Clark, looking lively in bright pink golf shirt and toting a giant, plastic Dunkin' Donuts take-out cup of iced coffee.

Danny replied, "Three hours of sleep!" and raised his hands above his head.

The previous night, seventy-nine members of the seventh- and eighth-grade band performed three pieces at a minor league baseball game, the Pawtucket Red Sox, the Triple-A team of the Boston Red Sox, "We Are Family" ("Our own, personal national anthem," Mr. Clark said), the "Raiders of the Last Ark" theme and "The Star-Spangled Banner." They wore bright emerald green T-shirts that said, "In Memory of Eric" on the left-hand side, a contrast to the dark green shirts they wore last year when they were in mourning. They played to the hoots and applause of their parents in the stands and later mobbed the white and fuzzy team canine mascot Paws for photos and hugs. They saw the school's name up on the Jumbo Tron, bought gobs of junk food during the game and purchased large, foam Paws claws. The three busloads of middle schoolers made it home after 11 p.m., following the PawSox's 5-1 loss to the Chicago White Sox's farm team, the Charlotte Knights. As I watched the sugared-up kids get off the buses and climb into their parents' cars, I couldn't imagine that they would be settling down to sleep any time soon.

Connor Jenks, a freshman tenor sax player at Algonquin Regional High School and Big Band graduate, was sitting in with the Big Band this morning. He was going to fill in for Harry on "Kaleidoscope" because Harry couldn't make it to Saturday's service. Connor, the older brother of a Big Band trumpet player, quietly sat in "his" seat which was now Ethan's seat. Ethan said nothing about the change.

"Mrs. Green emailed me yesterday, and she's expecting you to play two tunes. Which ones should we play?"

They played "Back to the Basement" with aplomb during this rehearsal. This was a definite contender, a vivacious, celebratory piece as was the Big Band standard, "Groovin' Hard" which they had played gloriously. The kids seemed to be thoroughly enjoying themselves. The trumpet section looked fiercely unafraid. That fierceness transferred to "Tiger of San Pedro" where the trumpet players elevated their horns to punctuate the song at just the right moment. The piece itself was exciting to the ear. "Tiny Capers" was a bump in this parade of sound as the band's confidence waned a tad. The quality of their playing was going in the wrong direction as they went deeper into their set list, containing charts they hadn't pulled out of their battered music folders. "Play That Funky Music" was in rougher shape in comparison to the likes of "Groovin' Hard." It had a rushed quality to it. Before cueing them to start "In the Doghouse," Mr. Clark quipped, "Let's see if anybody has practiced this." It was wildly uneven. "That needs work," he said. "That needs *work!*"

The first named storm of 2013, Tropical Storm Andrea, was steaming up the east coast during the first week of June. In Southborough, which would later receive flash flood warnings, it was intermittently rainy and in the 50s. In the Trottier auditorium on this first Friday morning of the last month of school, it was damp and chilly. Not especially good weather for the student council members to run out to the buses and escort the bus drivers into the auditorium to give them hot coffee and doughnuts for Bus Driver Appreciation Day. With large umbrellas held aloft, the student government members walked the drivers, via the auditorium's side door, to the tables laden with goodies. An additional bonus, was listening to the Big Band's final rehearsal before Eric's service. It was also a great distraction from the nerves.

"We're going to be appreciating some bus drivers in a while," Mr. Clark told the students as they entered the auditorium and took their places in the pit, in front of the stage where they would play the following morning. The students tuned as their director swept up to the rear middle section of seats, travel coffee mug in hand, to determine if he could hear them as they seized the first measures of "Sweet Home Chicago" and attempted to own them. "Individually, you are playing well. As sections you are playing well. But you're not listening to one another. This is a different room than the band room."

He walked to the front of the center bank of seats and heavily plopped himself down onto the table, accidentally knocking over his coffee mug, spilling it. "Oh! It's a sad day!" The coffee sadness was short-lived, doused when the kids started "Play That Funky Music," *More! More! Let's go!!* In between his jabbing and pointing of the air, Mr. Clark leaned forward and struck an imaginary cowbell at a stern clip, locking eyes with Richie who was manning the actual cowbell.

As student council members, their faculty advisor and the vice principal gathered next to the auditorium's side door, Mr. Clark said he didn't think the Big Band needed to rehearse "Kaleidoscope" this morning. They proceeded to "In the Doghouse." "Start at thirty-three. It's a buildup all the way to forty-two. Each new layer something new." However, students weren't counting, some were dragging, some were rushing, which was vexing Mr. Clark. "No! No! No! No! Road kill! Halfway is dead!"

By 7:50, bus drivers in their yellow safety vests and long-sleeved jackets started trickling in. The Big Band was playing "Dance Like No One's Watching" before shifting to "Late Night Diner."

"Relax! Don't rush!"

"Groovin' Hard" yielded appreciative applause and some whoops from the drivers as they shook off the raindrops. "Guys, I got you covered. You don't need to go to home room," he said to the kids. By 8 a.m. the student council members had already left but the Big Band members were still playing. They were on "Tiger of San Pedro," and like they had on Thursday, the trumpet players all lifted their trumpets in unison. They had finally internalized Mr. Clark's directives. Finally.

CHAPTER TWENTY

As One

‖: It poured for several consecutive hours during the early morning
hours of Saturday, June 8. The remnants of what was, for a
fleeting moment, Hurricane Andrea, lashed the area. It was spitting
precipitation. In front of the Trottier Middle School, a granite bench
had recently been installed atop a concrete slab not that far from the
roped-off yellowwood tree. It was inscribed with the words: "Life is
not a matter of milestones, but of memories. In loving memory of
Eric C. Green." A large stone, threaded with the color green and an
orange tint—Eric's favorite color was orange—had been placed in
front of the newly-planted tree. The stone came from one of his
classmate's yards. Later, it would bear a plaque which would read,
"Yellowwood Tree Planted by the Friends and Family of Eric C.
Green."

Inside the Trottier cafeteria, an army of Big Band graduates in
green "In Memory of Eric" T-shirts and khaki pants were helping
parent volunteers set up. The room exuded warmth, with bright
oranges and yellows in the Gerbera daisies on the round tables.
Long tables lined one wall and were covered with breakfast fare
made and purchased by band parents. The fancy black shoes worn
by Mr. Clark—who was in a black suit and a new emerald green

shirt, no necktie—could be heard clacking around the hallways, in and out of the band room and around the stage. He issued rapid-fire directions in a manner which suggested he had excess nervous energy he needed to expend. This was the most high-stakes performance these kids had ever experienced. Four of Eric's friends were slated to give speeches. The children were plagued with dry mouths, perspiration and jumpy stomachs. Gretchen Hartnett, who was going to speak on behalf of the parents, was so worried about whether she'd be able to make it through her speech that she asked me if I'd be willing to step in and read it should she become too emotional. I agreed to do it if she gave me the signal. Eric's parents, Suzy and Peter, were expected to speak but hadn't yet arrived.

Inside the band room itself, the atmosphere was somber and as charged as a college campus during finals week. At 9 o'clock, Mr. Clark shut off the lights to get the attention of the seventh- and eighth-grade concert band and Big Band members. "You *cannot* screw this up! You *cannot* fail. It's going to be awesome. The only bad thing that happened today, that's going to happen today, is that I lost my coffee." The children, sitting quietly in their seats, responded with polite yet stilted laughter. "We're going to relax. We're not going to worry about anything." It was as though he was talking to himself as much as he was to the students, many of whom said they were frightened that if they made a mistake or choked up, they would dishonor Eric in front of what would be a packed house in an auditorium with a 502-seat capacity. Brandon and Noah, the two Big Band boys who'd be playing both the songs dedicated to Eric, as well as giving speeches, seemed the edgiest, as did Lauren who couldn't stop thinking about her solo.

The plan was for Mr. Lavoie and Mr. Clark to make opening remarks, followed by the seventh- and eighth-grade band playing "A Kind and Gentle Soul" and then family and friends would speak. After an intermission, the Big Band would play "Kaleidoscope" followed by the yellowwood dedication outside and a reception in the cafeteria.

Pacing in front of the band room, Mr. Clark spoke softly. "There is no right way to respond to the ceremony today. If you need to cry, cry. If you feel like laughing, laugh. You'll play your best. If you need to take a break, take a break. The same thing goes for the audience. They might not applaud right away. They might burst into applause. They might throw fruit. If they do, and it's juicy, take a bite." He was in full-on nurture mode, a protective backstop there for his kids, regardless of how today went.

Meanwhile, in the auditorium, Mr. Clark had his Vienna playlist playing over the loud speakers waiting for the Greens to arrive. By 9:30, the time when the event was to begin, Peter Green was seated with family members, but Suzy wasn't. There was no way this was going forward without her. Ten minutes later, in a black dress layered with a dark blue blazer, Suzy, the backbone of this event, took her place next to her husband. Word was sent to Mr. Clark who signaled for the seventh- and eighth-grade band to take their seats on stage. Rod Stewart's "Forever Young" was playing. It had randomly popped up on Mr. Clark's iPod.

Mr. Lavoie, in a black suit, a white shirt and a white tie, looked morose as he walked to the unadorned, light maple podium on the right-hand side of the stage. "I am very proud to be here with you today," he began. "… Today is a celebration." He thanked what he called the "remembering Eric Green community" that brought the hundreds of people together in this room after months of discussion and planning while supporting one another through a difficult time. "We are fortunate to live, work and grow up in such a place."

"This is going to be a wonderful ceremony," Mr. Clark echoed in his brief opening remarks just before he introduced the first public performance of the ballad written for Eric, "A Kind and Gentle Soul." "Suzy said to me that Eric had a kind and gentle soul and when I told [the composer] James Swearingen that, he said, 'We now have the title of our song.'"

The initial soft notes were a little shaky as this light and slow-building piece opened, but the strength of the playing blossomed once those first measures were out of the way. By the time the xylophone's high notes and the soothing strains of the clarinets entered, the students had gained their footing. The piece took a sad sojourn, just for a few measures, before it began to swell with full, reverent sound, featuring a floating flute line throughout and ending on gentle xylophone plinks. Facial tissues, which had wiped away tears leaking out of the eyes of many in the audience, including mine, were clutched in hands as attendees applauded for a full thirty seconds after the three-minute piece concluded.

Mr. Lavoie and Mr. Clark handed out water bottles to the students on the stage as Gretchen headed to the podium. Gretchen—a very tall woman with thin-rimmed oval glasses and straight, shoulder-length blond hair—was wearing a flowy, light green patterned blouse. She read her speech in the comforting way a mother might read a bedtime story to her child, but in this case, she often spoke directly to Eric, specifically about how the parents of Eric's friends frequently saw him in the lives of own children.

"As parents of Eric's friends, classmates, teammates and bandmates, I speak for us all here when I say that we all know that he is actually very much *still here* with our children and taking good care of them every day. I once told Suzy this past year, almost on a daily basis, as parents of these boys and girls, we smile and sometimes tear up when we see that he is still working his magic amongst so many of these children." Her voice strong, she wasn't going to need me to rescue her. "You know what I am talking about. We've all seen it and had it happen. You suddenly see something or your child says something or looks at you in a certain way, and you say to yourself, '*That* was Eric. Right. There.' Do Peter and Suzy know how many things still happen because of Eric? Would Eric know how many things are still happening because of him?"

The green ribbons and bracelets. The green socks. The Eric Green Xbox characters on his friends' game systems. His initials carved into a tree by his friends during a hike they took on his birthday. The playing of "Taps" on Eric's trumpet on Memorial Day. The Boy Scout and Little League positive attitude awards in his name. The Pinewood Derby car named The Green Machine. The decorations his friends put on the Christmas tree next to the boy's grave. The friendships, between children and between adults, forged in collective grief that had Eric at their center. The simple statement from a boy: "Mom, you don't understand. *Everyone* thought they were Eric's friend." Gretchen addressed all of these things, telling Eric directly, "The world is such a better place because of you." On stage, several of the children were crying. One girl was red-faced and quietly sobbing as Mr. Clark brought her a bottle of water. Sniffles could be heard throughout the auditorium.

In discussing the music the school had written for Eric, Gretchen shared this:

"A few weeks ago, I was chatting with Mr. Clark and when I told him that Suzy had asked me to speak about Eric and how I planned to focus on how we have all seen and heard things this year that reassure us Eric is still here and always will be with us. He smiled and nodded his head and said, 'I do know *exactly* what you mean. I see it every day at school. And *that* is Eric's kaleidoscope.' He then said, 'Do you know how a kaleidoscope works? A kaleidoscope works when you put beautiful things inside this container, inside this prism and then you fracture it. You break that light apart and it splinters into a bunch of smaller, beautiful pieces and the light just goes on. That was Eric and that's what he is still doing to these kids.'"

Four Trottier eighth-grade boys, all of whom helped plant the tree on the school grounds, spoke next.

In a high-pitched, boyish voice but a confident tone, Thomas called Eric the students' "moral compass" and observed, "Many students regarded Eric as the kid you wanted to get to know better." After describing a trip they took to a Southborough friend's farm that devolved into a battle with rotten fruit being hurled about, Thomas, the shortest of the group of the student speakers, in his navy golf shirt and ironed red pants, said that when they think about Eric, he hopes it's in the way Dr. Seuss meant when he wrote his famous words, "Don't cry because it's over. Smile because it happened."

Speaking for the children who played on soccer, lacrosse, baseball and basketball teams with Eric, Brandon—who stood tall and spoke well but possessed a very young face and a mouth full of braces—said Eric was the one who was always smiling and cheering on a teammate when that player messed up. And when Eric's friends took to the turf for an indoor soccer game the day after Eric died, with green duct tape wrapped around their sleeves as a sign of their mourning, Brandon said Eric was there in spirit to lead them to an unexpected win. "Eric stood out because he always gave 110 percent."

It was Ryan's job to explain to the gathering how and why the group came to pick the yellowwood tree. Noting that the yellowwood has a long life span and could very well outlive Eric's friends, Ryan, a tall, thin sporty boy with narrow, oval glasses and a deliberate speaking style, said its longevity "will feel like a part of Eric is still growing up next to us."

Noah was the final Trottier student speaker, designated to talk about Eric's love of music. The Big Band drummer, standing perfectly straight and silently praying his voice wouldn't crack, also shared some anecdotes about Eric, including one about Eric bugging his father for an iPod and another about hungering for Chipotle fare, which the boys ate one weekend afternoon after seeing the Boston Pops in concert with the Greens. "Other memories of mine are Eric's sleepovers," Noah, in his green band T-shirt and tan pants and closely-cropped haircut, said. "Some of the latest times I have stayed up have been at Eric's house. We would always watch movies before bed. At Eric's twelfth birthday party, we watched *Dumb and Dumber*. We joked about which characters in the movie were most like the people at the party. I wasn't the last person to go to sleep, which was a mistake. Apparently, I had slept through the huge beanbag in Eric's basement rolling over me. Several times."

Peter and Suzy rose and headed to the podium. It felt as though the audience was holding its breath. As a parent, my heart ached for them. It must have been hard enough for them to sit and listen to all of this, to see those boys, never mind to get up on stage and speak. But unlike the weeks and months leading up to this day, when Suzy was a frequent presence and voice at Trottier, Peter spoke for them both. His thin brown hair parted to one side, Peter stood jacketless next to the microphone, a patterned, light green tie pushed right up to the crisp collar of his powder blue shirt. Taller than his slight wife, Peter seemed crestfallen as he spoke with his surprisingly deep voice that echoed throughout the auditorium. He latched onto Gretchen's theme of seeing Eric in the events of daily life. The previous night, the Boston Bruins narrowly completed a sweep of the Pittsburgh Penguins in order to reach the Stanley Cup playoffs, winning 1-0. However, it was the heroics of Bruins player Zdeno Chara in the closing minutes of the contest that caught Peter's eye, particularly when Chara stuck his arm out and prevented the Penguins from scoring. It was Chara's never-give-up attitude for the benefit of his team that prompted Peter to think of his son. "Little things like that make me think of Eric," he said, his voice breaking. He gulped down some air and steadied himself.

"This morning, it was cold and drizzly, and I needed a coat to wear," Peter continued. "I reached into the closet and grabbed an overcoat that, honestly, I haven't put on in maybe two or three years but it was the only thing I could find to wear. You know, here we are, in June, and I'm putting on a winter coat. I reach into the pocket of my coat and I pull out a pair of gloves. And I pull out a single napkin. And it just so happens, it was a napkin from Chipotle." Laughter and applause burst forth, a temporary relief. A big exhale. "I think all of you know it was Eric's favorite restaurant, so I know he's here with us in spirit because if that wasn't a sign that Eric is here, I don't know what it is." He held the creased tan napkin aloft, a talisman.

"After nearly eighteen months, we still continue to feel the terrible sorrow and loss of Eric's death," Peter said, acknowledging that the support offered by local organizations and friends demonstrated "a neighborly love that is truly amazing."

What elicited the biggest reaction from the crowd? Peter's explanation of the 4 x 6, color photo of Eric on the front of the event program. In the center of the image, surrounded by gentle ripples of water, was Eric, facing to the left, his brown hair made glossy by water, a smile spread across his face as a gray dolphin kissed him on the right temple. Five months before he died, Eric and his brother Alex traveled down to Florida, and with their father, went swimming with dolphins in Key Largo. The photo served as a reminder to Peter "that, like a dolphin, Eric was smart, he was brave, and he was social. Dolphins are known for helping others and Eric is well known for his kindness and his generous spirit." The day Eric died, January 12, 2012, dolphins began beaching themselves on Cape Cod. During a one-month period, over one hundred dolphins died and seventy-one were stranded alive, according to the National Oceanic and Atmospheric Administration. Scientists had no explanation for the unusual event. Peter offered a hopeful hypothesis: "It was as if those kind and magnificent animals wanted with all their hearts to come to Eric's aid ... I would like to believe that those dolphins that did lose their lives in the early part of 2012 joined Eric in heaven where they are joyfully playing together in the warm waters of a tropical paradise. Nobody knows for sure why dolphins beach themselves. It remains a mystery. Likewise, we may never know for sure why Eric died, but thanks to all of your love, kindness and generosity, we will always remember how Eric lived, and for that, we are eternally grateful."

It was excellent strategic planning to have scheduled a break after the Greens addressed the crowd. The weight of those speeches, of the sad beauty of "A Kind and Gentle Soul" was extraordinary. "There were moments when we were edging toward feeling like a wake, edging toward funeral," Mr. Clark told me later. A little breathing room inserted between the concert band piece and the speeches was absolutely needed for the members of the Big Band before they played "Kaleidoscope." Privately, Mr. Clark was very concerned about their emotional state. "I was worried about the kids. I was worried that they were going to be okay. This performance seemed so different from others. I just wanted to make sure they were taken care of."

The children retreated to the band room to regroup. Once inside, members of the band let loose their emotions, including Lauren who was a self-described wreck after the seventh- and eighth-grade band finished "A Kind and Gentle Soul." She felt sick to her stomach. Teary-eyed, red-faced and panicky, Lauren kept repeating, "I can't do it! I can't do it!" She was upset that she had forgotten the trumpet plunger she needed for "Kaleidoscope." She had to call her mother to ask her to deliver it to the band room. Mr. Clark was doing his best to calm her. Then an idea popped into his head. "Would you mind if I talk to the audience about you being nervous?" he asked Lauren. "Trust me. I can read an audience." When Lauren didn't answer right away, he added, "It would be a good idea to say, 'Yes,' but I won't do it if you don't want me to."

"I trust you," she replied, though she wasn't sure if she was going to have enough air to blow any of those notes.

The Big Band filed into the orchestra pit in front of the stage.

Most of them looked down, as if no one wanted to accidentally make eye contact with anyone who was going to trigger an emotional flood, including the Green family. Noah, who would be playing drums, was still trying to compartmentalize his feelings after giving his speech. He said he approached the tan and black Pearl drum set with "shaky nerves," adding, "I was trying not to get overwhelmed by the emotion. I really had to concentrate on what we were doing." The pianist who volunteered to play this piece, Olivia, had been worried because "people were focused on making it perfect." The normally confident alto sax player Owen said, "I didn't want to play a wrong note." Then there was Lauren, her wavy, long, light brown hair tightly tucked behind her ears. She would not glance at Mr. Clark as she climbed the riser in the back row to stand alongside her fellow trumpet players. Fidgeting again with the Claddagh ring on his right hand, a nervous tic of his, Mr. Clark faced the crowd and introduced "Kaleidoscope." The students learned the next piece, written for Eric "in difficult circumstances," he said. "The level of dedication and sheer heart" of the students in mastering this piece, will be obvious. Mr. Clark continued, "Mr. Morales wanted to do something that's kind of different because Eric was kind of different."

Before he started, however, he said, "There is a young lady," referring to Lauren, who was scared about doing her first trumpet solo, especially in this song. But, he was *certain* that she would have all the support of those in the room when she does it. No matter how she did—which, given her emotional state beforehand was a big question mark—the crowd would have her back.

It started with Mr. Clark snapping his fingers. *One. One, two, one two.* He silently drew a large circle in the air in front of them. That warm, round ball of sound. For the first fifteen seconds, which feature the trumpets cascading in crisscrossing lines of sound, things were a bit unsteady. The trumpets weren't uniformly strong, the students' musical confidence wavered. After watching the uneven progress of this piece for weeks, I was worried. By fifteen seconds in, the pianist, the quiet yet elegant stick of a girl Olivia, laid down the haunting and moody melody on the shiny black grand. It was as though a kaleidoscope had clicked into place in their minds. When the fluttering horns returned, I could hear their strength blossoming. By the one-minute mark, I kept saying, "Wow" to myself. This did not sound like the same kids who, just two weeks prior, had no idea what to do with this piece.

The complexity and volume of the tune surged just before Lauren took in a deep breath for her solo. She hit the first note. It wasn't the loudest note or delivered with absolute certainty, but it was even, as were all the other ones she nailed for the rest of her solo, maintaining a glass-smooth delivery throughout. "I could feel the whole band saying, 'Okay Lauren, you got this,'" Mr. Clark said later. For a full ten seconds, applause and appreciative shouts for Lauren drowned out the band. Relieved, she wiped her mouth with the back of her right hand, quickly glanced out at the audience, exhaled through her mouth and cracked a tiny smile. There was still a lot of territory to cover. "Kaleidoscope" was far from over.

At the three-minute mark, the whole band seemed to have gotten past its jitters and became enveloped in the mystery of this other-worldly chart just as the meat of the song transformed into a sassy, bopping piece, punctuated by the returning horn flutters. The soli section was, nearly across-the-board, excellent. That isn't necessarily the case with every Big Band solo or even with most of them. In fact, there are times when students perform solos even though their playing isn't as polished or winsome as their bandmates. Not so today. Of the saxophone solos, Ethan's was the most deeply felt, soulful. His emotional connection to the piece and everything for which it stood was clear from the squint in his eyes and the dangle of his green bracelet on his left wrist, never mind the notes emanating from his sax. The soli section wrapped with a one-minute opus from Jesse whose creamy guitar licks blended with this tune, as the muffled trumpets *wah-wah-wah-wah*-ed in the background. Jesse was in another place emotionally, musically, as he strummed his blue Fender, his mouth hanging open, a thousand-yard stare in his eyes.

Signaling the final melodic shift, Mr. Clark shouted, *Go!* Olivia played her evocative bridge that led listeners back to those pulsating horns, calling to mind the shifting images in a kaleidoscope—the colors, the movement, its ever-changing lens—as the composition ended on an urgent point. The sound of the horns collapsed into one another, like the intricate mosaics inside of the kaleidoscope that change with a tiny flick of the wrist replacing the previous beatific image, an image that slides into memory, never to be replicated in exactly the same way.

They stood as one band to acknowledge the thirty-second standing ovation the crowd gave them, feeling elated, grief released. Mr. Clark waded into the crowd, took Lauren's right arm, just after she heaved out a giant sigh that reverberated throughout her body, and raised it in triumph.

CHAPTER TWENTY-ONE

Swan Song

The goodwill created by the Eric Green celebration remained in the halls, classrooms and the air for several days after Father Flynn blessed the yellowwood while students, parents and Trottier faculty gathered on the damp grass in front of the school, water soaking through people's shoes. Afterward, inside the cafeteria, it was womb-like, protected, full of love, peace. Children stuffed their faces with sweets. Parents were smiling so much that their facial muscles started to ache. "When it was over, there was a huge sigh of relief," said Mr. Lavoie. "We got a lot of positive feedback from it. It brought closure. And I think the kids were great."

The Northborough-Southborough school superintendent was moved as well. "I was absolutely blown away," Superintendent Charles Gobron said. "I actually started crying. How do you even put a price on that morning? It was unifying around what's important in life."

"So many people came together for a joyful celebration, so many beautiful things came out of it," Suzy Green told me. "It has helped us heal."

Mr. Clark agreed, "It was an amazing day. It did what it was supposed to do." Reflecting on the feeling in the auditorium during the service, he said, "There was, like, this energy that was deposited in the room, an emotional imprint on the room."

Relief and kudos were all over social media as well, particularly Twitter.

From a former Big Band trumpeter who played alongside Eric, "Eric Green concert was truly amazing #daymade"

From a member of the seventh- and eighth-grade band: "all you need is a kind and gentle soul." This was followed by a green heart, something that populated many a Twitter feed and Facebook status update.

Another seventh- and eighth-grade band member said: "Hope we made you proud today Eric [*she inserted stars emoji here*] I miss you so much and I hope you're [happy] up there [*green heart emoji*]"

A third concert band member: "Every time I look at my trumpet, I think of you Eric [*green heart emoji*]"

That student musician published another tweet: "They say family is forever, and I really hope that's true because I'm sure going to miss band [*green heart emoji*]"

A Big Band member posted an image of a green and white sticker with two white arrows making a circle around a green heart that contains the initials "EG" in the middle and "A Heart of Green" written along the white circle. The hashtag: "#RememberGreen"

The local newspaper, *The MetroWest Daily News*, published a story days after the event. Beneath the headline, "Southborough's Trottier Middle School celebrates life of beloved student," reporter Brad Petrishen wrote, "Through tears, laughter and music, Trottier Middle School Saturday celebrated the life of Eric Green, the popular seventh grader whose sudden death devastated the school community last year." Petrishen also live-tweeted the ceremony and posted a short video of "A Kind and Gentle Soul," noting that it moved him to tears. The news story pleased a number of students including one who posted on Twitter, "That article on Eric Green in the newspaper just made my day [*five green heart emoji followed*] #resteasy."

There was little time for the Big Band members to soak in this bath of affection as they began their Tuesday rehearsal in the auditorium. Between this day, Tuesday, June 11, and the end of the year, they had three more concerts capped by Jazz Night next Thursday evening, where they would play sixteen songs and be joined by a professional saxophone player.

Unlike the times before other performances, Mr. Clark started out the rehearsal uncharacteristically easy on his charges. "So ... con-cert tonight!" He was unusually happy. "Be here by seven. Wearing black would be great."

Mr. Clark walked around the auditorium at nearly a stroll, not his normal, manic pace that consumes him before performances. He asked them to play "Funky Music." During that run-through, the kids played loudly. Very loudly. Guitarist Jesse seemed very excited to be charged with hitting the rusty-looking cowbell. Brad, meanwhile, was reverting back to the trumpet section's timid posture from earlier in the year, clenching with his body crouched behind the stand. His eyes screamed with worry, even during this relaxed piece. Although Mr. Clark didn't notice Brad's frightened demeanor he did notice that Jeffrey's and Kyle's trumpet bells were aiming toward their music stands. "Figure out a way to lift it up," he said, charging up the aisle toward the pit. Gesturing to the trumpets and trombones he calmly noted, "Some of your notes were flat. Some of you are off. Who wants to solo in 'Sweet Home Chicago'?"

"I'm feelin' it," Jesse said, nodding his head as he hunched his body forward over his Fender.

It was no surprise when Ethan raised his hand. "Sweet Home Chicago" was his kind of piece, tailor-made for his saxophone. Saxophone player David put his hand up, and seeing the fellow sax player next to him volunteer, Chris shrugged his shoulders then half-heartedly, bashfully put his hand in the air as well.

When they started playing the Blues Brothers' standard, not everyone had fully bought into its laidback mood. "Could you rush any *more*? Guys, re-*lax*!" Mr. Clark started clapping out the slower rhythm. His slow clap echoed, prompting the kids to giggle. Then was confusion about solos, but Mr. Clark tried to settle them. "Don't overthink it." The kids seemed to relish the chance to get out of their heads, to not think.

♪

"Do NOT play!"

Mr. Clark spent the moments before the final end-of-the-year instrumental concert distributing bracelets. Anyone who needed an Eric Green bracelet could fetch a new one from the giant bags Suzy Green had provided for the students. Although green was still prominent in ribbons, hair ties and neckties—Mr. Clark was in a forest green shirt and a green-striped tie with his black suit—other colors were starting to emerge. Ethan, for example, was in a peach-colored tie.

As Mr. Clark mildly barked at the musicians not to play their instruments, to save their energy for the concert ("Don't play! Why do I have to say that *again*?!"), violinist Natalie and bassist Cassidy sat together on the side of the room animatedly discussing their weekend sleepover. Natalie's braids along either side of her head made her a portrait of innocence, clashing with the fierce microbursts emerging from Mr. Clark ("Unless you are tuning, do … *not* … play!"). Feeling playful, he grabbed the shaggy-looking curly brown wig and dangled it above the heads of the girls in the front row in the band room, who squealed.

After a bittersweet performance, because for most eighth graders it would be their last at Trottier, the final group, the Big Band, settled into their seats in the pit. Mr. Clark spoke without a mike. He didn't need one. "So, do you remember when everything was *groo*-vy? When everything was funky?" he asked the crowd, introducing, "Play That Funky Music." "The most important instrument in this piece is the cowbell." Bassist/drummer Richie showed it to the crowd and shared a rare half-smile. But there was one more element to add before they began. "I made a promise to put this on when I conducted this," he said. A thick, mangy little animal emerged from beneath the front row of seats. It was that wig. With great difficulty, Mr. Clark pulled the gigantic, gravity-defying wig onto his round head. It looked as if it was applying pressure to his neck and temples. The audience and the members of the Big Band guffawed and scrambled to get a good photo, with some of the kids in the audience running toward the front to get a better shot of the band director. Mr. Clark raised his arms and cued the Big Band to begin. It was hard to pay attention to much else other than the beast atop his head. Thirty seconds into the song he yanked it off. The audience groaned disappointedly. To pacify them, Mr. Clark whipped around and sang some of the lyrics. Loudly. Eighth-grade orchestra violinist Kimberly appeared by his side. She was clutching the shiny, pink bob-style wig with bangs she grabbed from atop the television in the band room. Kimberly shoved it into his hands. "Why not?" Mr. Clark responded as he pulled the second wig onto his head. This one fit better than the first and looked strikingly odd, framing his bearded face. He wore it for the rest of "Funky Music," then turned around, held his arms aloft and flashed the rock-on sign with both hands as his eyeglasses slipped to the tip of his nose.

It was hard to deftly shift from the cowbell, the curly wig and the pink hair to "Kaleidoscope." Lauren wasn't distracted by the shenanigans. She was biting her nails and looked nauseous. Her cheeks, pink, were a stark contrast to the rest of her now-pale skin. She avoided looking at anyone as she prepared for her second-ever solo in four days. It didn't appear as though it had gotten any easier, even with the emotional pressure of getting it just right for Eric removed from the equation. Her solo was very good, the breath smooth and strong. The other soloists, Chris, Patrick, Derek, Ethan and Jesse were, likewise robust. The long and difficult composition was executed with genuine pleasure but not the heart and the ache they'd infused into the notes at the Eric Green event, when they delivered their best rendition.

"Dance Like No One's Watching," was good as well, but "Sweet Home Chicago" was better, amazing, actually. Mr. Clark got the crowd to slow-clap along with him as Jesse and Ethan delivered knock-out solos which, in the end, led to a loud, standing ovation.

Afterward, as the students gathered their belongings from the band room, there was a lot of hugging and saying, "Goodbye." Danny, a seventh grader, was embracing everybody, including Ethan, who wasn't all that much of a hugger. Lauren received a lot of loving squeezes and high-fives. An eighth-grade flutist for the concert band, her eyes filling, stood in the band room doorway. She looked from left to right then blew a kiss and quietly said, "I love you all."

♪

Mr. Clark had been at Trottier for twelve hours already when rehearsal for their final performance began in the semi-dark auditorium, the thunder rumbling outside lending an ominous feeling to the moody room. The kids had gone home, presumably ate dinner, and were driven back to the building to rehearse for Jazz Night with their guest musician, a top American saxophone player and faculty member at the Berklee College of Music in Boston.

Mr. Clark was in typical pre-performance mode, worrying about everything. "Were there shadows across the faces of the students when they stepped on stage?" he asked me, not really waiting for me to answer. He was fretting about a number of things including how Danny, who was curling his lips inward across his teeth and pursing his lips, would fare given he had braces put on his teeth that afternoon. *Were there enough microphones on the stage? Were they in the right places?*

When Walter Beasley arrived—escorted by Deb, the parent liaison—Mr. Clark hopped off the auditorium stage to greet him. Walter, once called "the heir to Grover Washington Jr.'s throne," was tall and broad, dressed in an orange-striped golf shirt, tan pants and light brown suede shoes. With a shaved head and a thin mustache, Walter had a leather sax bag in his hands and a silver chain bearing a green stone around his neck. Sax player Ethan took private lessons from Walter, who had christened him with the nickname "Cool Ethan."

As the Big Band members started playing the opening of "In the Doghouse," Walter raised his eyebrows in surprise as Emma, a tiny, mostly silent seventh-grade pianist with shoulder-length dark hair, played her first bold notes up and down the ivories. Walter leaned forward, then stood up to get a better view of her as her playing formed the backbone for the piece, prominent in the first notes, supportive and omnipresent throughout. "So, would you like to play a solo on that?" Mr. Clark asked Walter.

"It's amazing to hear," Walter said as he advised the band to "pay attention to the floor" of the piece, the rhythms. Gesturing to Emma, he said in his deep voice to Mr. Clark, "That's tight, right?"

Mr. Clark had the students play the beginning part of "Doghouse" again. Pointing to Emma as her fingers moved along the keys of the upright piano, Walter said, "*That's* your floor. *That's* what you should be following." He asked alto sax players Chris and Owen to play along with Emma, then suggested that they work on the "hitch" he heard in the sax playing. "Everybody," Walter said, "jazz is based on *doo-ba, doo-ba* ... Don't be ashamed. Just say it."

When they commenced "Doghouse" for a third time, the students peeked over their music stands, seeking out Walter's eyes for approval. They tried the piece again, this time by having Walter jump in. The kids nervously sped up their playing, beneath his solo. "Don't do that," Walter said.

"Late Night Diner" was shaping up to be *the* piece of the night, with Ethan and Walter doing a call-and-response sax soli section. Walter closed his eyes and let loose, as though wading into a pool of bliss. When it was Ethan's turn to jam while his band director and private teacher looked on, he appeared uncharacteristically uncomfortable. While Walter's freely emotional musical outpouring seemed to cajole the other students out of their comfort zones, offering up a bit more of their musical souls after Walter had given them permission by example, Ethan seemed reluctant to follow suit.

After hearing them play "Kaleidoscope," Walter was complimentary not just about that piece, but about their playing, overall. "Last year, you were very good. This year, you're awesome. ... You sound like a group of old men and old ladies."

The following morning, hours before Trottier's third annual Jazz Night, Danny was still complaining that his new braces hurt. Plus, the neck strap from his bari sax had been digging into his neck, he said. Danny wasn't the only one ailing. Trumpet player Patrick was at home, sick. "Everybody keep your fingers crossed," Mr. Clark said. Patrick was, at that moment, acutely sick and wracked with abdominal pain, but Mr. Clark hoped it would pass by nightfall, like a storm front.

"I do not want you to play much, or at all," Mr. Clark said when the students settled down during their morning rehearsal. "Play easier. Play softer, play more gently." He pointed at tiny Henry in the trumpet section. "I'm calling you out. If Patrick's not here, you don't need to play louder to compensate. Now, with a normal performance, it's like a sprint, three songs. You can go all out. *This* is a marathon. I don't want anyone coming here *after* 6:30. And why is it better for the audience to see less of you before the show? It's all about ego. It's more impressive to come out as a group."

This seemed like it was going to be a discussion-heavy rehearsal. "During intermission, you are not allowed to leave here, the band room. We've been working ten months to get to this point. Ten. Months. Bring your A game."

Near the end of rehearsal, as they were working out their solos, Richie slipped into the room and took his place in the rhythm section.

♪

By mid-afternoon, the Weather Channel app on my iPhone made an alarming sound. It was an alert for a severe thunderstorm warning effective until 2:45 p.m. and a flash-flood warning until 9 o'clock. I opened the app and assessed the hour-by-hour forecast. A thunderstorm, apparently not of the "severe" variety, was expected to visit Southborough between eight and nine.

♪

By 6:15, forty-five minutes before show time, Mr. Clark got the word: Patrick didn't have a stomach virus. He was being rushed to Children's Hospital in Boston because he needed an emergency appendectomy. Fellow sixth-grade trumpet player Brad was home with strep throat. Danny's mouth full of braces still ached. "It's a good thing redundancies are built into the band," Mr. Clark said, unconvincingly to me. In spite of the missing band members, tonight was going to be about moving on. After the long year of sadness cloaked in green, a couple of kids opted to wear different colors, like Ethan who again wore a peach-colored necktie, although two green Eric bracelets were still dangling from his wrist. Mr. Clark also wore peach in the form of a new shirt as he tried to exude a sense of calm, withdrawing behind the closed double-doors to the band room bearing the sign, "Current Big Band members only."

Mr. Clark expended his surplus energy well before students began arriving. He set up tables in the lobby for refreshments at intermission as well as the donation table, all of which were decorated in light blue and yellow. Boston Marathon colors. Proceeds from the evening would go to the One Fund established two months beforehand to help those injured by the Boston Marathon bombing. "We are one Boston," the Jazz Night program quoted then-Boston Mayor Tom Menino as saying. "We are one community. As always, we will come together to help those most in need. And in the end, we will all be better for it."

News that Patrick wouldn't be able to make it quickly spread, as band members, wearing their concert black, entered the room, prompting discussions ranging from the purpose of the appendix ("It's a vestigial organ," Mr. Clark explained, saying he had had his removed in his 20s.), to other surgeries. The students were cleaving to one another in clusters around the room. Several eighth graders— Ethan, Jesse, Lauren, Brandon, Noah and Aaron—circled around one another as if beside a campfire. Danny, who appeared to be trying to get Lauren's attention, hung around the outer edge of their sphere. A group of seventh-grade boys beckoned Danny to join them, but Danny didn't respond, content to hold Lauren's phone and sit next to the eighth graders. Jesse and Ethan were jamming—Jesse on the guitar, Ethan on the sax—as Jesse tried to recruit Ethan into his rock band Indignous. Riffs from AC/DC songs, in addition to snippets of "Sweet Home Alabama" and "Stairway to Heaven" came from Jesse's guitar, as other musicians joined in. Bassist/drummer Richie was sitting near but not quite with his fellow eighth graders, shielding his face with his hand and turning away when bari sax player Josh tried to take photos of him. The seventh-grade girls were near the front of the room, gathered around Ashley, giggling over something on someone's iPhone.

By 6:45, the Davidson brothers, Harry and Henry, arrived and Mr. Clark informed Henry that he was lead trumpet tonight. Later Henry said, "When Mr. Clark told me I'd be lead trumpet, I told him, 'Oh no! I can't do this!' But Mr. Clark's like, 'You're gonna be fine.'" As the tiny boy attempted to absorb the news, the band director sent the brothers and Josh out to the stage to make sure their music was open to "Back to the Basement," so they could just walk out on stage and start playing. "I'm gonna open up the house once the Davidsons get off the stage," he said.

The students finished tuning. The air in the room became electric. Mr. Clark shut off the lights to get their attention, and with as much emotional restraint as he could muster, said, "We started this in September, focusing on this. We're playing 16 tunes, something's going to go haywire."

I left the band room to take my seat in the auditorium, off to right, the seat I'd occupied during almost all of their performances throughout the year. The crowd was decent-sized but nowhere near the full house in attendance for the Eric Green event. The house lights, which were usually on but dimmed during most concerts, were noticeably darker. The lights on the stage, reflected by the white foldable acoustical sound shell around the trumpet risers, looked bright and hot. Into that spotlight, and only about fifteen minutes behind schedule, Mr. Clark and his Big Band stepped as the audience of family, friends and Big Band alumni applauded. No introduction. No words. Just them and their music.

One, two. Rapid snapping of fingerpads that would be split and bloody by the time the performance was through. *One, two, a one two three and* … the 2012-2013 Big Band began its last concert with every member who was present contributing to the opening explosion of sound in "Back to the Basement" to a wildly rapid tempo, a heartbeat working overtime. The trumpets, missing two members of their ranks, sounded surprisingly polished during the measures which prominently featured them at the one-minute mark, so different than the September days when kids were trembling behind their stands. The soli section went on for over four minutes and featured all boys. The loudest and most fearless solos came from the band's leaders. Not a hair out of place and his wire-rim glasses perched on his nose, Ethan delivered a stand-out solo. Jesse, tucked over to the left of the horns and the right of the drums and bass, invoked a light, twangy touch that perfectly complemented the shuffle's attitude. The final solo, from Noah on the drums, was ten seconds of lightning-fast rolls and frosty strikes on the ride cymbal. With less than thirty seconds left in the piece, Mr. Clark pulled the music back, only to build it up and crash it into the stage.

"How about this sixth-, seventh-, and eighth-grade band? Whaddya think? Whaddaya think?" Mr. Clark said into the microphone, addressing the audience for the first time, keeping his remarks short. He had all night for his quirky maestro commentary. Before announcing the next piece, "Tiger of San Pedro," he told the audience that Patrick, who would normally be spotlighted in this chart, wasn't there because he was on his way to Children's Hospital to get his appendix out. Ignoring any emotional pangs folks might have experienced from having a top trumpet player's spot empty, leaving an uncomfortable empty spot on the stage for the second year in a row, Mr. Clark donned his game face. Brisk piano notes and vertical oscillation of the pellet-filled shaker set the Latin-themed "Tiger" off. The piece was a speeding freight train barreling through notes. Until what was supposed to be Patrick's solo. His bandmates played what normally would've been the background music, beneath his trumpet. It was very noticeable that something wasn't right. Given the loud, bombastic way the Big Band played this piece, it sounded plain wrong to hear those twenty seconds or so of underplaying. And nothing else. Once they got past Patrick's would-be solo, they picked right up again through Noah's pounding, electric performance on the drums to the ending pounce. Playing that song, at that pace, must have been exhausting. The band had fourteen more charts to go.

At least the next selection, "In a Mellow Tone" did not possess the insistent and driving tempo of "Tiger," although it still proceeded at a fairly rapid clip. And, it wasn't mellow. This was Brandon's solo moment. Mr. Clark, a trombone player himself, opted to highlight this. "It's hard to pick out Brandon. He's hard to spot," he joked, pointing at the boy he'd nicknamed The Sequoia, who usually looked fairly timid while playing. Mr. Clark also noted that it was his birthday. His fourteenth. "He's gonna kill me," Mr. Clark semi-whispered as he laughed before leading the crowd in singing, "Happy Birthday." Brandon's solo was full of character and the much-sought-after warm and round quality of which Mr. Clark spoke so often. Carol's piano notes before the concluding horn blasts were like cherries on this sundae of a song. "Brandon!" Mr. Clark yelled, cueing the audience to give him another round of applause, gesturing to the boy.

During "Tiny Capers," the dynamic 1960s-ish tune, which the band played well, I felt bad for little sixth-grader Henry who, with no prep time, had to deliver Patrick's part. The poor boy barely got the notes out, and those that did emerge weren't always the correct ones. Luckily, it was a short piece.

"Kaleidoscope" was, overall, solid, but not nearly as good or as emotional or as intense as their premiere. Sections where the horns were required to flutter at different octaves didn't. Instead, they crashed. Lauren, whose solo was a victory over nerves at the Eric Green event, fell apart halfway through this time. It almost seemed as though she was holding the trumpet to her mouth but nothing was emerging from the bell. While Chris nailed his sax solo with precision, Ethan's lacked the normal Ethan-like intensity and soul. Jesse's solo was very quiet at the beginning—it was hard to tell if it was him, his guitar, the amplifier or the microphones—but grew in intensity as it proceeded. At the chart's conclusion, Lauren was teary-eyed and red-faced, biting her lip. A fellow trumpet player, who looked concerned, offered her a bottle of water.

The introduction of Walter as the guest artist took some of the performance burden off the kids at just the right time. In a gray suit jacket over a black shirt and pants, Walter eagerly dove into "Late Night Diner," attempting to engage his protégé Ethan in a musical give-and-take. Ethan's playing initially seemed quiet and withdrawn, at least for Ethan, mirroring what happened with his solo in "Kaleidoscope." As they stood together, Ethan about a foot shorter than Walter, Walter swayed as he played, clearly enjoying himself. Ethan, however, looked terrified. The children were just starting to lose some of their oomph, particularly those in the trumpet section. They really needed an intermission.

Inside the band room, Mr. Clark was trying to keep spirits high. Applauding his band's performance, he said, "That was awesome!" He checked on Henry and playfully joked about whether the boy needed oxygen. Danny put his hands to his cheeks and said, "My mouth is *killing* me!" As the kids broke loose and started goofing around, eating Doritos and crackers, Mr. Clark showed me his own wounds. The fingerpads on his middle fingers and thumbs had split open from all the vigorous snapping. "In an hour, this will all be over," he said to me, his eyes moistening. For the kids, especially the eighth graders, the finality of it all, would sink in during the following week, during the last two days of school.

When they returned to the stage for the second half, Walter thanked the audience for attending and for supporting these young musicians:

"It's so important that you feel that what they're doing is special, because it is special. What Mr. Clark is doing, I've never seen before, only once, and that was my own music teacher in California who taught me life lessons, he taught me the life lessons I learned through music. … The life lessons we learned in band, working as a team, enabled me to do what I'm doing in my career."

"Groovin' Hard" kicked off the second half but it didn't have that trademark Big Band spark or burning drive that it usually did. The rendition they performed at the Eric Green service two weeks earlier was explosive. Tonight, Mr. Clark looked like a magician, trying to manifest energy out of thin air, twisting at his hips while stretching his arms out and splaying his fingers out as though casting a spell. The band did manage to grab hold of it for the final third of the piece, just after the big sax soli. Were they getting tired, physically? Were the horn players' chops too weak to make it through sixteen selections? "Groovin' Hard" was their best piece. This didn't bode well.

If Mr. Clark was, in fact, a magician, his spell to inject the kids with a new burst of energy finally kicked in during "Dance Like No One's Watching." Between the fiercely hasty drum beat that was pushing the band forward and Walter's sax improv, it seemed as though the kids suddenly had shots of espresso coursing through their veins. "In the Doghouse" marked their second wind. They sounded like their glorious selves, having fun, jitters jettisoned, jazz attitudes well beyond their years reacquired. It was wonderfully rowdy. Whatever was ailing Ethan was now gone because he got his mojo back on his solo, just in time, too, because his showcase tune for his final Big Band concert, "Finding You Here" followed, sounding slower than usual though still marked by elegant piano playing and a gauzy, dreamlike tenderness in Ethan's sax solo.

Any anxiety that had been holed up inside Mr. Clark's sleep-deprived body was gone, enough so that he allowed himself a goofy, rehearsal-like tangent when he introduced "Cute." "I'm gonna guarantee that if you're over a certain age, you're going to know something that Neal Hefti wrote. Okay? If you're over 30 and I go, *Na-na na-na na-na na-na na-na na-na na-na na-na* ..."

"Batman!" several in the crowd responded.

"Exactly! Right? See!" Pointing to the middle schoolers behind him he said, "They have no idea what I'm talkin' about. Oh, by the way, the original Batmobile just sold for $4.3 million. And it probably doesn't even pass the, what's that fuel test thing? Anyway, all right, so this is a tune called ... oh, he also wrote the song for *The Odd Couple* sitcom, okay, but really, his greatest musical achievement was giving the Basie band those incredible arrangements to demonstrate what you can do with time. We're going to play a tune called 'Cute' and I think after you hear it you're gonna agree that it can be called nothing less. And, this piece is gonna feature one of our drummers, Noah. Can you even see the drummers back there?" The thin boy stood up and smiled shyly. "Oh! *There* he is! There he is. I think that's one of the reasons Richie took up bass, so he could come out and be seen."

Richie picked up the cowbell as his bandmates pulled out "Play That Funky Music." Mr. Clark took the microphone and asked Richie to hold the bell aloft, telling the audience that it was vital to the success of "Funky Music." Surprisingly, Richie raised the bell and grinned broadly. Despite the habitual tardiness, the loss of his spot on several tunes because he wasn't at rehearsals, at least he seemed to be relishing his final concert or was doing a good job pretending. Even still, Mr. Clark wished he could have done more to help his student with whatever Richie was struggling.

The time for the Big Band's swan song, "Sweet Home Chicago," arrived. Danny looked pained. On several levels. Mr. Clark looked as though he was starting to slip into his June sadness, the sadness that comes with the end of a school year. "It is truly a joy for me to get to work with these guys," he said. "I'm gonna miss this band in particular." The festive romp that was "Funky Music" transferred to "Sweet Home Chicago." Mr. Clark egged the audience on, turning to face them, raising his hands above his head and clapping in time. The crowd eagerly complied. The song, a monument to attitude and power, was fueled by an entire year's worth of work during which they plowed through grief and heartache. The resolute clapping and the faith of their band conductor pushed them to its final blast, which led to a standing ovation. Just when I thought the kids were about to keel over, Mr. Clark had them play the last dozen measures again.

Then came the celebration.

The band members embraced one another with intensity. Mr. Clark found Lauren and gave her a fierce hug. Four high school freshmen, who had sorely missed the Big Band since the conclusion of their eighth-grade concert in 2012, formed a human tunnel for the Big Band members at the end of the band hallway, elevating their straightened arms and touching their fingertips to form an upside-down-V. The last one through the tunnel was Mr. Clark who was greeted like a rock star by the teens who had all grown taller than him over the past year. They later reminded everyone that they were still kids when they began smearing cupcake frosting on one another's faces. The lobby quickly became hot and stuffy as parents and family members demanded group photos and selfies with Mr. Clark. One student's grandmother was so moved by the concert that she grabbed both of Mr. Clark's hands and thanked him. One of the Big Band members told his mother that he didn't want to leave.

CHAPTER TWENTY-TWO

After the Fire

𝄢 At 10:15 p.m., on the eve of the last week of school for the
2012-13 year, I saw this Facebook post from a friend who lived
near Trottier:

Fire at Trottier – saw trucks heading in – heavy smoke in corridors still – Marlboro covering Southborough station.

Comments to that post came forth almost immediately.

"omg. Is it out? Where was the fire?" one concerned Big Band
mom asked.

"Fire is out – heavy smoke still remains, not sure where fire
was," the original poster replied.

At 10:16, I sent a text to Mr. Clark, "Rumor going around
among parents that there was a fire at Trottier."

I hopped onto Twitter and began searching tweets for any information I could find and forwarded this to Mr. Clark:
"@ScanWorcester: Southboro: Trottier Middle School. Units o/s
with fire in the music room. Heavy smoke conditions."

Was the band room on fire?

Mr. Clark, who usually has his iPhone at the ready, took ten
minutes to get to my text and, upon reading it, wrote back, "What?!?"

I texted him that a locally-run web-site, Southborough News

had a bit of info. I sent him a screenshot of it. When he told me he couldn't read it, I told him to go on Facebook, where he was friends with many parents of current and former Trottier parents. It was then that his iPhone died.

My cell phone rang. It was a panicked Mr. Clark calling me from his home phone asking me what I knew and whether he should head over to the school. His voice was trembling. I told him I didn't think it would be a good idea for him to go since he couldn't do much and he'd likely be in the way. But sitting back and allowing things to happen wasn't his style. He got off the phone with me and called a former student who lived nearby to see what she saw out her window. He called his parent liaison Deb. He phoned Mr. Lavoie, the principal.

News that the fire had been in the "music room" spread quickly. A Big Band parent of an eighth grader said on Facebook, "This is so bad. Smoke filled rooms doesn't bode well. This school can't take much more." A few minutes later, she added another comment. "My heart aches for these kids. They need the last week to be routine after all they've been through."

At precisely 11 o'clock, Mr. Lavoie sent a mass email to Trottier parents:

> *Dear Parents,*
>
> *This evening, the Southborough Fire Department had to put out a small fire in the chorus room.*
>
> *There is smoke damage, but it is not extensive.*
>
> *I have every reason to believe that school will be in session tomorrow as scheduled.*
>
> *I will keep you abreast of any changes – Thank you!*
> *Mr. Lavoie*

The band room *wasn't* on fire. The fire that started was in the chorus room, adjacent to the peninsula of the band room. I later learned that an electric keyboard began smoldering, which left the left side charred.

Early the next morning, Mr. Clark texted me, "The smell is the worst, but it's getting better. Chorus room is pretty trashed. Band room is fine."

"Fine" was relative. While it was true that the chorus room was trashed—black soot in various areas, footprints tracked through said soot along the floor—the band room was not fine. In a strange bit of timing, the band room had already been cleared of chairs and set up for a special election—on the last day of school—to fill the U.S. Senate vacancy left by John Kerry when he became U.S. Secretary of State. The band room was one of the town's polling locations. The morning after the fire, it reeked of an acrid plastic and a chemical odor that irritated the throat. Walking into the darkened room, the smell didn't immediately smack me in the face, but when I stood in there for a few minutes, it got stronger and made for uncomfortable breathing. (After I left Trottier, remnants of the odor felt as though they were lodged in the back of my throat.)

Standing beside me, sipping a large Dunkin' Donuts iced coffee, Mr. Clark was talking about his band room sanctuary—the one he spent a great deal of time showing me back in August, explaining the significance of every artifact—and his fears that it might have gone down in flames. "I couldn't imagine the band room being gone." All around us, the people hired to do fire clean-up were setting up very large fans and loudly dragging things around. There were several high-powered fans stationed throughout the music corridor, in the auditorium and by the school's front doors. The auditorium, where there would be two days' worth of awards ceremonies and performances, was infused with a slightly less offensive odor than the music hallway.

The end-of-year events had Mr. Clark in his AV geek mode as he was seen running up and down the aisles from the sound booth in the back of the auditorium where he adjusted volume, to the stage where he adjusted microphones for the student and faculty speakers who spoke of the sadness of leaving and of the challenges faced by the eighth-grade class, for the participants of the comedic eighth-grade lip synch event, for the singers and musical performers. The first day's ceremony honored extra-curricular successes, including those in music. Referencing the recent appendix removal, Mr. Clark gave trumpet player Patrick a medal for making the Massachusetts Central District Band. He also bestowed most improved designations on trombone player Brandon and drummer Noah, a spirit award on trumpet player Lauren and MVP on sax player Ethan for their work in the Big Band. A well liked social studies teacher, Mr. Holland said, "I really believe it will be quite a long time before this eighth-grade class is forgotten. You have encountered more than your fair share of challenges." He added that throughout this year they had embodied "the triumph of the human spirit."

Mr. Clark carefully selected the music to which the eighth-grade class marched, for the final time, into the bitter-smelling auditorium—the sentimental "Home" by Phillip Phillips—as they took their seats of honor on the stage. This assembly, for academic achievements, featured speakers and performers, including Lauren singing and her pal Ainsley, a member of the seventh- and eighth-grade band, accompanying on an acoustic guitar. For a couple weeks, the two had been rehearsing Coldplay's "The Scientist" in the band room, seeking Mr. Clark's musical advice. "I went to his room during studies and breaks and he helped us with the chords," Lauren said. "One day during lunch, we played it for him. He cried and said, 'That is better than Coldplay's version.'" Near the end of the last awards ceremony, Lauren sat on a stool on stage, Ainsley next to her holding the guitar. Before Ainsley played the soft and spare guitar chords, Lauren took the mike and dedicated the heartbreaking ballad to Mr. Clark.

> *Nobody said it was easy.*
> *It's such a shame for us to part.*
> *Nobody said it was easy.*
> *No one ever said it would be this hard.*
> *Oh take me back to the start.*

Mr. Clark had been trotting up the aisle toward the sound booth when he heard Lauren's dedication. He whipped around and pressed his right hand into his chest. I could hear him sharply suck in his breath as he eyes welled behind his glasses.

The final gathering of the Big Band occurred the day before Lauren's poignant song, before "We Are Family" rang out over the loudspeakers as the eighth-grade class exited the Trottier auditorium one last time, before one student consoled Mr. Clark saying, "Don't cry Mr. Clark. It's going to be okay."

On Tuesday morning, booted from the band room because of the special election, the Big Band members hung out in the auditorium, passing freshly distributed yearbooks back and forth for everyone to sign, including Mr. Clark, who had his own yearbook that he was also sending around. Kids were laughing and embracing after reading what they wrote. Mr. Clark threw in wry commentary, like when Brandon simply wrote his name inside Mr. Clark's yearbook. The band director looked up and said, "Really?" A recording of their Jazz Night performance—a copy of which Mr. Clark gave to each band member—was playing over the auditorium speakers.

There was a strange atmosphere in the room, not counting the whir of the giant fans and the still-present burnt smell. All that was left was goodbye.

Mr. Clark graciously accepted end-of-year tokens from the kids that would further decorate the band room, but his favorite items were the handwritten letters and cards. Those went into that special box he kept at home, something that would most definitely be grabbed in the event of fire.

It was time for the students to go to homeroom. As they left, most gave Mr. Clark one more hug, even Jesse, who rarely gave hugs. When the last lingering stragglers walked past the whirring fans, Mr. Clark looked up the aisle at their backs and said quietly, "Then, that's it. Stupid kids."

Epilogue

I received a text from Mr. Clark as another school year was coming to a close: "I would NEVER change anything to avoid feeling the sorrow I feel at the end of each year. EVER. The love and joy of everything leading up to it FAR outweighs it. This quote is too strong for this situation, but it's kind of the idea, 'Grief is the tax we pay on loving people.'"

After watching the Big Band for a year, after speaking with students, parents, teachers and Mr. Clark, after researching jazz music, learning a great deal about music by virtue of watching it being made, and repeatedly listening to recordings of Big Band performances to discern nuanced differences, what did I learn? Did the members of the Big Band finally find closure with Eric's death? Did their participation in the Big Band help them heal?

I believe the student musicians did indeed find solace, notably at the conclusion of the Eric Green celebration service, mostly because they had to play through their pain and do so together. They had to face that pain at a young, tender age, accept it and process it through their instruments. There was no running away and pretending it wasn't there. I could hear their naked, emotional bravery when they played at that service in June 2013, when their sorrow was intermingled with relief that they had emerged on the other end of a year with a triumphant performance in front of Eric's family, friends and the community. Playing "A Kind and Gentle Soul" and "Kaleidoscope" on that early June morning was an epic feat for these children, particularly for those in the Big Band as the original jazz composition was an incredibly difficult one. The Big Band had to push through dense layers of emotion to reach that moment. They had to work harder than they thought possible, own their individual parts as well as the accompanying sentiments that lurked alongside each measure on their sheet music, beneath the dedication, in bold lettering, to their deceased classmate. And, when they did that, when they played those pieces, the looks on their faces—relief, pride and "can you believe we just did that?"—were extraordinarily satisfying, especially for me, a mother of an eighth-grade drummer who spent the 2012-13 school year trying to make peace with his own complicated feelings. Being part of that Big Band, at least for my son, was a nourishing, restorative experience. I'm not sure that every child in this particular band could necessarily say that—I'm thinking of Richie and Martin, whose experiences were vastly different—but it's fair to say that a majority of the members likely could.

The children of the Big Band overcame many other obstacles throughout the year ranging from personal struggles (with confidence, with divorced parents, with anger issues) and health woes which felled members of the band (like Patrick's appendicitis on Jazz Night, another student's serious concussion), to external events like the Boston Marathon bombing (whose impact resonated loudly throughout the greater Boston area), and the closing of the band room after the Trottier fire. Although the band room hadn't been on fire, the idea that it could have been taken away from them stirred up uncomfortable feelings. Throughout the year, I had to keep reminding myself that these musicians were still children, some very young children. I firmly believe that they wouldn't have been able to play so stunningly during Eric's service or win musical awards at UNH or MAJE had they not endured the tough, tense early months at the beginning of the school year, those days when rehearsals were not always fun, when their benevolent band director's face looked frustrated and sometimes angry. Mr. Clark motivated these kids like a winning youth football coach who pushed his charges, sometimes forcefully, to perform at the level where he wanted them to be by June because he believed in them even if they didn't believe in themselves. He started in the fall with a stretch of difficult rehearsals where the groundwork was built and expectations were explained.

The band emerged in June as a proud, award-winning group. Mr. Clark helped them become a band. A unit which had one sound, one giant heart. While it was the children who produced that mature-sounding, sassy music, it was Mr. Clark, who, although he stood in front of them to direct their playing, was really behind them the entire time, his hands on the small of their backs, gently guiding them forward even as he occasionally had to roar to keep them moving. When they turned around as they were departing Trottier, he was left behind in the band room with tears in his eyes.

After the 2012-13 academic year was over, many of the students who went on to the high school were surprised when they experienced a sting of longing for that Trottier band room. It was the same feeling experienced by other older, former Big Band students who, as the cliché goes, didn't know what they had until it was gone. It was the same nostalgic pang that was hanging in the air like ripe fruit when the 2010-11 Big Band reunited on Memorial Day 2015. It didn't take long before it dawned on the 2012-13 Big Band members I observed that if they continued playing jazz music—which many, like Jesse, Josh, Harry, Lauren, Farah, Angelina and Natalie, did not—it would never be like it was with Mr. Clark in his band room. In the back of their minds, they always knew this, but it didn't seem real until they were freshmen in new schools and faced music directors who weren't Mr. Clark.

These children, by and large, were enriched by their experiences in the Big Band. They were encouraged to plunge into the world fearlessly. They clung to one another through trials and triumphs in the turbulent terrain of middle school, rarely anybody's favorite life passage. They sustained strength from one another, inspiration and camaraderie. To these particular Big Band members, music was a lifeboat and Mr. Clark their captain, a sometimes cranky and gruff captain, but always, to the core, loving and more than a little goofy.

For me, I learned the difference between a bari sax and a tenor sax. I learned words like "embouchure" and that "chart" is a synonym for the word "song." I learned that, for all his bluster and in spite of that twisted music stand that sits atop the instrument cages in the band room, Mr. Clark is a softie, something that I didn't know for certain until I observed him during the year. I witnessed his dedication as he attempted to process his own grief, cope with his constant worries about the students' mental states and his regret about not being able to connect with Richie and Martin. I saw Big Band children who made musical hash of a piece during one rehearsal, then play it with adroit and breathtaking emotion a mere two weeks later. I cringed when each member of the trumpet section had to play a measure one by one—when most could not because they hadn't practiced—but smiled with surprise when I heard them later acknowledge that they had known they needed to work harder and were proud of the music they eventually produced. I saw a girl who had not done a solo during her first two middle school years do one under the most stressful of circumstances. And she soared. During this year I saw love and heartbreak. I heard gorgeous music. And I felt joy ... except during those explosive diarrhea jokes. Those I could have done without.

Acknowledgments

There are so many people for whom I am extremely grateful and without whom this book could not have become a reality. The support I received was tremendous. Many people were willing to speak with me and share photos and videos with me, things that proved invaluable to my writing process. Thank you all.

This project would not have been possible had Jamie Clark not been on board. Jamie was incredibly forthcoming in the face of the torrent of queries I sent his way during interviews, in texts, in emails and in phone calls. He opened up his world to me, introduced me to family and friends, and insisted, frankly, that I become one of his many friends, despite my professional, journalistic insistence that we couldn't be. He wore me down. He's like that. Relentless.

The other people to whom I owe a debt of gratitude are the members of the 2012-13 Big Band who allowed me to follow them around, take notes and then pester them with questions. Most of the band members consented to speak with me individually, some of them twice. Their voices were vital to this book. Using their real first names, I want to thank these students for consenting to interviews: Ben G., Jonah, Owen, Jamie, Bridget, Nate, Jon, Selena, Nick L., Kevin, James, Matthew W., Merry, Sam, Kiara, Andrew, Sophie, Max, Will D., Chloe, Curtis, Kevin and Dustin.

Big Band parents were a rich source of information and support. Throughout the writing process, they agreed to interviews and diligently answered my questions. Deb Scaringi, Gretchen Hartnett, Mike Hartnett, Deb Keefe, Julie Jenks and Karen Travins were great resources.

The book project began in the tragic aftermath of the death of Eric Green. His mother Suzy Green graciously gave her blessing to this project. She sat down with me for several hours and discussed the worst period of her life. She was kind and generous and for that, in the face of her tremendous loss. Suzy, you are an inspiration.

The Trottier Middle School principal, Keith Lavoie, a cautious man, gave the green light to my project and gave me permission to haunt the middle school halls. He also spent hours digging through documents to answer many questions, and consented to multiple sit-down interviews. Fellow Trottier faculty members and Southborough educators were kind enough to spend hours speaking with me about the school, the music program and Mr. Clark including: Robin Boucher, Carolyn Alzapiedi, Steve Brady, Lisa Klein, Tom Griffin, Martha Bachman, former Northborough-Southborough School Superintendent Charles Gobron and former Southborough elementary and middle school principal Linda Murdock.

The Clark family welcomed me with open arms and a boatload of frankness during our interviews including: Colleen, Meghan and Bridget Clark, as well as Maureen and George Clark, K.C. O'Brien and Mary Ann O'Brien. Many of Jamie Clark's friends and former students sat down with me in person or spoke with me over the phone to tell me tales, including: Matt Newton, Erich Ledebuhr, Channing Moreland, Steph Bacon, Craig Callahan, Bill Cleaver, Kelsey O'Hare, Matt and Alisa Pietro, Jocelyn Pietro, Julie and Danielle Doherty, Torie Shakespeare, Adam Klein, Connor Jenks, Dillon Ford, Brian Keefe, Sarah Schoen Damiani, Scott Morrill and Meghan Hornblower,

I owe a great deal of thanks to my eldest son Jonah, a member of the Big Band, who gave consent to allow his mother to observe his last year of middle school in the band room. I know this felt like an invasion of sorts, an encroachment of what had been "his" territory, outside of the maternal gaze. But he was able to rise above his fears that Mom would be an embarrassment. Thank you for your faith in me that I would be able to document this year of your life in a way that would make you proud.

During the writing process, I was blessed to benefit from the wonderful input of my friends Gayle Carvalho, Deb Scaringi and my uncle, Lawrence O'Brien. I was able to workshop chunks of this book through courses I was taking at Bay Path University as part of the Creative Nonfiction MFA program. Anthony D'Aries and Mel Allen, two of my instructors, gave me much appreciated direction and notes, as did my fellow classmates.

The writing and researching of this book took place over the span of three years. They were three very challenging years for me personally. My family provided me with much-needed moral support, forming the backbone of my cheerleading squad. I extend boundless thanks to my husband Scott and my children, Abbey, Jonah and Casey.

And finally, thank you to Nancy Cleary for believing in the power of this story and making sure it was published.

Sources

J.W. Pepper: The descriptions of the Big Band pieces that were attributed to "a website" came from J.W. Pepper.

Jazz: I consulted several books to educate myself about jazz history and jazz education including: *Teaching Music with Passion* by Peter Loel Boonshaft, *The History of Jazz* by Ted Gioia, *The Jazz Standards* by Ted Gioia, *The Jazz Language* by Dan Haerle, *This is Your Brain on Music* by Daniel J. Levitin and *Jazz 101* by John F. Szwed.

Mr. Clark: When I started this project, Mr. Clark gave me a long list of books that inspire him which I read as I researched this book including: *The Hobbit* by J. R. R. Tolkien, *The Last Lecture* by Randy Pausch and *The Five Secrets You Must Discover Before You Die* by John Izzo. Films he insisted I watch were: *Mr. Magorium's Wonder Emporium, Mr. Holland's Opus, It's a Wonderful Life* and *Saving Mr. Banks.*

Southborough: I perused a book on Southborough history, *Fences of Stone* by Richard E. Noble and consulted annual town reports and reports from the town clerk. I also referenced a number of articles about events in town from the local newspaper, *The MetroWest Daily News, The Boston Globe* and a local blog, MySouthborough.com. I referenced: the 2014 *U.S. News & World Report* high school rankings and *Boston Magazine* for information on Algonquin Regional High School; the *Boston Globe's* analysis of Massachusetts Department of Elementary & Secondary Education MCAS scores; U.S. Census Bureau data analysis from the web-site American FactFinder; and Southborough tax information from an online Massachusetts Department of Revenue Division of Local Services Municipal Database.